FRIENDS FOR A LIFETIME

The Saga of a Sixty-Three-Year Quaker Love Affair

By Don and Lois Laughlin

This Book Can Be Found At
Amazon.com/books
They allow you to review a few pages to
see if it is worth your time.
Comments can be made at this site.

ISBN 978-0-9834859-0-2

Library of Congress Control Number 2011936860

Library of Congress subject headings:
High School Romance
Love and Marriage
Sixty-Three-Year Togetherness
"Till Death Do Us Part"

Published by Springdale Press
Iowa City, Iowa.

ACKNOWLEDGMENTS

Five close friends of Lois' and mine were steadfast consultants from the beginning of my delving into her journals. Three were from Venus and two from Mars. No one should imply from this ratio that it takes three of one to equal two of the other! They all brought individual talents to the task.

Bill Deutsch, Margie Lacey, Larry Marsh, Erica McLane and Ardith Tjossem were essential contributors to the many decisions concerning which of Lois' journal entries were appropriate and necessary to the story. I owe all these (friends in all cases, Friends in some cases) a huge thanks for their time and expertise.

My daughters, Naomi Laughlin-Richard and Martha Laughlin, gave me continual support and critique of what I was trying to portray. I owe them more than I can ever repay.

Suzan Erem, **http://www.lastdraft.com**, has been an invaluable help in the whole process of writing, cutting and rewriting. She helped decide whose voice, and when, and with what information, was heard. I am heavily indebted to her.

Choosing pictures from family archives, Scott Laughlin-Richard, **www.scottlr.com**, designed the front and back covers to depict some events in our lives. My sincere thanks to him.

THE UNEXAMINED LIFE IS NOT WORTH LIVING

Socrates

WHY WRITE THIS BOOK?

This question is appropriate, since I have never written non-fiction in my life, and my age precludes ever amounting to much as a writer.

Lois had always said, "Please don't read my journals." I had mostly honored that request throughout our lives, but after her death I opened her journals and began to read. I was surprised to find the importance of some things I had only vaguely understood. Her interest in writing, or publishing, was a lifelong urge that never got fulfilled. She was an "A" student in the writing classes she took from time to time from the University of Iowa, but was never satisfied with what she tried to produce for publication.

As I read deeper into her journals, I realized she had a lot to say about her life—joys, frustrations, problems, satisfactions and dissatisfactions, and the solutions she settled on in response. She expresses freely her deepest feelings, both joyous and distressing. She had a lot to say about me—often wondering if I was the problem or the help. I'm sure she would say "both" from time to time. I slowly came to realize that her journal writing might be the writing she wanted to do. If she ever got published, I was the one to make it happen.

So, these are the reasons I write—help Lois fulfill a lifetime dream and throw our life experiences to the wind in case someone else is watching.

Her great bent for honesty, openness, and completeness dictated that she record in her journals more than I might be comfortable with. If I am to honor her adherence to these principles how can I delete what I am uncomfortable with? I was complicit in her feelings throughout our lives together, so I must share responsibility for my contribution to her intimate life.

Together, we reveal the inner workings of one marriage. There is probably no other like it in the world.

Don

CONTENTS

INTRODUCTION

This is the saga of a 63-year love affair. The love rose to many peaks, slogged through many swamps, and brushed off many pests as the years progressed. It survived to the end but went through many times of neglect and disappointment. Like many young people in the war and post-war years of the 1940s, Lois and I married very young and under precarious conditions. We were naive and inexperienced but we had unlimited faith in the future and in life on this planet.

I grew up with parents who did not discuss their marital relationship under any circumstances. I never saw them fight or even heatedly disagree. I didn't even realize that married people could have problems and solve them. The words "depression" and "frustration" were not in my vocabulary at the time we married, but I became intimately acquainted with them within the first few decades of my life with Lois.

But as I think back on my parents, I realize there were telltale signs of distress. I remember my mother's "sick headache," which occurred every once in a while. I read later that that was the term used by women of my mother's age as a reason to be excused from sex. And I unwittingly learned the art of denial at a young age. I surely brought this art to our marriage.

Lois came to our marriage with a load of self-doubt and personal insecurity. One time, we took a bus from Whittier College (near Los Angeles, where Lois was a student at the time) to the home of a minister we both knew. We had an appointment for him to help us plan our wedding and arrange the ceremony. When we got off the bus a few blocks from his home, Lois got cold feet and we walked many blocks while she overcame doubts about committing her life to our marriage.

Lois' doctor, a woman whom she grew to love, would later call Lois a "diminutive" person. Whenever Lois came to her office, she would describe her symptoms as "unimportant." She made herself as insignificant as possible. She always complained when someone wanted to take her picture, even though she was quite photogenic. Of our sixty-three wedding anniversary celebrations, all were conducted privately except our fiftieth. She appreciated being recognized but never pushed herself into the limelight.

Her journals, which span from high school to age eighty-three, reveal her lifelong struggle with herself to maintain her self-respect and to live a productive life. Even when writing to herself, her struggles were understated. The life she was handed often didn't meet her definition of a productive life. She aspired to be a writer and to participate in more intellectual circles than a mother of six in rural Iowa in the 1950s and '60s did. The happiest months of her life were during the summer she was accepted into the Iowa Writers' Workshop.

We found our Springdale home, where we would spend most of our life together, in early summer 1959. It was an old four-bedroom farmhouse on a four-acre lot with an old barn accompanying it.

One day in the mid-sixties we had spent the morning with the kids cleaning the yard and raking and piling up old boards. We burned the pile and watched it until it was little more than embers. The pile was twenty feet from the old garage, which was used only for storage—garden tools and boxes of household stuff we seldom used. The day was calm and clear so Lois and I left ten-year-old Naomi in charge and went to do errands. But the day changed. A light wind came up, stirred the embers and blew some of them onto the garage. It went up like a kerosene torch.

From 1940 to 1944, our first years, we had kept in touch by letter with only two visits. In that building was a box of our earliest letters with which we had developed our love affair over those four years and two thousand miles of separation. Now our real-time records of that love affair were burned with often only corners and parts of pages left.

Sometime in her late-seventies Lois spent many hours going through the box of burned letters retrieving as much of the sense of them as possible. In her journals she called them "Burned Letters." We've used some of what she perceived to have been in the letters to help write this story.

When in Iowa, as a high school sophomore, she wrote many letters to Anna Mae, her best friend at home in Oakland, California. Kids in those days had a habit of keeping letters and these eventually found their way back to Lois. Many are included in this writing.

It has been my observation that for many people who marry it is not just to a person, but to a family as well. This is a beautiful and stabilizing fact for most societies throughout the world. Lois' journals are replete with references to her family and mine.

Lois was the youngest of four. Her siblings stayed in California where they had grown up. Her brother Kersey, 15 years her elder, married a woman named Burt and settled in Alameda. Her sister Teresa, 12 years older, married Ralph and settled in Berkeley, and Naomi, eight years older, married Bob and settled in Chico.

Lois wrote less about my family. I had one younger brother Jerry, living in Texas, and one sister Margaret and her husband George who settled in Toledo, Ohio, until they retired to Estes Park, Colorado in 1990. We had six children, and their stories are woven into our lives as intricately as our growing up and finding each other. Their joys, loves, challenges and in two cases, premature deaths, are as much a part of our love story as those first letters we wrote and then lost and our last days together holding on tight for every last moment Lois and I could live and cherish.

This is that story.

HOME   349 Alcatraz Ave

CHAPTER 1

LOIS' CHILDHOOD YEARS IN CALIFORNIA

Lois:

I was born May 24, 1925, in Oakland, California. I don't know much about my father's employment before I was born. He may have been a fundraiser for a college at one time and he may have been a school teacher for a while—the information I could glean was never clear.

From my earliest awareness we owned three houses. The Lawton Street house was in another neighborhood a mile or so away. A big, two story stucco box, it remained remote from my life as long as it was filled with renters who paid. During the Depression years it was obvious that sometimes they couldn't. Serious and angry talk of "back rent" and mortgage payments due are a kind of constant murmur in the background of my memory. The .25-karat diamond solitaire I wear is a rent payment. I don't know how I know this, or how it came to be mine, but children from those days knew how to use resources at hand, and Don and I used this stone for an engagement ring.

The two other homes, a bungalow on the corner of 349 Alcatraz Avenue and Hillegas Street and the flat next door 345 and 347 were my home until I went to college. The flat had been converted from one two-story house where our family lived before I was born.

Mother and Dad, both of whom were born and raised in Iowa, arrived in California in 1919 with three children. By 1925 they owned a wood and coal business (which went broke) and three houses.

We lived in the bungalow until I was eight. I loved its dark brown shingles and cream-colored trim. It had a front porch and a low brick wall to climb or sit on while watching people get on and off the streetcar across the street. The front room had a big bay window, looking out, not onto the bay but onto the ever-interesting Alcatraz Avenue. There was also a fireplace with L-shaped window seats built in on either side, which formed a kind of shallow alcove apart from the main living room area, a great place to play house or hospital on a rainy day.

The dining room also had a fireplace, and one wall had "plate rails" above wainscoting. Elegant, but simple. My mother loved nice things, but seemed to lack a gift for making any special display. We always lived with what was there, as is, no frills. One wall in the dining room contained a large built-in buffet with glassed-in cupboards above and below the serving shelf.

The sleeping porch along the back of the house, with windows on three sides, had a door into each of the bedrooms. The toilet had its own little closet, separated from the big bathroom.

Don:

Shades of the future! Little could Lois know that the first home we would own would have no bathroom—only a toilet in the corner of an upstairs bedroom. Early settlers had no concept of the "bathroom" and made do with what they had—hot water from the kitchen stove and a galvanized tub close by. Privacy was voluntary. In the twenty-first century, our grandchildren would be freaked-out to think of living in a home without one or two bathrooms! As people acquire wealth, luxuries inevitably become necessities.

Lois:

In the kitchen along one wall were tall cupboards with narrow doors to the ceiling. The stove took up most of another wall and the outside wall was occupied by the sink with about four feet of counter space and the cooler at one end. We did most of our eating around a drop leaf table with a center drawer at each end. When I was little my big sister Naomi confided in me that a thin slot of opened drawer under the oilcloth could get rid of some horrid foods like lumpy oatmeal (one of my mother's standards). The room was a busy traffic area with a door from the back hall, one from the back entry, one into the pantry (a large walk-in closet with more ceiling-high cupboards), and another swinging door into the dining room.

It seems a long time that I slept in a crib pushed up against the window seat in a corner of the dining room. Orange juice (home squeezed), so good, so cool, mixes with memories of howling with pain from mustard plasters on my chest and back. Family stories abound of my three bouts with pneumonia. They blur into one memory for me of cold stethoscopes on my shivering chest or wet pads of cloth stained yellow that were cold yet burned. At one time I was considered potentially brain damaged from prolonged high fever.

My parents tried hard to make me well and strong. One of their efforts included cod-liver oil in a large brown bottle kept on the bottom shelf of the cooler. I was not cooperative. A morning ritual was to place two kitchen chairs together to make a bench with their backs forming a head and foot. Dad would force me onto this little bed, hold me down and hold my nose while mother poured a spoon full of oil into my mouth. Usually, in the struggle, some of it dribbled down my cheek or chin, but some always went down my gagging throat. A warm stained and stinking wet washrag was always given to me to wipe my face as I got up from this degrading incident. This brief but horrible scene continued for a long time. I know it lasted into my first years of school, because the belched-up after taste occurred in classrooms.

My parents hated this as much as I did. It was so important that it was never mentioned, but never neglected.

I remember one time being held and rocked by my sister Teresa in the chair beside the library table in the front room. She told me we were closer to each other than to our mother because we had the same mother/daddy blood, and mother's was different. I liked that idea.

Teresa was twelve when I was born and has seemed always to be my best mother. But she went away to college when I was four and didn't come back to Berkeley until she and Ralph and their two little boys returned from Boston, MIT to UC Berkeley about 1941 when I was sixteen. Then, although she had demanding and difficult males in her household, she often had me come to their house, and she sometimes bought me a beautiful sweater or something else nice to wear.

When I was five I sat on the piano bench with Naomi while my brother Kersey and Dorothy were married in front of the fireplace. There were several other people there but it was a somber celebration. Kersey was twenty, and mother didn't approve of this marriage at all.

Don:

There is a remarkable contrast between the relationship of Lois' mother to her son, and Lois' relationship to her sons. Both of our boys were married in large, formal church weddings with strong support from us for the wives they had chosen. We did not have the strong, narrow religious definition of behavior that her parents had. She was always conscious of the verbally violent conflict between her mother and Kersey when she was a child. She was determined that this not be part of our home.

Lois:

Before this marriage, Kersey lived at home in the dark bedroom behind the front entry. When he was home, he and mother had terrible arguments, yelling, screaming at each other in great anger. Kersey swore a lot and usually went out banging doors. If dad was home he never said a word. Kersey could have gone to Whittier College. He was offered a trip on a freighter. (He always loved boats.) But after high school he got a job with the American Trust Company and worked as a teller in the big marble bank downtown. He chose the "fast" crowd, bought a tan Model A with a rumble seat, smoked Camels, and drank. What were my Victorian Quaker folks from rural Iowa to do with such a rebel? Born in 1910, he was a child of the "roaring twenties."

Our sleeping porch had a door into each of the bedrooms behind it, one to the room where my sisters slept and the other into my mother and dad's room. This porch was my room. It was just a bit wider than the length of my cot-bed and I don't remember any other furniture in it.

From the porch I would hear my father sing after I had gone to bed. Why wasn't I ever allowed to stay up? Dad was proud of his rather nasal tenor. Sometimes Naomi played piano and they practiced hymns or church choir pieces together.

My sister Naomi had a flare for drama. One night we were home alone. She was doing dishes in the kitchen; I was in the big bed where my sisters slept. The hall light cast familiar shadows on the wall and I was easing into sleep. Suddenly I heard a piercing, high voice. "Lois, I've gone craaazy, I've gone craaazy" came from a hideous creature weaving across the floor by my bed, a huge shadow writhing on the wall behind it. Naomi had covered her arms with big white dish towels and the monster she had become continued to moan. I disintegrated and began to cry hysterically. It was only a few moments before she realized that I was truly unable to control my terror and took off the costume to become herself again. I suppose she comforted me. I have no memory beyond the stark shock of it.

Another time Naomi came pounding up the steep dark stairs from the basement washing machine, crying and gasping as she showed me her hand and arm covered with white blisters. In fear and pity I ran to the kitchen yelling for mama. It was bright in the kitchen, mama began to laugh, as the soap suds began to dissolve and turn to water dripping from Naomi's arm. I even begin to see it as a good joke, but too scary for me to enjoy. My sympathy had been exploited.

We owned an Essex, a muted gray-green two-door sedan. When mother needed a car during the day she drove Dad to work and went to get him again in the evening. Nobody liked the Essex. It was kind of low class, ugly, no style. Mother especially hated it and drove it badly. With mother we never drove through an intersection after a stop; we bucked, jerked, and sometimes before we got across we stalled and began all over again with grinding gears. Late one afternoon a man came to look at the Essex. He gave my mother fifty dollars and drove it away without bucking. Mother took the money into the bathroom and buried it between some towels in the cupboard with the drop down doors. That night family members discussed keeping secret all the money we had in the house.

Sitting on the bed, I often watched my older sisters, now in their teens, and Roberta, (a special friend of Naomi's who seemed to be at our house often) look at themselves in the mirror, bemoaning their noses, eyes, chins or hair. They ate peanut butter on soda crackers, laughed and chattered together, but I wasn't really with them. Sometimes I was forcibly removed, shut out from fear of the feather in the doorway, or by the door shut tight against the piece of cloth wedged into the doorframe above my head. I must have been a pest, probably doing my best to be noticed, possibly succeeding but not knowing the right things to be noticed for. How could a preschooler relate to the things that people eight years older than I were interested in?

Don:

     As a child Lois was so fearful of feathers that one placed on the sill of a door kept her from entering the room. Her older sisters used this phobia well. Even as an adult, she had an unreasonable fear of feathers. On the farm she had to steel herself to gather eggs from under setting hens. Butchering chickens for our meat supply was never a pleasant job although she was skilled and efficient at it.

Lois:

     We often had company – aunts, uncles, and cousins. People came to dinner—mostly church folks. When Teresa was in college, girl friends and boys came. She was pretty and popular and had several would-be suitors.

     Our neighborhood was in the Oakland flatlands, not in West Oakland where the poorer blacks and Asians lived, but not in the Piedmont district where well-to-do businessmen lived, or in the Berkeley hills only a mile or two north of us where the university professors lived. The houses were solid, well built, but not very modern. Stucco or cedar shingle siding were common. Many were probably built around the turn of the century.

     Iceboxes were more common than refrigerators, and some, like us, still had only built-in coolers with a screen on the outside wall for ventilation. During the summer it was a treat to climb up on the bumper and scoop chipped ice from the back end of the truck while the driver was delivering the fifty-pound block to Mrs. Johnson's kitchen.

     One of the best summer events was the frequent arrival of the little truck, precursor to the pickup, loaded with sweet corn. "Alameda sweet corn. Ten cents a dozen." It wasn't till years later, when I moved to Iowa, that I realized Iowa's famous farm crop was not sweet corn.

     I believe our neighborhood could be considered lower middle class, although an MD lived a block away and Mr. Nelson, of the big white house across the street, must have been a professional of some kind. But most were probably employed as clerks, like my dad, or laborers, like Frank Johnson on the telephone lines.

     My folks had graduated from William Penn College, in Oskaloosa, Iowa. Dad had taught school in Chama, New Mexico. (I can't imagine him as a good teacher.) I think they considered themselves a notch or two above our neighbors in education and culture.

Don:

     William Penn College was a family tradition. My dad attended for a year or two, my sister and brother attended and I was a graduate as was my son, David. Deriving its name from the Quaker founder of Pennsylvania it had a strong Christian bias. During the years I attended it also had a strong Quaker peace testimony. In later years it became William Penn University and an important component of higher education in Iowa.

Lois:

The neighbor kids almost never came to our house to play. I was frequently in theirs. I had few toys and no games until I received a Monopoly set. Hanna, a large doll, a large wicker doll buggy, and a large red tricycle and my beloved golden teddy bear were my only toys. Peter, our fox terrier, was perhaps my best toy. She, yes, she was misnamed, would ride in my doll buggy, sometimes staying in it while I pushed it around the whole block.

We Woods didn't really know our neighbors at all. The social life of my parents consisted almost entirely of people from First Friends Church in Berkeley, several miles away.

Between the gutter boards, which have now become cement curbstones, and the sidewalk on Alcatraz Avenue there was a narrow dirt space filled with weeds or grass, depending on the care of the property owner. There was a big English walnut tree in our space, spreading shade in the summers and dropping lots of nuts in their thick green hulls in the fall.

My folks were very inconsistent in their love for mankind. One chilly Sunday morning as dad backed the car out to the front of the house he discovered a lone man, a tramp, picking walnuts up and stowing them into a bag. Dad went kind of berserk, he ran towards him, shouting, "Dirty wop, get away, wop thief!" Wops for the Filipinos, Chinks for the Chinese, Japs for Japanese, and kikes for the Jews were common words, from dad, especially for people whom he looked down upon. Naomi would cringe and gently remonstrate, "Daa-ad." After Pearl Harbor I know dad used the term, "dirty Japs," easily.

The Takahashi family were members, or perhaps only attenders, of our First Friends Church in Berkeley. I think one of them was an oculist used by my parents. I suppose they were deported to the camps after December, 1941. I never heard of any special care our good folk in family or church took for them.

Two blocks away, on my way to school, was a Catholic elementary school. Catholic and public school kids usually ignored each other. We all used the same penny candy store and occasionally rude words, shoves, and tongues stuck out were part of waiting a turn to buy a caramel B-bat or bubble gum. The ancient couple who lived in rooms behind the tiny grocery-candy counter were like automatons, never having any personal reaction to whatever shuffling and words took place in front of their glassed in candy counter. One time, long, cylindrical balloons that stretched to amazing lengths when filled with water, became an instant seller. When I took mine home my parents made it immediately clear that this was not a toy and it disappeared. I don't remember them scolding about it, or giving any explanation as to why it was not a toy. Some activist parents must have banned their sale. It was a short-lived fad.

During these years in fourth, fifth, and sixth grades I became an accomplished thief. I went home for lunch and very often snitched a few pennies or a nickel from mother's purse as I left for the afternoon. It was terrifying work, done very fast, and with great concern that the amount taken was small enough not to be noticed. I don't understand why I didn't ask for a nickel or even a dime, but I never could. Mother was often on the telephone when I finished eating. I would go into my room for a few seconds and then, coming back through the folks' room I would stop by her purse on the dresser and do the deed! Sometimes she would hang up just as I was opening her purse, and I would abort the job. As far as I know she did not ever know what I was doing. The burden of guilt was heavy, but I did this for a prolonged period of time. I was able to ask for a dime to go to an occasional Saturday matinee, but I was never a member of the lucky ones who went every week. I knew kids who had an allowance and the freedom they had with money was awesome. The subject or possibility of an allowance never came up in our house.

I have often said that I come from Berkeley or San Francisco area. Who ever heard of Oakland? But I'm sure it is a snobby class thing with me. When Teresa and Ralph moved into the Berkeley hills and became part of the UC campus because of Ralph's professorship in the physics/metallurgy department, I was inordinately proud of my connection to brains and education.

I lost my tonsils when I was nine or ten years old. I was always a sickly, skinny kid with a chronic cold. My parents did their best to make me healthy. There was the cod liver oil ordeal in the mornings. Then I wore brown goggles and took a series of sunbaths under a warm yellow light in a doctor's office. I had to drink the "top milk" from the quart bottle even though it made me gag. I came home from school early in the afternoons, until fifth grade, to take a nap. And as a further effort of care the doctor recommended that the tonsils must go.

Don:

When all considerations are made it must be admitted that her parents were eminently successful in bringing her through an unhealthy childhood into a healthy adulthood. There were times, in her grade school years, when they seriously considered putting her into a TB sanatorium. As a young woman she was always aware that her lungs were her limiting factor, but she never gave in to her special condition. She walked regularly—often a mile a day—into her eighties.

Her first hospitalization, except for childbirth, was at age 78 when both knees were replaced with metal joints.

Lois:

In college I learned that my frequent attacks of runny nose and eyes, often with sneezing so prolonged my throat got sore, were called hay fever. I had never heard of allergies before this. This was particularly interesting to me because my brother, fifteen years older than I, also came down with a terrible head cold almost every Sunday, a stressful day in our household.

On the day my tonsils were to be removed I had strict orders not to eat anything. It was the first time in my life I had not been urged to eat. Summer vacation had begun, and early on a Sunday morning, the air still chill enough for a sweater, I joined many other little kids and their mothers in a surreal setting in the yard of a Seventh Day Adventist Church. I had never heard of people who went to church on Saturday. In the yard were a sandbox and a couple of swings, some weedy grass surrounded by larger patches of bare dirt. We were a subdued bunch. We knew we were going to have our tonsils cut out. We knew we would be put to sleep and would wake up with a sore throat and could have all the ice cream we wanted when we got home.

Mothers sat on backless benches or leaned against the swing frame, talking with each other or semi-playing with their kids. It was eerily quiet, kids and moms alert when the woman in white came out of the church basement and called a number. A mother and child would then follow her into the mystery. By noon there were only a few of us left to pretend to play quietly in the barren yard, and our silence was heavy around us. Strangely, not one child or mother cried or grew hysterical through those long, tense hours.

After the noon sun had gone far enough west that some tall trees on the side of the yard made some shade and coolness, the woman in white called for number 21. Mother grabbed my hand suddenly and we followed her through that awesome door. Into a dark hall and a stench I learned later was ether, then into a room made of sheets, each one hanging from the ceiling. There was a row of four or five of these rooms made of white sheets, each one with moving bits of feet and legs exposed at the bottom. This first room was filled with wooden folding chairs, and on each one a pile of clothing. What happened to the person who wore those clothes? I felt the resigned terror of one who knows of nothing to do but cooperate with those in power. I was appointed to a bare chair and mother stripped off my clothes and put on my nightgown that she had mysteriously produced.

Then I was lying on a white table, frantic for air, suffocating from a strainer over my nose, and being told to count to ten.

Dad came in the brown Studebaker to take us home. It was dark; I was choking and heaving with nausea that brought nothing up to relieve it. The pain in my throat was more horrible than I had expected. I was put into our folks' bed with the high scroll-top head and footboards. It felt especially hard to be there. My sister,

Naomi, said there was blood on my face. I dozed into painless peace for unknown periods of time, then woke to misery, and urged to drink and swallow.

But drinking and swallowing was torture. I felt gypped that I was unable to eat some ice cream. I had been promised all I wanted of something I loved so much. We would buy ice cream at the Safeway a block away on College Street, and since we had no refrigerator, ice cream had to be eaten immediately. I don't remember enjoying some ice cream even the next day. I hope I did.

I have wondered about that Mormon surgical clinic in a church, obviously a temporary setup. How many physicians were there? Did they do as many as thirty kids that day? Did any child have complications that required more care? If so, was there medical care at the church over night? Don's dad told of his tonsillectomy on the kitchen table in the farmhouse. I think of surgical clinics in much of the world today where even the water supply is scant and polluted.

This clinic may have been a Mormon missionary medical service for folks in Oakland during the depths of the Depression. It was surely cheaper than the hospital. I have no idea what criteria qualified me for the service. My dad was not unemployed, he had a steady income and owned property. My folks were penny squeaking scotch about spending money for personal needs or wants. How come mother was never in the hospital, even for tests, during all the months she was sick? I hope they paid their fair share for my tonsil removal, and I'm grateful it turned out well.

Then there was the music. My earliest memories of music are lying in bed at night listening to Daddy sing: "Sing Me to Sleep" and "When the Dawn Flames In the Sky." Naomi played the piano, or perhaps Kersey did sometimes. He was the best musician in the family. Sometimes he stood between the double doors joining the front room and the hall and tap-danced. And of course, hymns at church and Christmas carols in season. Don't think we sang them much at home. Singing "My Rubber Dolly," "The Man On The Flying Trapeze," "My Grandfathers Clock," "Tell Me Why," "Believe Me If All Those Endearing Young Charms," "Won't You Come With Me Lucile." Where did I learn these old standards? My mother never sang. Daddy sang in the choir and was a member of the community Orpheus Club of men singers.

We had a battery-charged radio in the corner of the dining room in the 349 bungalow. It was where my crib had been when I was very sick. When we moved into the upstairs flat next door at 345 we had an electric radio up on the mantel over the bookcase. After school I listened to Stewart Hamblin and his cowboys. Mother listened to the Metropolitan Operas on Saturday afternoons. Milton Cross was the commentator. Mother's taste was finer than mine.

Every spring, Peralta School (K-6) had a May Fete. One year the theme was "Sleeping Beauty." In the auditorium/ gym one day the girls in my class were told to pretend they were Sleeping Beauty waking up to the music. I knew exactly how

Sleeping Beauty felt, and as I lay on the hardwood floor stretching and wondering at being in the world, I WAS Sleeping Beauty. Those moments were the apex of the whole event for me. I was chosen to play the part.

In school I also learned to love the carol, "While Shepherds Watched Their Flocks," which I hated when we were learning it. "Lady April" will also stay with me till I die.

Don:

Music was very important to her throughout her life. She never got enough to be well satisfied. She had a recorded collection of the protest music of the sixties, which she played often while working in the kitchen. Peter, Paul and Mary were among her favorites, but she had others, too. Lois encouraged her children to learn to play music. We bought a piano for Ruth at an early age, and she and several others learned to play it well. She saw to it that all of our kids who wanted music lessons were sent to the best teachers in the community. Martha excelled at the guitar and Lois learned it too—they played together whenever Martha was home.

Lois loved guitar music, and as she got older complained that her fingers wouldn't work freely enough to cover the scales she wanted. As the empty-nest-syndrome settled on us, she loved to play her guitar and sing, but always by herself. Even my presence was sometimes enough to cause her to quit.

She also had a lifelong passion for drama. While on the Scattergood School staff she sometimes took a part in a student/staff play and thoroughly enjoyed it. Later she joined the Iowa City Community Theater and tried out for a few minor parts, but never landed anything significant. She was so determined to be part of a theatrical group that, for a time, she volunteered for menial tasks just to keep in with the group.

She enjoyed the University of Iowa Theater and we sometimes bought season tickets to a series of presentations. If the schedule permitted, our out-of-town guests were often taken to a play while here. She enjoyed discussing, with anyone who would participate, the meaning and innuendoes of a drama we had just seen.

Lois:

At my sister Teresa's house there was a fabulous record player which could play a stack of records in the correct order. Her house was where I listened to classical music for the first time. (Mother's operas didn't penetrate, sadly.) Beethoven, Tchaikovsky, Mozart. They had a record of Paul Robeson singing which sent me into a trance. "Sylvia's eyes are like the night..."and "Sometimes in the Twilight Gloom apart" I can still sing. The Peat Bog Soldiers and other songs of the communist International they had, as all good underground communists should. Richard Dyer Bennett, a counter-tenor singing English folk songs also fascinated me.

No one knows how much music means to me. I never, seldom, ever mention it, but I need it, get hungry for it.

I can't make music. Did that idiot woman who received my 50-cent piece every week for how long, one year, two, make music seem unapproachable? Never do I remember a sense of progress, of improvement. I think I "practiced" fairly regularly, always with frustration at lack of perfection.

I know I received no reinforcement from either parent. But these were terrible years. We all must have been under strain. Mother was bedridden, was dying. Who got meals? Did laundry? It's a blank to me.

But I do remember this moment: I am practicing music and in the bedroom mother and dad are talking very seriously about what to do with me when she is gone. Gordon and Florence Lowe will take me in. And I am silently sobbing and shaking and pretending to practice as I hear snatches of this conversation.

Religion played an important, if sometimes ambiguous, role in my childhood. I've recently followed an occasional impulse I've had for years. I've gone through an old hymnal and picked out some songs that have been important to me, sometimes much too important for mental health, I now believe.

It's no one's fault. Perhaps my genetic make up and the circumstances of my life caused me to take too seriously the sermons and songs. Don, who heard and sang the same messages, says he didn't give them a thought afterward. Alas, I was not so casual. From earliest memory, a melting melody could clobber me. When I was a guilt ridden, half orphaned, lonely adolescent, longing for love and someone to love, the pseudo-gospel tunes we sang in weekly youth meetings, called Christian Endeavor, came close to finishing me as a person. In my efforts to "be good," not knowing what "being good" was, I came near to disappearing. Being good boiled down to hardly existing, not doing or trying anything.

The only "not doing" that may have given me a shred of self-power to build on was my "Not" answering altar calls to come forward and be saved. But, of course, my inability to surrender or my wickedness in withholding myself, only led to more guilt. A heavy load for a young girl.

There was the time many years ago when I went with a carload of kids to a revival meeting in Iowa Falls. I was impressed by the big auditorium where it was held. The ending was, of course, an altar call, and the organ plaintively playing "Just As I Am," the preacher making his pleas and prayers for our salvation, the intensity of the atmosphere, tore at my innards. I did not go forward. No one in our group did. Coming home, the group was relaxed, flirty, playful, loud, glad and relieved to be free. All except me. I was a tangled knot of guilt and confusion.

I must've been about fifteen when we were driving home one time from a young people's conference in the car with our pastor, Gorman Doubleday. Again I was lonely, sad and confused while the others seemed so carefree and together. I sat in the middle of the front seat next to the driver. Suddenly I was shocked to feel our minister, the driver, stroking my face, where my budding and horrifying sideburns were becoming visible. Then his hand was on my knee for just a moment as he whispered words to me. I have no idea what he said, I'm not sure I knew even then. But they were complimentary, supportive, and amazing to me. Here we were, just released from being hammered by religious, spiritual admonitions and reminders of our wickedness, and the minister, the minister, was doing physical things. It gave me a jolt, but also a spark of hope that perhaps I was not totally unattractive and unfit for human contact. I was grateful for the incident.

Sadly, a few years later Gorman Doubleday became an item in the East Bay newspapers. He had been using a mirror that enabled him to peek up the skirts of women in the university library stacks. Well! Shades of Sinclair Lewis's Elmer Gantry.

There is a film, "The Night of the Hunter," which features another evil preacher. In that story I heard "Leaning On The Everlasting Arms" for the first time. Done in that pulsing, evangelizing manner, with accompanying organ sustained notes and ripples, the song becomes a model of religio-corruption in my mind. Yet, always the "and yet," it is a tune I sometimes sing to myself. That long drawn, plaintive eeeee can be a good blues.

Again, back to my hymn book. Those hymnals had no spirituals in them. Was black folk/religious music considered low? Irrelevant to white Protestants? And what about gospel—the good news? Hymns are usually solemn, sedate rhythms and words praising or thanking the deity. Some of, much of, the music is monotonous. Few great Odes of Joy here.

Another element of gospel is the sensuous aspect, almost sexual sometimes. I've often thought of this. I've listened to some modern gospel, written for and by the conservative Christian groups, and I'm struck by the erotic feel and the contemporary language of pop love songs found in them. Sometimes at first listen I can't tell the difference between the two. I call this music pseudo-gospel, because for me it's a sentimental, feel-good, substitute for deeper spirituality. I tread on thin ice here, not wanting to disallow joy and exuberance in spiritual experience. But I have too many miserable memories of groups mesmerized by speech and music, and when I see the rocking, waving upheld arms, dancing, swooning, even talking in babble, (Apostle Paul's tongues) of some religious services, I become profoundly distrustful of the sources causing such behavior. When does it become exploitive and dishonest?

I'm a private dancer in the kitchen, a wallower in sentimental lyrics and melody, but I'm aware of what I'm doing, in control. Perhaps control freaks are forever denied the joy of utter surrender.

I've made a list of some of the songs I sang that were/are a part of me. Probably the tunes, the simple melodies, grabbed me more than the words, certainly true when I was young. One of my few memories of my mother and I touching is of my leaning against her in church, feeling cozy as we looked for the hymn number. Dad and Naomi were up in the choir. It was special to sit close to her and feel peaceful.

I've grouped the songs into seven categories. Of course, most songs can fit into more than one. My list: 1. Solemn Praise. 2. Jolly Praise. 3. Comfort. 4. Prayer. 5. Commitment. 6. Surrender—altar calls. 7. Appreciation of Nature.

When I was in junior high and high school I knew by heart at least one verse of all these songs, all of the verses for some. By the time I had left college I had so repudiated my childhood religious tortures I would not sing these hymns or choruses. I steeled myself against this kind of music as I had come to believe it was manipulative. A piano's trills, the lilt of accidentals, the pulsing chords and melody from an organ, and the voices singing harmonies—I loved it. I hated it. It was a powerful part of my life.

I was determined that our children would not have to overcome such pain. Now I regret that they have none of this heritage.

I have now worn many more years and find myself occasionally humming or singing words to these songs. And when the words are unbelievable or offensive to my current beliefs or lack of, I get a kind of inner grin, realizing that it simply doesn't matter any more.

I'm a singer who cannot sing, but one who loves to sing. I've never been able to carry a part different from the dominant melody unless I'm next to a person who can carry me. My range is considerably less than an octave and the quality is thick, husky. But when I sing these songs the rolling accompaniments are still in my head. That makes me sound so much richer and fuller! I have to laugh when I hear the tape and realize that technology does not yet catch the music inside my head! "I sing because I'm happy?" I don't know. I'm just going to do this singing thing because I want to. I want listeners to know the messages that have made me part of what I am. What I have loved and also hated and mistrusted? And it embarrasses me to do this, but I will be glad to have it done and tucked away.

Here is where I end my story. NOBODY has to listen to the singing.

Sometime soon after our mother died in September 1937, Winnie Bellamy came to live with us in our upstairs flat. Winnie was a tiny, bony, homely spinster who had lived with her widowed sister, Carrie Palmer. They were members of the Berkeley Friends Church with us. They were affectionately but derisively known as the Apple Sisters, and I don't know why. They may have been in their fifties, possibly even sixty. I thought of them as one thinks of the pyramids, so ancient and permanent that age in years has no meaning.

Winnie was always nice to me and made some efforts to become close, to share thoughts. I was always standoffish and she must have had a lonely, cold time of it in our house. She cooked, kept a neater house than we had ever known before, and did laundry in our kitchen deep tub under the removable board countertop next to the regular kitchen sink. She would have had to hand wring all of the laundry before she sent it flying out over space and the garage on the pulley clothesline from our one person back porch. I hope Dad paid her more than her room and board.

Winnie lived in the dining room/wall bedroom, and not one element of her life ever left that room. She was unobtrusive to the point of invisibility. She stayed with us about two years.

During the summer of 1939, Roy and Edna Wood visited California with their daughter Faye, husband Keo Rash, and their little toddler daughter. They invited me to live with them the next school year, while I was still young enough not to have boy problems. That was the message I received. Ralph and Teresa also visited us with their two little boys, Neilen and Glen. We must have been a busy household. Where did everyone stay? Was Winnie still at our house?

When Ralph and Teresa went back to MIT, I rode with them as far as New Providence, Iowa, where Roy and Edna lived. It was my first time out of California.

Don:

Life has a way of throwing curves that are sometimes fortuitously beautiful. Lois had two other invitations to spend the school year away from her father, as he seemed to want. Both of her sisters invited her to live with them—Teresa in Boston and Naomi in California. My mind wanders over a bleak and desolate landscape of possibilities had she chosen one of those opportunities. In all probability we would never have met.

I remember serious discussions with friends in college on the subject of whether there is one specific person meant for me or whether people normally chose from a bevy of personalities. At that time I think I seriously thought there was only one for me, and that I had met her at an early age. As an octogenarian, I think otherwise, but rejoice in the series of events that were not of our making.

The "Engine Man" on His Throne

Courtesy of the Iowa State Historical Society—Iowa City
The A M Wettach Collection

Planting corn with horses

Courtesy of the Iowa State Historical Society—Iowa City
The A M Wettach Collection

CHAPTER 2

DON'S CHILDHOOD YEARS ON THE FARM

Don:

I was born December 6, 1922, to parents living on a rented farm in east central Iowa known as "the Carter Place" because a Mr. Carter owned the farm.

I have only a few memories of the place. One time my dad was trying to bring a wagonload of stove wood up a hill from the timber where he had been cutting. He had a team of horses, but one of them was young and not yet trained to pull heavy loads. The older horse, when given the "cluck" signal, would strain gently into the yoke and pull for all he was worth, but couldn't pull the load alone. The younger horse only jumped and pulled sideways and added nothing to the pull the wagon needed. I was on the wagon seat with my dad. We got down and walked to the barn to get a pitchfork so that he could "encourage" that horse a little more. I remember being a little frightened by the prospect of what was going to happen, but with a lot of verbal encouragement and a few light pricks on the rump, the young horse jumped up and down a few times then leaned into his collar, and with all four tugs tight now, the load began to move.

My only other memory of the Carter Place was that my younger brother, Jerry, and I would ride a tricycle and kiddy-car pell-mell around the dining room table and out into the kitchen, around that table and back again.

I must have been four or five years old when we moved to the "Shepherd Place" in Hardin County, Iowa. It was located on the leading edge of an ancient glacier coming down from the north, where the glacier had stopped and deposited its tons of rocks and stones. Every year Dad had to clear off stones that had surfaced during the winter. They were of all sizes, from those that took a crowbar to move, to the twenty pounders. We had a "stone boat" to haul them away, a flat wooden platform with two runners underneath so that the rocks had to be lifted only a few inches to get them onto it, made the backbreaking work as easy as possible. A team of horses dragged the "boat" from rock to rock and then off the field.

All corn or bean ground—that is ground planted to corn or soybeans—had to be plowed with a moldboard plow. It was heavy work that took many days in the fall and spring with lots of horse hours involved. As soon as we picked the corn, fall plowing began and went on until the ground was too frozen to turn over. Farmers tried to get as much fall plowing done as possible so that spring planting could begin on time. Of course, hitting a submerged rock was something to avoid. It could break the point of the plow and stop work until repairs were made.

On the Shepherd place we lived a mile and a half from a one-room school. I started there in first grade. There was no kindergarten. About twelve kids were enrolled in the first eight grades. I walked to school and when Jerry was old enough we walked together. In the dead of winter, when the snow was deep and the winds had been high enough to pack it hard, dad would come get us in the afternoon with a team and bobsled. He could cut across fields, driving over the fences on the crusted snow with the horses walking safely two or three feet above the ground.

Our dad had bought Jerry and me a Shetland pony when I was seven years old. Dolly was the delight of our lives and she became a part of the family. We always rode her bare back with only a bridle for gear. She knew all the tricks of small horses. A startled pheasant taking off from deep in the grass was always a noisy beating and thrashing of wings until it was well airborne. When Dolly was at a dead run and that happened, I swear she could do a square corner sideways. She'd send me, of course, straight ahead. If I broke no bones, and it seemed I never did, I then had to retrieve the pony and get back on. Shetlands are high strung and easily startled, but calm and highly pettable when all is well. Their main goal in life is to eat whenever they can. Once the excitement was over, Dolly always went where the grass was the greenest and started doing what she did best, as if nothing had ever happened.

When we first acquired Dolly, her back was about head high for me and we had to be either lifted on by someone or find a fence to climb, then jump on her back if she would stand close enough. Dad put Jerry and me on her back once so we could ride her to school but we fell off on the way and couldn't get Dolly to stand for us to get back on. We had to walk her home and Dad put us back on.

But times on the farm were not always funny or embarrassing. Sometimes they were tragic. One time, a cow somehow ended up in a lot with about twenty sows, each weighing about 300 pounds. The cow was giving birth when Dad found her. It was too late. The sows had gotten the smell of blood and placenta and nothing could stop them. He tried to fend them off and get the cow out of the lot, but he was outnumbered and outweighed. No one heard him hollering for help. He lost both calf and cow. It was a real financial loss to a struggling young farm couple who needed every asset they could hang onto.

We moved from the Shepherd place to the farm that Dad bought, ten miles away near New Providence, when I was in third grade. On this farm, during the 1930's, I finished my childhood and grew up.

As a kid I lived an independent life with no knowledge of the Great Depression my parents and the country were feeling. Once shoeless days began, my chief concern was avoiding thistles in the grass and boards with nails. It took only a few days for the leather-bottom feet and the necessary calluses to develop. We had few toys but we had lots of space, and old boards and old metal from which to make things. My young childhood days were carefree and semi-irresponsible. I had the run of two large barns, smaller out buildings and all the animals and weeds and paths one could hope for. Jerry and I and friends were limited only by our imagination, and we had plenty of that.

I did have chores to do each morning and evening, before and after school for most of the year. But the summers were my own, even with chores, which were not a burden. It was so satisfying to be a part of the family effort and my contribution was always appreciated by my parents; I was a partner in the business. Besides, all my friends were in the same boat, and we could commiserate with each other about our daily mishaps.

Young children shouldered much responsibility for milking and chicken chores. Helping feed chickens and gather eggs was one of my earliest jobs. Our chickens were free ranging so the hens laid eggs in outbuildings and weed patches—anyplace they could find seclusion and make a nest. My job was to find those nests and pick up whatever eggs had been laid during the day.

Chickens were not always friendly. Usually the hen was not sitting on the nest, so I didn't have to argue with her. But sometimes she was. In that case, all I had to do was slip my hand under her and pull out the eggs. It was often that easy. But female chickens are programmed to return to the nest each day or so and lay an egg. Eventually it occurs to her she has enough eggs in the nest, and it is time to sit on them and make them hatch. So she sits faithfully for twenty-one days. Her only activity during that time is, once a day, to get off to let them cool briefly and to turn the eggs, one at a time with her beak. Once done she settles back onto them to anticipate the brood of chicks which will soon be surrounding her. Hens often sit on ten to twenty fertile eggs at a time. Once a hen has decided to sit on her eggs she was called a "broody" hen. Broody hens are very defensive and will peck anything that gets close. They strongly resist being robbed of their eggs.

So back to my problem. The peck of a broody hen can draw blood, so I had to respect her mood. If I had a heavy shirt or jacket on I could go under her so fast she couldn't get me. With a gloved hand over her face I could protect my bare hand with the eggs on the way out. It often didn't work, but one way or another I always won.

I've always thought of September as the perfect time of year. It represented the time when the hot summer was over, the days were cooler, and crisp nights were a welcome change. The crops were in and mostly harvested by September, but the major crop, corn, was still a big unknown. And corn picking was still ahead.

I still believe September should be the first month of the year. It is the time when an easier phase of life is just beginning. Vacations are over and it's a more relaxing time with so much work behind and with time now to enjoy the fruits of one's labor. School is beginning again and kids are involved in new classes and relationships. It's a new beginning for a whole segment of society. Back then it was a time for farmers to look forward to some leisure. With nothing to do in the winter except milk the cows and feed and bed the livestock and keep the water troughs thawed out and working, there really was time for reading and working on things neglected during the busy summer days. My dad read the whole set of Zane Gray cowboy books one winter.

One of my great September pleasures was to pick a bunch of grapes from the patch beside the driveway as I headed out to bring the cows in for milking—one of my early childhood chores. The grapes were sweet and juicy and ice cold from the late night frost. I could spit the seeds wherever I wanted. As I walked the long lane to the far pasture, a Meadow Lark kept a few fence posts ahead of me singing at the top of her lungs on each one. She was a beautiful flash of yellow and black in the low morning sun. I felt as carefree as the early morning birds as I headed down the lane on my first morning responsibility.

One barn on our farm was a large two-story wood structure with space on the ground floor for horses on one side and milk cows on the other. There were stalls for three teams and stanchions for eight cows. Down the center, between the stalls and stanchions, was a wide alley used for getting hay to the animals. At the east end of the alley was a chute in the ceiling for hay to come down from the mow above. Back then, loose hay was the prevailing storage method. Baling, available by the late thirties, was little used for home consumption. Loose hay was labor intensive and required large haymows because it was not compact. Our mammoth haymow stored both loose straw for bedding and loose hay for cattle feed. By fall it was filled to the roof, and by spring it was so bare that some floor boards were showing. There were times in early summer when enough floor was bare to make a wonderful place to roller skate. I skated alone, or sometimes with a friend, gliding around the floor and collapsing into piles of straw at the sides. Rough boards were a challenge that we either navigated with skill or jumped. At other times, the large half empty haymow with steep piles of bright yellow straw towering twenty feet up the side of the mow, made, for a friend and me, the side of a mountain with "gold in them thar hills" to be prospected. Loose straw had short pieces of binder twine strewn throughout it from the drying process. They were almost the color of the straw and a prize to find. They were our gold. In the half light of the mow, the afternoon sun burst through knot holes in the wall of the barn and pierced the dust clouds from our climbing. As we prospected for gold, those narrow dusty beams moved steadily up the mountain side as the western sun sank lower.

Jerry was my kid brother by a year-and-a-half. We were very much alike and shared many common interests, yet kept a different set of friends most of the time. He was more mechanically inclined with an interest in engines of all kinds. My interests were electrical—radios and auto wiring. I once wired a romantic red bulb into the dash of our family car.

Riding the school bus home with a friend, Jerry spotted an old car sitting in a farm lot. He passed it many times and finally realized it wasn't being used. He stopped off to dicker and found that it could be bought for five dollars. After many days badgering dad he got the signal: "If you can get it started you can have it." Dad gave in.

Jerry gleefully rose to the challenge. The next morning he loaded a battery, tools and a tire pump onto our school bus. Later that evening a barely running 1926 Chevrolet coupe came rolling into our drive.

Risk was not in short supply and we sometimes took it just for fun. Occasionally a neighbor boy would ride his bike over and with Jerry we would have a bumblebee fight. We would find a particular old board half hidden in the grass from which was coming a low buzzing sound. From a small hole in the grass beside the board we could see the big yellow and black bumble bees coming and going. We knew there was a nest, a colony, but how big was a mystery. Arming ourselves with a solid, light board a couple feet long and a few inches wide we kicked the cover board aside and faced the hoard.

There was another precaution that we were keenly aware of. A dead bumblebee is as good a stinger as a live one. We surmised that they always died belly up with their stingers projected upward. Bare feet were the height of stupidity for this campaign.

Bumblebees are a fascinating insect. They are closely related to the honeybee, but do not store large quantities of honey—enough for a day or so only, and then go hunting for more. They do pollinate flowers but on a more limited scale than honey bees. Swarms of up to fifty bees live in holes in the ground—sometimes dug by other insects or even animals—or under rocks or limbs or boards. They have an SUV-like body—short wheel base and high center of gravity. Unlike the honeybee, their stingers are not barbed so they can sting as many times as is convenient. They use this feature well. They are not a belligerent enemy, or an enemy at all, and do not attack humans unless disturbed.

Kicking off their cover obviously disturbed them and they responded as we knew they would. We were ready. They flew well but not fast and were so visible that it was easy to keep them located. Their massive bodies made a distinct thud as the board made contact. The only problem was, at first they had us badly outnumbered and the air was loaded with attackers. We swung fast and kept keenly alert. Mid-air swats were usually a knock out. It was better to hit them on the fly where there was no danger of breaking a board by hitting the ground too hard. Usually, before these gladiatorial contests, we had the foresight to have a spare board on hand in case of a break. Gradually their numbers dwindled and we began to relax. At last we had nothing left but a rehash of the marvelous victory.

What a difference seventy years of living can make. This story of my irresponsible young days seems appalling to me now. No thoughts of environmental responsibility then. No thoughts of my relationship to the natural world then and to bees in particular. The world of the early twenty-first century is not the world of the middle twentieth century. We now know so much more of where we have been and where we must go.

Those days were full of planning and dreaming. In the wintertime I hunted and trapped and felt the real independence of an early pioneer. More than once each winter a friend or I would be sent home from school because we smelled too much like the little black kitten with two white stripes down its back that we had trapped that morning. One best friend, Bill, and I read stories of the north woods of Canada and Alaska, and our only life's ambition was to become a lone trapper in the wilds of Alaska and run our trap lines for miles. By summer, we were cowboys and Indians. My mother made a beautiful Indian chief's headdress for me. It was a band of red and yellow cloth with turkey feathers sewed into them to make a crown around my head and down my back. It was my pride and joy for several summers.

I subscribed to catalogs of Western riding clothes and cowboy-style gear and saddles of all prices. Cowboys wore leather chaps over their Levis to protect their legs from rough brush as they rode the range, and boots for protection from snakes. I needed a pair of chaps. Of course there was no rough brush that I would be riding through, but they would look so neat. From old worn out binder canvases my mother made a pair of chaps. They weren't leather, but even though the canvas was old it was stiff and served the simulation perfectly. It was hard to cut and even harder to sew. She may have been unwilling to use her sewing machine because the canvas was too heavy for it and she didn't want to damage her machine, so it was hand work all the way. But she did it and I wore them proudly.

When I wasn't a cowboy or a trapper, my boyhood imagination turned to airplanes. I never saw a real one until I was in high school. But I pored over pictures whenever I could. The National Geographic, on display in the tiny library shelf in the one room schoolhouse, gave me much to think about. I built a miniature airport in one corner of the yard and fantasized flying in and landing in the dirt runways I scraped out. When I was older, I built model planes of solid wood. I had a small turning-lathe to shape the fuselage, and carved and sanded wings and tail surfaces until I had what I wanted.

Those were the days when cereal box tops brought real toys. I saved the tops from Wheaties boxes until I had enough to get a balsa and tissue paper, rubber band plane with a wingspan of fourteen inches. It was winter when I finally got it assembled, so instead of the wheels in the kit, I fashioned skis and used the snow banks for take-off and landing. To this day, I have a couple of cold-sensitive fingers from the frostbite I got while winding up the rubber band with bare hands.

The hardware store in Eldora was a favorite wishing well. Each fall the windows were decorated with cornstalks, pumpkins and branches of fall trees and displayed guns and every kind of hunting equipment one could want. When I was ten, I picked out the rifle I wanted—a 22 caliber, bolt-action repeater. My Dad promised I could have it when I turned twelve. So for the next two years, every time we went to town, I checked it out to see if it was still available. It always was, so I eagerly saved every penny I could stash away. On my twelfth birthday I put my money down and became the proud owner of a new shiny rifle. For the next few years, I spent many hours polishing the walnut stock, keeping the metal blued and the barrel clean.

Dad taught me how to be safe with the gun and I followed his instruction. I never had an accident, but one of my best friends, Larry, did. We had been hunting squirrels in a timber near his place and hadn't bagged a single one all morning. I left for home while he continued to hunt on his way back to his house. As he crossed over a fence—a particularly dangerous operation—his gun went off and a bullet went through his hand. It was an impressive lesson for all the boys in school—obey the safety rules and unload your gun when climbing a fence.

I have no idea how much my parents sacrificed during those Depression years to give my brother and sister and me the material things we required to grow up. But it is clear they gave us all the spiritual sustenance we needed for a happy and sheltered childhood.

There were only a few times when the protective shield my parents built around us cracked and I could see some of the sacrifices they were making. There was a time when a car salesman would come to the farm to talk to my dad for hours and try to convince him that he could afford a new car. He wanted one so badly that he finally agreed. The dealer had a new frosted-green Chevrolet on hand—price: Eight hundred and fifty dollars. Down payment was ten dollars and he made it. The car was delivered and the family sat in it, caressed it and smelled it, but a couple days later reality began to set in. Dad knew we couldn't really afford it and called off the deal. The shiny new Chevy was returned, and we made do with our old car. Even the down payment was returned.

Tax time was another tough time. Taxes came due in March and required us to sell a load of corn, or a cow or a couple of pigs ahead of prime, to cover the bill. Sufficient cash flow to cover a debt like that just didn't exist. My mother kept detailed financial records in a narrow, tall, lined account book. She penciled in every sale of eggs and every loaf of bread she bought and in a separate column she entered every one or two cents spent on sales tax on every item.

My dad was my mentor. He was always right. I respected his judgment and knew exactly what he expected of me. I don't remember lectures on smoking, but I knew for sure I was not supposed to. He didn't smoke and that told the whole story. In spite of that, I did have one smoking experience with a neighbor boy. When the corn was way over our heads and the silks were dry in the fall, we ventured into the field, and with toilet paper and dry corn silks we rolled our own and lit up. It didn't seem to do anything for us, so we left it behind.

As I grew older my responsibilities and status grew. In high school I was part of the local 4-H program. Each boy had a livestock project that consisted of choosing an animal—hog, beef calf, dairy cow, poultry, and taking care of it, feeding, bedding, training, currying, and manicuring. The county fair, in late summer, was the climax of the project unless it was good enough to make the State Fair. In that case it took more grooming, more training and more time. Unruly calves in the show ring could be disqualified. They weighed in the neighborhood of a thousand pounds, so a small boy on the end of the halter rope couldn't coerce one into doing anything—they had to be trained to do as you wanted. The secret was to start when they were small, when you could handle them, and never let them realize, as the feeding and the year went on, how much bigger than you they were becoming.

Farm animals, and especially kids' livestock projects, presented a strange phenomenon: there was care, concern, and even love, but it all ended as a piece of meat on the table. Young boys and girls gave all their attention and energy to the animals in their care. They became pets. Their pens were kept clean with fresh straw bedding, and they could count on feed as regularly as clockwork. In the winter, ice was broken off their watering pails every morning and evening. I couldn't have treated my best friend any better.

My projects were always beef calves and hogs. The school year started with the added glorious experience of going with my dad to visit farmers in the county who specialized in raising calves for the 4-H shows. We wandered the fields and feed lots inspecting every 200-pound calf we could get close to. It was always in the fall when the weather was clear and the sun warm in the middle of the day. We went only on dry days so we didn't slosh around in mud. It was always an experience of high hope. Every fall, before the work and expense began, I fantasized about the huge sale of a prized animal that would bring a triple price. My dad taught me what to look for in a calf that would do well as a feeder and as a show calf—deep body, straight back, well-muscled shoulders and straight well-placed legs, and many other features. We looked at their eyes, their ears, their tails, and their ancestry. Purebreds were more expensive and out of my class. My livestock had not only to present itself well in the show ring, but even more importantly had to have the possibility of making some money. Mine always did, and each year added to my bank account, so that at the end of high school I put myself part way through college.

It's hard to remember how impossibly large some things may seem to a twelve-year-old boy. Take for instance a twenty-acre cornfield ready for the first cultivation.

Corn in the thirties was "checked." That meant it was planted in rows forty inches apart, but also in rows forty inches apart at right angles to the first set of rows. You could sight down the rows from either the east-west direction or the north-south direction. This was accomplished by stretching a wire along one side of the field, staked securely at each end, where the planting was to start. This was a smooth wire except for a knot precisely every forty inches. It rode in a forked mechanism at the side of the two-row planter. The wire slid through the fork, but when it came to a knot it pulled the fork back which released three seeds into the ground in each row. So the planter moved down the field—click, click, click planting three seeds in both rows every forty inches.

With good moisture and sunshine to warm the soil it took about seven days for the corn to pop through the ground. "Well, you can 'sight' that west field this morning," my dad would happily announce when the first plants showed up.

Within ten days, the first cultivation began with the corn running in close competition with foxtail, morning glories, button weeds and anything else that grows between rows. As soon as early breakfast was over I arrived in the field with my team and one-row cultivator. With one horse on each side of the row, sitting on a seat that straddled the row, one foot on each side of the row in a stirrup that allowed me to guide the shovels as they churned through the dirt, I began my day. With only the sounds of the jingling harness and the swish of the black soil beneath my feet, it was easy to realize I wasn't in the field alone. Crows, jays, meadow larks, robins and red winged blackbirds were delighted with the new prospects for food that crawls and jumps from the newly turned-up soil. I felt useful and at peace. The sun felt warm on my back as I headed north down that first row. Still, that eternal field was ahead of me—I knew I would never live long enough to see it all plowed.

One morning, on the second cultivation, when the stalks were about a foot high, I "fell asleep at the cultivator." After about ten stalks of corn were clipped off beneath the ground, the extra, fatal crunching sound woke me up. I don't know if it was my intrinsic dishonesty or naivety that prompted me to stop the horses, and go back and set all those plants in the ground. They looked green and straight as I climbed back on the cultivator and called "gid-up."

Fortunately for me, I was the one who cultivated that field for the third and last time. But suddenly, at a certain spot in the field, short, yellow stalks were flowing underneath. I knew exactly where I was and what had happened. I was well old enough to know that plants without roots have no way of getting water and die within hours. Kids are a great help on a farm, but they are not always a one-hundred-percent asset.

The thrashing rings of the thirties in the Midwest were not simply "intentional" like some these days, but a true cooperative with a sound economic basis for existence. They were eminently successful. They sprang from the need to get the acres of oats harvested and the grain into bins and the straw into barns or piles during the warm, dry late summer months before the snow began to fly. Before the advent of the combine, it was an operation that could barely be accomplished single-handed. The financial investment in a thrashing machine was far too much for small farmers, and unnecessary. A machine that could thrash for one farm was big enough to thrash for ten. Cooperation was the answer. The work needed a crew to haul the bundles in from the fields, and a crew to pitch bundles from the shocks on the ground onto the hayracks of the haulers. It needed people to haul the grain and scoop it into bins. It needed individuals to man the power source and individuals to supervise the separator. These were all working at once and almost continuously from the time the dew dried off the fields in mid-morning to almost sundown.

A group of five to ten farmers, whose fields were in close proximity, formed a Thrashing Ring Co-op. If they were able, they put in enough money to collectively buy a grain separator and a steam engine to power it. Sometimes they borrowed for part of the capital outlay.

A grain separator was literally a thirty-foot long thrashing machine—early ones were wooden and later ones metal. It separated the oats from the straw and chaff by feeding the bundles from the field wagons into a set of rotary knives and beaters. The oats fell three feet onto shakers, sieves and blowers to get the chaff separated out, then worked their way to the bottom-center of the machine. They were augured to one side, elevated above the separator into an automatic half-bushel recording scale, then out to a waiting wagon. The straw was blown the length of the machine to a large blower feeding a fourteen-inch tube to get the straw into a barn or large stack. Each farmer decided where his straw would go.

"Setting" the separator and engine was a precision process. The "separator man," using a simple bubble level, cleared the chaff from chosen spots and leveled the separator both sidewise and lengthwise to keep the oats moving smoothly through the machine—one man with a spade dug some wheels in while others he blocked up. Two men, working together, looped the sixty-foot flat belt over the single large pulley ten feet off the ground on the separator and around the large pulley, also ten feet off the ground on the steamer. The "engine man" took great pride as he backed the black monster carefully away from the separator to tighten the belt to precisely align his engine with the belt and separator. With the engine set, and the wheels blocked, he gently tapped the throttle and the belt began to move. Every pulley on the separator came silently into rotation. If the big belt stayed on, alignment was perfect, if not it flew off. As the engineer pushed the throttle firmly forward the big knives began to slice the air, shakers began to shake and blowers to blow. The two synchronized machines settled into a steady low roar and the days work began.

The black steel steam engine was powerful, slow and heavy. The ten-foot-tall rear steel drive wheels crushed everything in their path. The one-third-as-big front wheels were steered by heavy log chains. Each farmer provided a pile of lump coal near where he knew the engine would sit. The engineer, sitting like a king near the firebox door at the rear, cranked the heavy cast iron steering wheel to keep the engine in place when on the road.

The steam engine pulled the separator from farm to farm, and used its belt-drive capability while thrashing. It stayed at each place long enough to thrash that farmer's acreage of oats and then moved on. Some farms took a day, others took more. I used to thrill at the sight of the rig coming to our place. It moved slowly but steadily down the road. The coal-fired boiler puffed alternately noisy black smoke and quiet white steam. Every rise in the road required more power and the black monster responded with deep chug, chugs and clouds of black smoke. When it came under the overhanging trees of our driveway and up the slight incline, it shook the limbs to the trunk and enshrouded them in black coal smoke. It was an awesome sign of progress and of the big workday ahead.

Farm wives and daughters were an integral part of the whole. My mother was a good cook, as were all her friends, and meal planning for threshers began long before harvest time. The women even canned some fruits and vegetables early in anticipation of the coming annual event. Schedules were a bit iffy because weather was a major determiner of work. The grain in the fields had to be dry for the machinery to work. The women planned meals a few days ahead but were always aware that a sudden rain could postpone the big day. Once they were sure the meal was really going to happen they baked the pies at the last minute.

Thrashing-ring meals were more than just a meal. Young men (and old, too) were happy to be in the company of the young women (and old, too) who were equally conscious of being watched. My dad was anxious for his wife to be known as a good cook and gracious host. My mother was anxious to impress the men who would take a detailed report of her meal and table home to their wives. My mother worked hard, conscious that her reputation was at stake. She found dozens of things to worry about. Mashed potatoes without lumps were an absolute necessity, so she would beat boiled potatoes into a creamy smooth texture. Gravy of just the right thickness and taste complimented the potatoes. She chopped fresh cabbage from the garden into a large round wooden bowl, and flooded it with sweet cream sauce and set it aside in the pantry ahead of time. If the season was right, sweet-corn-on-the-cob was a real treat. These farm people were not vegetarian—in fact I never ran across the word until many years later. Anyone who tried to live without meat would be strange indeed. Roast beef and fried chicken were served on the table in large, piled-high platters.

It took great skill to put on a large meal with twenty or so hungry eaters, getting it all together at the same time, with some dishes appropriately hot and some appropriately cold. My mother was a master at this, and it worked out every year. After it was all over, she could pick out details that she wished had been different, but never found any major flaws. As night came on and the big engine out by the barn slowed to a quiet hiss, the jingling of horses and the yelling of men ceased. Mother would be tired, but happy and proud of her day as she smoothed the tablecloth where hours before sweaty men had crowded around. She reveled in the remembered mingled smells of working men, fried chicken and baked bread. My eight-year-old sister, Margaret, worked the long day beside my mother in the kitchen, stirring, setting aside, arranging utensils, stacking plates and all the many little things that had to be in place for a very important meal. She knew her way around and had learned many of the meal-making rituals. Margaret's light blond curls and happy smile made her a favorite for teasing among hungry farmers.

The crowning close of the season was the traditional ice cream supper. We met at one of the farm homes for potluck supper followed by more ice cream than was good for anyone. While the women got supper in order, the men cranked out the ice cream. Refrigerators were not common in the 1930s, but one of the neighbors had an ice house and sold ice through the summer. It was ice sawed from the frozen lake in the middle of the winter and packed in sawdust for the summer. A large suspended scale and pair of ice tongs hung beside the door. The block size you needed was chipped from a larger block, picked up with the tongs and weighed and sold. It was a near-zero energy enterprise. I don't remember commercial ice cream existing at all, at least not among our family or those of the thrashing ring. Ice cream freezers were an essential tool on every family's list. Standard recipes abounded, but one wife had a recipe for a sweet white ice cream—I loved it. Most were a rich cream color. The process took several minutes of steady hand cranking, then the welcome feel of the mixture beginning to congeal. The process ended with all of the kids who could crowd around licking the paddles. I remember being embarrassed by my dad's excess. He was a master ice cream eater. It didn't hurt him, and everyone else did the same. The talk, as we ate, was of horses and engines and yields of oats—whose did the best, and where the weedy spots were.

An early September morning in Iowa also had its own peculiar characteristic smell and sound. Corn was everywhere, and wet from the dew and frost, had a wonderful, indescribable pungent smell of its own.

We picked corn by hand. It took a very nimble, steady rhythmic motion to grab the ear on the side of the stalk, and with a steel hook on your cotton mitten, open the husk, grab the ear, twist it off and throw it into the wooden wagon with a bang. As one hand threw the ear the other was reaching for the next one. Husking mittens had double thumbs so that when the face of the mitten wore out it could be turned over and the back with the new thumb doubled its life.

The wagon, pulled by a team of horses, had one side built up four to five feet higher than the other. This made a bang board that the picker hit with every ear he picked. There was no question which neighbors were in the field that morning. The sounds were easily identifiable and carried for miles over the quiet morning air.

The horses were often trained to stop and start just enough to keep the picker beside the wagon. But many others were told by the picker to stop and start. Corn picking was a vigorous job for a month or two each fall. If a person was right handed, his right arm, which did all the twisting and throwing, was soon feeling the strain. The fall was usually spent with an increasingly sore arm and wrist, sometimes even to the point of having to stop for a day or two for recovery. Early morning cornfields were always wet from heavy dew, but as the season progressed from fall to winter the dew changed to frost. Within minutes after starting to pick, one's cotton mittens were soaked and icy.

Sometimes a husband and wife team could pick two hundred bushels a day. This usually meant a daughter or other family helped with meals and child care. The fall corn picking season was undoubtedly the most physically active time of the year for the men while food preservation took long, hot, summer days for the women.

As the sun rose steadily above the horizon, rhythmical pounding on the bang boards increased as more farmers arrived in their fields and began picking. For most farmers, picking corn was not the only day's activity. Cows had to be milked, and hogs, cattle and horses fed before breakfast. After breakfast, the horses were harnessed and hitched to the wagon and then went jingling to the field of waiting, frosty corn.

The wagon usually held fifty to sixty bushels of corn and was often filled by noon and scooped off by hand before dinner—the noon meal. The more affluent farmers had elevators that were powered by an electric motor if the farm had electricity, and by a small gas engine if it didn't. Usually, accompanying this equipment was a lift for the front of the wagon so that the corn poured out over the wagon end-gate directly into the elevator hopper.

For the noon break, the horses were often fed and watered without unhitching. They ate their oats and munched on hay while the farmer ate his meal. As the sun sank low on the western horizon, the second load came in. This time the horses had to be unhitched, unharnessed, watered, stalled, and fed before the farmer was ready to do chores and eat supper.

A good corn crop meant cash in the bank; some cribbed corn was actually sold for cash sometime during the coming year. Once the crop was in the crib, everyone wondered what price it would fetch. Family get-togethers with other farmers always meant a lot of talk and guessing of the future of corn prices. Oats and hay were mostly fed on the farm to chickens or cattle with a small portion used for the horses to do the needed work. Most of the corn produced on the farm was used to fatten hogs and cattle. If it was a poor crop, it meant that corn had to be bought or the hogs or cattle sold before "finishing" and that meant a lower price.

Ear corn, as opposed to shelled corn, was stored in slotted buildings. The horizontal siding was spaced wide enough to let air in, but close enough to keep ears of corn inside, and the yellow corn was readily visible from outside the red painted structure. They were long narrow buildings designed for maximum movement of air through the corn. Warm, dry, fall days furnished perfect natural ventilation so that corn harvest could start early, when the corn was wet, but be dry enough for mold-free keeping before winter set in. No fuel of any kind was used in those days for drying corn. As the fall days progressed from early September into late October, the yellow line on the sides of corncribs rose steadily, day after day, as the telltale mark of how harvesting was going.

The September days were long and the nights short, and life was demanding and productive. One could always see the results of his or her efforts and that was satisfying. Happiness, in those days, was defined not by gadgets and leisure, but the satisfying accomplishments of mind and muscle.

When we were a little older, Jerry and I, with our grandfather's help, built a light, two-wheeled surrey with shaves to fit Dolly. It was made from old buggy parts with no springs and a plank-board seat wide enough for two. The wheels were standard steel-rimmed buggy wheels. We sometimes rode together and sometimes one or the other of us had a friend visiting who rode with us. The demise of the surrey came about one sunny day that should have been a day like all others. We were both on the surrey and on the way home about a quarter mile away. Something startled the pony, which was a pretty standard occurrence, and she headed for home on a dead run. No amount of cajoling or pulling on the lines could slow her down. She rounded the curve into the driveway with no problem, navigated the corner of the yard with no problem, cleared the windmill and headed straight for the open barn door. That particular door was a heavy-duty door and wider then many. The pony cleared easily, but not us or the surrey. The wheels stopped when they hit the sides of the barn, but Dolly went on. The harness was stripped, the wheels smashed, the shaves broken in halves and the surrey splintered to shambles. When the dust settled, Dolly was calmly eating hay with harness parts still dangling from her neck.

The sunrise chore of bringing in the cows for milking was not always a pleasant job. We had a small twenty acre pasture adjoining the barns and hog lots. My dad often pastured the milk cows there during the summer. It was good pasture of alfalfa and brome grass and maybe some timothy mixed in. Pure alfalfa pasture can be very dangerous for milk cows. They love it and can easily overeat. It has a tendency to produce bloat in the cow's stomach, which can increase internal pressure and kill the animal. One solution when using pure alfalfa pasture is to carefully limit allowed grazing time on it. This takes good management and is risky.

A much more acceptable solution was to plant some non-bloating grasses with the alfalfa so that it is impossible for cows to eat too much alfalfa because they can't select what they are getting. My dad used this practice and never worried about bloat in his dairy cattle.

But timothy and brome grass can grow to three feet high or more in the summer, and that was the problem. Grass of any height in the early morning is always uniformly covered with dew. If you don't touch the plant the dew stays put, but the least shake and it all falls off.

Over a period of weeks of grazing the cows had made their own paths throughout the pasture. They branched out from the gate near the barn to the far end of the pasture like branches from a tree. The seven or eight cows grazed between the branches and were scattered over the pasture. My first attempt to get them into the lot was to stand in the gate and call them. Sometimes this worked and they would slowly stop grazing and wend their way to the barn. But usually it didn't work—they simply stopped grazing, looked at me and went back to clipping off the grasses.

Cows don't chew what they eat at that time. They bite off pasture grasses and deposit the bites in one stomach. Later, at their leisure as they lie resting, small amounts are coughed up, chewed, and swallowed into another stomach. As a youngster, I loved to watch this process. A few minutes after a cow lies down, you can see the cud coming up her neck. She chews it a while, then you can see the bulge sliding down her throat as she swallows it. She waits a few seconds and another cud comes up. She chews, swallows, and half dozes the morning away.

If the cows chose not to respond to my calling, I was faced with the miserable prospect of going out into that sea of waist high, chilly grasses to round them up. If I followed their paths carefully I could sometimes get them in without getting soaking wet. Usually I couldn't. Instead, they grazed until I got behind them and shooed them toward the gate. That usually meant cutting between their paths, and of course, shaking all the available dew onto my clothes.

Cows are by nature a very curious animal. If some unknown object—machinery or strange animal—arrives in their pasture, they will always gather around to sniff it out. Sometimes an object driving by on the road beside the pasture—like a load of new hay—attracts their attention and they gather at the fence and follow it as far as possible.

But their attitude is far more than just curiosity—they are ridiculously playful. I think they realized this morning ritual was at someone else's expense! Too many times I got them up to the open gate, but not through it, and they stood there waiting for me to shoo them on in. As I came up soaking wet and ice cold within a hundred feet of them, they would put their heads down, kick up their heels and with their tails straight up, head on a dead run for the far ends of the pasture. I could almost hear them yelling "Let's high-tail it out of here." In mocking derision, they went back to calmly grazing—looking up occasionally to see how I was taking their prank. I didn't see them laughing, but I knew they were.

I didn't take it well. Their behavior made me furious—soaking wet and cold because of their devious behavior. First, they could have, of course, come in when I called them. Second, if that wasn't to their liking, they could have stayed close to the paths and come in as I got reasonably well behind them. I could have stayed on the paths and kept dry. Lastly, even if they forced me off the paths to get closer behind them, they could have gone through the gate and not prolonged the agony by forcing me to conduct a second roundup.

I always did get them into the barn eventually. These were milk cows and as the time got later, their udders grew fuller and the pressure reminded them that relief was available in the milking barn. What they didn't know was that their waterloo was awaiting them. The milking barn was a set of eight stanchions with a feeding trough in front of the stanchions. The animals willingly put their heads through the stanchions to get at the grain they loved, at which point they would be locked in. They ate while being milked. It was a good arrangement—they were comfortable, got fed, and my dad, Jerry, and I would sit on our one-legged stools and milk them one at a time.

But I had an uncontrollable problem. I was so furious; I was literally shaking with anger. And I took it out on the stanchioned cows. I was the only one there at first, so I had the herd at my mercy. I did terrible things to them before sitting down to milk. The first thing I did was to twist a tail or two until it really hurt. Their heads were locked in but their rear ends were free to dance about. And the tail twisting really brought dancing. As I cooled down, to some I gave a kick or two and then calmed down enough to start milking.

This behavior was totally unacceptable for a good herdsman, and at fifteen, I knew better. Milk cows produce best if treated gently and never abused. I knew I was violating all the rules of good management. The guilt laid heavily on me as the summer went on. My dad remarked once about a cow with a crooked tail and wondered how it could happen. But my guilt stayed deeply hidden and a carefully guarded secret.

I worried and thought. I was angry and dismayed at myself for getting so angry. I knew I had to find a way to live peacefully with my cows. I gradually began to reason with myself that the cows were living up to the nature of cows much better than I was living up to the nature of a reasonable human being. I figured out that the early morning soaking didn't hurt me in the least—by the time the chores were done I was dried off and comfortable. Dealing with the idiosyncrasies of dairy cows was a normal part of farming, and I was the loser not to accept their nature with grace. As these thoughts gradually settled deeper into my consciousness, I decided I could change my attitude by simple mental effort. So I did. I found great peace and satisfaction in finding that I could get wet most mornings and sit down and milk without rancor. Cows have short memories, and I assume they soon forgave me for past sins. In any case they kept producing, and I kept milking.

CHAPTER 3

NEW PROVIDENCE DAYS AND MISTAKEN IDENTITY

Lois:

Aug. '39-May '40

This year may have saved my life, kept me out of an institution. I didn't bloom, but I budded a bit, and of course, it shaped my whole life to come.

Roy and Edna were so good to me in an offhand way, and I was never able to express how much I loved them and appreciated their gifts to me of being themselves and seeming to accept me.

September 1, 1939

Dear Anna Mae,

Wow what a beginning. Well, here I am in New Providence, Iowa. A great metropolis of 350 inhabitants. The whole school from kindergarten through high school has 123 members. The largest class having 18 pupils. I will be the 124 pupil. School begins Monday. We don't get a holiday for Labor Day. I'm awfully scared and excited. I have to rent my books and everyone carries a lunch pail except the poorest ones Bonnie said (more about her later), So I guess I will have to get a lunch pail.

I will go on a school bus and oh, how I dread getting on it all alone not knowing anyone next Monday. It makes me have butterflies flittering in my innards just to think of it.

The country here is just beautiful. There are little nothing lumps all over everywhere. People here call them hills, but they would probably call Grizzly Peak, Mount Fujiama (so you can imagine what high hills they are.)

The men are making hay now and my second cousins, Bonnie and Robert, and I go up in the hay mow and play in it. Oh, kids did you ever play in a hay mow or on a wagon load of it. It's just glorious. It smells so fresh and clean, and you can jump from way up high into it and not hurt yourself at all unless it's packed down a lot. Robert climbed clear up on the roof of the barn and jumped into it, but he's not a bit afraid of high places.

Oh I almost forgot. I went out in the fields where they were making hay and rode out in the hayrack. You have to stand up in the things because if you sit down they are so jiggly that you would get a splinter jiggled right into you, "I know," says the voice of experience. I can stand up without holding on now but every once in a while if it lurches forward I fall down kerplunk and then Bonnie and Robert and Enos the hired man laugh at me and call me a, "city slicker," which I am. When I was out in the fields I rode on the tractor while they were gathering hay.

Love again to everybody, Lois

Lois:

My first afternoon, two cousins a year or so younger than I, led me on a tour of the farm. They were sturdy, secure, knowledgeable and friendly as they led me in my new brown oxfords through the pasture where the cows were grazing. I liked them a lot. Suddenly my foot squished into a fresh cow pie; the toe of my shoe up to my laces was covered. We laughed and continued the trek although I was most anxious to wash off this stinky stuff. I was stricken when I cleaned that shoe in the basement washtub to find that it was permanently stained with a pale greenish/tan tone, lighter than the other shoe. It never occurred to me that I could tell someone about this. I knew I would have to go to school wearing those shoes. And I did. And no one ever mentioned them to me.

In September 1939 Hitler invaded Poland and I was aware that invasion and war in Europe were bad events for people. For me September was learning simple chores: gathering eggs and feeding chickens, walking into the western sun after school to bring in chopped wood and corncobs to feed the cook stove, learning that to ride the school bus you didn't need a token to drop into the glass box. There was no glass box.

Aunt Edna bought me a heavy, wine/brown tweed winter coat (I loved it), and my first heels, black patent pumps about an inch and a half high, worn with my first long stockings. These were heavy rayon affairs that wrinkled at the knee but girls wore them to school for warmth all winter. I also reveled in a navy two piece "snow suit" to wear for sledding and ice skating, neither of which I did very much, but the few times were special with cousins Bob and Bonnie, and other kids from school or church.

Don:

I clearly remember our first ice skating party. We were a group of church kids who gathered at the church and took a bus from there to Pine Lake. The ice on the edge of the lake had been scooped free of snow forming a glass-slick area about the size of a basketball court. A steeply sloped bank of fifty feet or so led from the parking area directly onto the ice. Lois, bent on making the most of her introduction to outdoor skating, led the pack down the path onto the ice. With first contact she went flat on her back. Then, with more caution and respect, she enjoyed the night.

Those kinds of parties always called for a bonfire on the edge of the ice where skaters could warm frozen hands and feet. Even with single digit temperatures, hot chocolate and warm relationships kept spirits high until time to reload the bus.

Lois:

My room had a south and west window, one looking onto the gravel road where the school bus came and the other onto a double row of pines that constantly whispered in the perpetual Iowa wind. I slept in a double bed that had a dark walnut headboard as tall as I, and a slightly lumpy mattress with no give to it. Along part of one wall was a three-drawer dresser with a marble top and a mirror taller than I. The bottom drawer was my place for books and school stuff, diary, letters. There was a small closet for hanging things. The room was really bare, with cream-colored walls and a small braided rug to step out of bed onto on freezing mornings. I loved that place.

I had joined a community where belonging to church and being a good farmer were primary requirements. Family history helped, too. I had become one of the establishment! Frequently, at church, some old lady would inquire about my dad, "How is he getting along? He was such a good singer. We were friends with him and Lucile in school." Sometimes there were anecdotes about my folks: Lucile's initials scratched into the window of the telephone office where the Kersey family lived; the double wedding of my folks with my dad's cousin Charlie Wood and Ethel. Remembering people and history with them surprised me. I hadn't realized my parents had roots, a life before California and our family. It gave me a feeling of belonging I had never felt before.

Uncle Roy's son Oscar and his wife Marjorie moved into the tenant house close by. All that year one or both frequently bopped into our house for brief visits. Oscar was a great jokester/gag man, and he and his mother made a good show. Cousins Bonnie and Robert often visited their grandparents and I sometimes went home with them for an overnight. This was a kind of bustling bunch of open family connections entirely new to me. Aunt Edna especially worried about her daughter, Aletha, Bonnie and Robert's mother, with her second marriage to a kind of ne'er-do-well but charming, Jimmy was good at reproducing. Bob and Bonnie had two little stepbrothers and a stepsister. I loved them all.

It was a year of social life and friends, Ruth Williams and Leslie Drier were my favorites. Church activities, (a revival), Christian Endeavor, drama club at school,

36

Friday night basketball games, junior-senior banquet, these were revolutionary fun to feel a part of.

And there was Don. So much for the girl not yet interested in dating and boys. I was stunned when the phone ringing in our kitchen was for me and a boy asked me to go to the movies with him, saying his name was Laughlin. Oh yes, I knew a Jerry in my class. Aunt Edna said I could go, that Laughlins were a good family. When a stranger came to the door, I was floored. It wasn't Jerry but a similar look in a shorter version, two years older and a senior, named Don.

Don:

She was a sophomore that year and I was a senior. Our paths around school didn't cross easily, but they did. I watched her for days whenever I could—watched her make friends with other kids and gradually meld into a small rural high school. She seemed happy and laughed a lot and was a natural cut-up. I was just the opposite, so I felt a strong affinity to someone of the opposite sex with carefree characteristics that I admired but couldn't achieve. She became popular with some students, and her voice, slightly deeper than most young girls, stood out. It was rich and full and mature. It was not a native Iowa voice. It represented a girl I had to get to know. It beckoned relentlessly.

I fretted for days trying to get up nerve and figure out how to make contact with her. Finally, I asked my mother for advice. She knew Roy and Edna Wood very well and approved of their young niece. My folks and the Woods had known each other since childhood and been members of the local Friends Church all their lives. They had probably talked about Lois many times since her arrival in late August. My mother said simply "Why don't you just call her up?" What an obvious and sensible solution, but so difficult to achieve!

When I made the call, I was so flustered I didn't make it clear who I was. I was sixteen that fall, and it was my first time making a formal date by telephone. We hadn't really met before this, and I was much more aware of her than she was of me. I had been watching her closely, but I don't think she had ever noticed me. So the call was to a stranger whom I wanted to get to know. I felt awkward but I was successful.

Lois:
October 20, 1939
Dear Anna Mae,

You've heard of Jerry haven't you? Well last Monday after school the phone rang and it was one of the Laughlin boys (and I thought it was Jerry) asking me to go to Eldora to the show with him. Well of course I went when Aunt Edna said I could. I was upstairs when he came and I came downstairs into the front room expecting to see Jerry but there was his brother Don. He is a senior. Whew, I must have looked awfully surprised but I went with him and had a swell time considering....... I didn't think much about it except wish that it had been Jerry. But the next morning when I got on the bus the kids moved over so that the only seat I could take was by Don. (the Laughlins are on my bus.) Wednesday night there was a Sunday school party and when the cars came for the kids at the church, two girls pulled out of the front seat of Don's car and made it very clear that I was supposed to get in by him so I did and then later on we all went out to the cemetery. The kids all made way for me to get in by Don and it was so crowded I was practically sitting on his lap. Well gee-whiz, now all the kids say that Don likes me but I don't see why a senior would like a dopey sophomore like I am. And I don't like him (well I like him and he is a keen kid) but I like Jerry so much more and Jerry likes Arlene Newton, a darling freshman. Oh gosh it's a terrible mess and I wish that boys would like a girl when a girl likes a boy don't you? How are you and Sam coming? I hope it's a lot better than Jerry and I, I get the heeby jeebies just to look at him and I just can't talk to him without stuttering like a baby.

Lots of love, Lois

Lois:

That was the year of Disney's Snow White, of Bing Crosby's White Christmas, of "Have you forgotten so soon/That lovely night in June/The graduation dance/The glorious beginning of our beautiful romance/All the gay diversions we planned in advance/Have you forgotten so soon? Have you forgotten so soon/The sun upon the sand/The moon of yellow gold/The things at Coney Island that the fortune teller told/Air conditioned movies that gave us a cold/Have you forgotten so soon?" Don't you remember/The witches party on Halloween?/Oh that grand December/The whitest Christmas I'd ever seen." Well, the whitest Christmas, the Halloween party, they were all true for me, and the rest all fit into my haze of romance.

In spring, on one of those evenings with lingering warmth but with grass still soggy under foot, Roger and Sam, two non-academic boys in my class, took me for a ride to Pine Lake, a state park a dozen miles away. How come I was allowed to go with them? They were not from the best families. I will always remember how Sam danced with me beside the car while Roger manipulated the radio. One of the few times in my life when I really danced. He was a natural and made me into one.

On the first of May I learned about May baskets when Aunt Edna sent me out into the yard in search of the boys who had hung the wilted flowers on the door and knocked and run. One of them was Sam.

Don:

May basket hanging was a once-a-year fun time for kids. The tradition was for boys to put together some kind of paper basket—sometimes a cone of decorated newspaper—or left over wallpaper—with a paper handle—and fill it with popcorn, candy and flowers; then under cover of darkness, on the first day of May, hang it on a girl's door knob—holler "Maybasket!" and run and hide. Usually by then the plum trees and dandelions were in full bloom, and made good additions.

Of course we boys made sure we were always caught. It meant an inadvertent cough or sneezing from behind our bush, before the girl gave up, and it was easy to stumble or run too slowly to make catching assured. We knew all the available tricks to make the hanging worth the effort and turn out as we planned. The hope was always to be invited in for hot cocoa and cookies and, of course, visiting.

Lois:

It may have been one of the first years in my life where, much of the time, I felt easy, accepted, and aware of the privileges of belonging to a group. I was also aware of the family a mile up the road from us. Rodney and his sister got on the bus after my stop. They lived with their mother in a house one-third the size of Uncle Roy's, perched on an eroded bluff above the road. No one smiled at them or moved over to make space for them on the benches. Usually they were ignored, invisible, non-existent. Overt cruelty or heckling surely occurred sometimes, but I was blithely glad to be unaware. They were outsiders and I knew exactly how they hurt. I did not do one thing all year to be friendly or supportive.

CHAPTER 4

OUR LIVES CONVERGE

Don:

In addition to being a very particularly poignant season of the year, for me, September has a very special bittersweet taste. I met a young girl in September and lost my wife in October—with sixty-three years between those two months.

There was a rumor in town in the summer of '39 that one of our neighbors had invited a young niece to live with them for the school year. I couldn't have cared less, until one morning the school bus made a stop that hadn't been on the route the year before. The couple who lived there were older and their children were grown. The girl who timidly climbed the steps and looked for a place to sit was obviously in a new situation. Peering through thick-lenses she surveyed the rows of seats. The kids all stared as she wedged into a seat beside an unfamiliar girl. People in a small, close-knit, rural community don't show much grace in welcoming a stranger. But she smiled in her confusion and I, sitting farther back in the bus, knew immediately that I had to find out what was behind that smile. It was a smile I was destined to love and never forget for the rest of my life.

Many years in the future, incomprehensible to a sixteen-year-old boy, I watched it fade and change to a plea for help. "But I can't help you die, Loie."

"Yes, you can" she said.

The school she had come from was a big-city, California school of several thousand kids. The one she came to was a small town, rural Iowa school of one-hundred-twenty. Even in my old age I can't fathom the emotional strain that life had thrown at a fourteen-year-old girl. She bore up well and her active sense of humor was her saving grace that kept her from succumbing to deep depression.

I was no help to her in my naiveté and inexperience. As we dated that fall and winter I sometimes sensed that all was not well, and often interpreted it as something between us that I could not understand or help. She got letters from her father, and she occasionally reported on them. She was sometimes melancholy and we would end up somewhat short on conversation during our evening together. We both learned later that it was a year of transition for her father and in all probability she had been sent away so that he could be free to court a woman to take her mother's place. He wasn't one to divulge his secrets to his young daughter. For many years she felt cheated of his confidence and love, and this non-relationship was an important part of her later mental health. She was in her forties when she came to terms with her relationship with her father and was able to accept him as a normal fallible man. I'm not sure she was ever able to forgive him for his inability to confide to her his need for companionship. She would have been perfectly capable of sympathizing with him and even giving him confidence and permission to pursue his life as he saw it. But this bond was denied her and it haunted her for the rest of her life.

Our high school days were happy ones most of the time, and our relationship grew steadily more important to me. I was so happy and excited to secretly go shopping for a gold, heart-shaped locket. It had a light, feminine chain and clasp for the back of her neck. Never before had a gift been so important to me. I gave it to her, with a tiny picture of myself in it, on one of our dates just before Christmas. We were with a group singing Christmas carols on a cold, clear, starry, squeaky-snow night and I found a moment when we were by ourselves to pull it out of my pocket. She was surprised and delighted, and I was certainly happy too. We had been dating for four months.

As important as the moment was for me, Lois remembered it differently.

Lois:

Letter of 1/4/42

I don't know what the gift was. The only gift I remember is a round silver compact about two inches across that had a tiny mirror, a powder cake, and a thin powder puff. Don gave that to me the Christmas of 1939 when I was living in New Providence.

I loved that little thing although I never used it, never having learned to powder my nose. But I remember the feel of it in my pocket, and the possibilities of glamour, or at least normal femaleness, that it symbolized. And it was a gift from a boy for me!

Don:

My mother's parents lived on a small acreage on the edge of New Providence, Iowa, about three miles from our place. It was a small, rural town of 300 residents including dogs. It was a "one-of-each" town—one grocery store, one hardware store, one blacksmith shop, one telephone office, one radio repair shop, one bank, one school, one church, one graveyard, and a one block main street.

It was all so different for Lois whose early years were spent among miles of houses in all directions. Dozens of businesses abounded within blocks of her house. Her familiar streets were paved—mine were all gravel.

Our telephone company, for example, was a true co-op. Members were patrons of the community and had one vote per member. Its lines ran out from the office in all directions for a radius of ten miles or so. Each line had two to ten families on it. To call a family on your line you hand-cranked a series of shorts and longs. A short was one-half turn of the crank, and a long was a whole turn. Of course all the phones on the line rang when one did, so privacy was nonexistent. The operator could also listen in if she so wanted—and she often so wanted. To call a neighbor on another line you dialed the operator—one short—and she patched your line through to the other line. She was the source of all community gossip and news. If you couldn't reach your party she could tell you that he had just gone to the hardware. Crank the hardware and ask for Jim to be put on the line. Sometimes the phone ring would be one long, long ring—maybe fifteen seconds. That was a public announcement of some kind. "Widow Mables' house is on fire—

all hands are needed." Or "the Jack and Jill has cheese on sale at half price till noon today." It was a community like thousands of others the world over—loving, prejudiced, caring, gossipy—where rumor becomes fact with the speed of the wind.

And unlike Lois' urban upbringing, I had no experience with people of other races as I was growing up. There were no black people living in town, or the county as far as I can remember, and whenever they were referred to they were "niggers." I remember my grandfather using the term—not in a derogatory attitude, but as the only way he knew to identify African-Americans. I never met a black person until I was in college. I don't recall that race was ever mentioned in our home for the first eighteen years of my life. Everyone was as we are.

My grandparents' small acreage had a barn and enough space and pasture to carry a cow for milking or a calf or pig for butchering. It was always neat and picked-up with all tools in place and clean and oiled. Grandfather had time to keep the place in good shape. Cockleburs and horseweed popped up if you turned your back for one rain. North of the windbreak was a large raspberry patch. It was a maze of canes and hard to navigate, but loaded with berries if you could get to them. I spent many hours each summer working my way through the brambles. It was a peaceful and delightful time, with no small part of the attraction to me being the myriad of wrens flitting about in the hot, lazy summer days singing at volumes far beyond what their size could warrant.

I loved to spend the night at my grandparents, to sleep in the summertime in the screened-in porch over the back door. My cousin, several years older than I, sometimes slept there, too, and we would hear owls in the trees that he would try to imitate and coax closer to the house. Breakfast was sour buckwheat pancakes and maple syrup, which I have never experienced except there at grandmother's table.

Lois never met her grandparents; I saw mine often, and many Sunday noon meals were at their house. My grandfather was a semi-retired farmer and a caretaker of the local cemetery. He was a short, heavy-set man with white hair and a white mustache he dubbed his "cookie duster." He was jovial and liked by everyone. He was diabetic and not one to make much ado about ailments. So he largely ignored the symptoms of that malady that showed itself often as sores on his feet that didn't heal easily, if at all.

In our small town, our grandparents were like second parents, only better, so it was all the more jarring when, one night after a long and luxurious date with Lois, I came home driving the only car in the family and saw my parents' house all lit up and the folks waiting anxiously for me. My grandfather had died.

Another memorable end to a date with Lois came one night when she decided she was dressed too formally to go to the movies. She was not one to stand on convention, and she didn't like tight clothing. So this fourteen-year-old girl, on perhaps our third or fourth date, didn't hesitate to make herself more comfortable. With a pluck here and a pluck there and a bit of squirming she reached into her sleeve and pulled out her bra. It has always been an amazing and mysterious maneuver to me whenever the few times I've seen it done over the past seventy years. It wouldn't have been any more surprising if she had pulled a white rabbit out of her sleeve, or even a purple kangaroo for that matter. It was not a sexy ploy, I knew, just a matter of comfort. I kept driving and we chatted on.

The annual Junior/Senior banquet was a gala affair and we seniors spent many hours planning and decorating for the event. As a senior, I could invite anyone I chose. Lois was not the only sophomore there, but there weren't many others. It was near the end of the school year and we both knew that her time in Iowa was getting short. We made the most of it.

Her school year in Iowa was a blip in her life and mine, but the consequences were forever. For her it was a year of vastly new experiences from her life before she came and the one to which she returned. For me the word "California" took on a new and exciting and heavenly aura—it was a place of pure romance. It was no longer a state, but a place out of this world which I longed to see and be part of because it held the girl I loved. I thought of it as a land of flowers and "milk and honey" where everyone was happy. It seemed infinitely far away, but I was infinitely confident that I would get there somehow.

I was pleased to know she felt the same way about me, but that entire year was a significant, sometimes painful and often joyful transition in her life.

Lois:

Thursday November 2, 1939

Dear Anna Mae,

Anna Mae did you ever go to a show with Jackie Cooper or Deanna Durbin or Bobby Breen etc. where they went to a camp or a school and were real popular and had a lot of fun and everything was just perfect except for one blot and that all cleared up, so that they had a perfect ending? And did you ever wish or dream that it would happen to you? Well, I did and yet never dreamed it could be true, but this last week has been just as exciting and thrilling for me as any movie could be, so I guess I'll tell you about it.

It all began last Thursday when Don (have you heard the name before?) asked me if I would go to the 4.H. banquet with him. The banquet was last night. I said I would go and that's all we said about it. I knew that Don had bought my ticket because my name was down on the list and I hadn't put it there. But on Fri. he looked me right in the eye on the bus and didn't even smile at me and I felt sort of terrible about it cause he usually embarrasses me he smiles so noticeably. Well on Mon. I began to get sort of worried because he hadn't hardly said anything to me and I didn't see how I would get into the banquet if he had my ticket and I didn't go with him. And Tuesday I really was worried cause he only said "Hi", the whole day long and you know that when you worry you keep thinking of more things to worry about and so by Wed. I was homesick, didn't think anybody liked me, thought he was sorry he had asked me and that it was all a horrible mistake and mess. After school on Wed. when he hadn't said anything about it, I decided to rush over to the office and get a ticket for myself and go with Polly and the rest of the girls and just forget the whole affair (or try to) So I bought a ticket from "Donnie" Reece, and rushed out and got on the bus. I had hardly gotten settled on the bus when Don who was sitting next to me said out of a clear blue sky "Is it all right if I stop for you at about 6:30 or 20 to 7.?" Of course I said, "yes." So there I was minus the 35 cents cause I can't take that ticket I bought back, cause if he should find out, and things sure get around this town, I would just die. Well then comes this dreamy part!!!

The theme of the banquet was "School Daze," and we had dunce caps for mint cups and report cards for place cards etc. and Don was toastmaster and teacher and he was sort of mad cause they made him sit at a desk all by himself up in front of us (there were about 35 of us) to eat and announce the speeches and everything. One of the first speeches was "Jeep" Wright I don't know his first name, everybody calls him "Jeepers." He spoke on "Dates" and began very seriously about Columbus and Washington, etc. and then he said (I can't remember it as funny as it was) "and now we come to the year 1939 and a beautiful (ahem) girl is lying on a beach in "Sunny California" reading in a newspaper with a boy named Don who is going to be a great farmer and who gets "A's" in all of his Agriculture projects now." "Well she decided to come out and see his hogs and she liked the monkey so much better that she decided to become official guardian of him." And Anna Mae, then Leslie, who is the worst boy you could think of to have as a relative, and I'm not fooling said, "What's her name?" and old Jeeps said "Why can't you guess? It's that awful Wood girl." Then everybody just roared and I was as red as a beet and so was Don and they just laughed more at us and then Jeeps gave some more examples of kids around there. Towards the end of the dinner all of a sudden the kids began singing "stand up, stand up, stand up Don and Lois, stand up, stand up, etc." And they kept singing it and singing it and Don put his thumbs down and I was so embarrassed that I can't remember what I did, but finally we had to stand up and take a bow 'cause they were just deafening us. I sure felt funny 'cause Don's mother was serving and she's my Sunday School teacher. She's actually nice and afterward she didn't seem to mind, but I felt sort of cheap and some teachers were there, too.

Don:

4-H activities were an important part of a high school education in a community that had few occupations other than farming and related businesses. Agriculture was offered all four years, but no physics, chemistry or languages. Any biology was closely related to farm animals and crops.

Farm Shop was a course offered for juniors and seniors. Some of the boys overhauled tractors or cars. Non-farm boys often made wooden furniture. We learned to weld and use power tools. One of the years I built a small, portable hog house which I used in my animal project. It was a boys' class only. We learned self sufficiency and to solve problems without help. It was an age when one didn't "buy" a solution to a problem. Rather you "made" the solution with your own mind and tools and hands.

The 4-H program was more than just raising livestock or crops. It was a society of like-minded and like-motivated kids. The girls had their projects, too, but they were not generally livestock. They were concerned with homemaking— gardening, preserving food for winter, sewing and making clothing.

The public school there at that time was an institution for propagating the society we were all involved in. Each gender played its part with little crossover in education toward the life of the other. We mixed for social occasions which were a vital part of our growing up.

Lois:

Well that's all that happened but I did have a good time and after stewing all week it was a lark although sort of embarrassing. It's awfully easy to be popular here Anna Mae, cause there isn't very much competition and so just about anybody could be popular as the dickens. I'm sure going to get an awful let-down when I go back to "Uni. I sure hope I'll be able to take it after this perfect year. Of course I'm no belle here but I'm no wall-flower either. Gee, I wish you could be here, I know you'd like it cause you'd be so well liked too, and they just have the keenest times ever. The trouble is they don't realize it, they think it would be fun to go to formal parties and dance and play kissing games all evening but they have much more fun here. I'm sure going to be a wall flower when I go back home because I've completely forgotten how to dance. There's only one thing wrong with the parties here and that's that the kids sometimes go out in cars afterward and neck!!! Last night after the banquet Don and I and Jeep and Nadine went out in Don's car and I was so scared that I was actually sweating but they were just swell and I liked Don all the better for it cause he didn't try to get very mushy at all. Just about all we did was chew gum and go through town honking like everything and then we rode all over the country and honked every time we passed a house and it was about ten o'clock, which was late to go honking through this town and the surrounding country cause every one goes to bed at nine if they're home.

Oh yes, I almost forgot to tell you. It snowed!! Just a little light feathery snow that was all melted away by 10:00 A.M. But it was snow and it was cold. Every morning the mop is frozen fast to the side of the house and pretty soon we'll be having our first big snow. I have to wear stockings to school everyday now and I'm always snagging the old things something terrible. I haven't got my snowsuit yet but I hope to soon.

Lots of Love and Such, Lois

December 1, 1939
Dearest Anna Mae,

I'm going to the show with Don tonight. To see "Stanley and Livingstone." We're going in Don's car. It's raining and it rained all night so the roads will be as slick as butter, but the folks said they wouldn't worry cause, "Don's such a careful driver Oh yes, I got my report card and I went up in everything except English and I went down in it and all in all my grades are just terrible ...

Lots of love, Lois

December 14, 1939
Dearest Anna Mae,

Merry Christmas!!!!! You're the first person I've said that to and I really mean it!!

I've been here nearly five months and it seems as if I had just been here a little while because the time has gone so quickly.

Yesterday when we got on the bus we all sat on the edge of the seats because they were so cold, (they are made out of that leather sort of stuff, you know) I said something about "I wish somebody would warm these seats," and Alan Pool, a little kindergardener, who had just moved over so Don couldn't sit by me (the piker) of course he thought he was being nice making room for Don but when Don nodded his head to move one way the stubborn little boy moved the other. Well any way he is a cute little kid and he said, "Well, why don't you wear long underwear like I've got on and then he pulled up his trousers and showed me it, and he was pointing out how it was made to fit tight around the ankle. I was awfully embarrassed and red and the kids that were on the bus just roared and Don practically rolled on the floor, I laughed, but oh, gee. What a life!!

Last Saturday night there was a 4.H. Banquet. I'm not a "4.H.er" but Don asked me and guests were "welcome." It was a wonderful banquet. There were about 300 there and lots of people didn't know lots of other people but everyone was so very friendly that it was a lot of fun.

Afterward, when Jerry took Arlene to the door he stayed a good half-hour, and Don after a lot of hemming and hawing and making me promise not to be mad, popped the question. It's awful silly, but a real problem in this town and this is what it was. "Do you think necking is wrong?" We had a real discussion about it, morals and beer and cigarettes and everything and I've made a friend! Anna Mae. I know that no matter what ever happens I'll always remember Don not as a "boy" friend but as one of the nicest, cleanest, most honest and straight boys I ever knew. Now, that must sound terribly gushy but if you knew how rare that kind of boy is in this town you'd understand how I feel. I hope I'll always be able to find one boy like him. I wish every girl could know a boy like that, it just shows that it pays not to be cheap.

Loads of love, to my very best friend, Lois

March 19, 1940
Dearest Anna Mae,

SPRING has come to Providence. Oh, I'm so glad. Sunday the sun shone and the first bees flew, they don't fly unless it's 50? or over. Everything is thawing out and the roads are soggy with mud and our car is stuck in the mud in our driveway and my stockings get splattered with mud when I walk out to the school bus but anyway it's SPRING! Of course snow drifts still hem the road sides and there aren't any flowers but little green twigs are beginning to sprout out on the trees so it really is spring. Oh, it's going to be wonderful when the days get really warm. Ummm.

School gets out May 17 or something like that but I don't think I'll go home before June or so, but I don't know.

Bye, Lois

March 20, 1940
Hi,

Today about noon Spring arrives officially at Providence. The sun is shinning shiny but it's awfully cold. Oh, I wish it would get really warmmmmmmmm.

Do you have a new Easter outfit? I won't be able to get one because of the sheep oh, they're simply horrid. We have 350 of them and at least 300 of them will have lambs! We've lambed about 50 of them so that means we're not done. Out of the 50 we've had 10 (four died) little orphans or weak ones. We have to keep them out in the brooder house and keep it really warm and feed them one ounce every two hours. Some are so weak we have to squirt it down their throats and then rub it down for them. We have to do all that to six of them every two hours and by the time we have six more we'll all go crazy!! It's really terrific! We have to stay home all the time.

Last Saturday the folks went to a Wool Growers Convention in Des Moines and I stayed home to feed the lambs. There were only three then and one died soon after they left. Saturday night I was tired and dirty as only lambs can make one and was sitting in the front room answering Lesley's letter, while the folks ate. They had just got home. Well, who should knock at the door (there's only one doorbell in the whole township) but Don!! I had a coal smudge on my face. I'd just been down to fix the furnace a while before- and I smelled like a barn!! He smelled pretty "baby beefy" himself though. He rode over on his horse Dolly. Isn't that a nice name for a horse? We just gabbed most of the evening but we played one game of checkers which he beat, and I tried to teach him how to play chess but I couldn't remember how a bishop can move so it wasn't a very successful game. The big dope didn't leave until 11:40 p.m. I was afraid the folks would come in and kick him out but they didn't say any thing about his lateness at all. The next day at S.S. though, he said he'd gotten home at exactly midnight and that his mother said he should have been home at least an hour and a half earlier. I secretly agree with her cause it just about killed me to get up the next morning and feed lambs. You'd think company would leave earlier wouldn'tcha?

Bye, Lois

March 25, 1940

Oh, I wish it would hurry and get warmmmmmmmm. I'm so tired of being cold, having to wear so many clothes just to stick my head out the door, and of going down and feeding hunks of coal (which don't burn) to the furnace!! Last week was just a false alarm I guess. Oh me, Spring has left us for a more charming abode.

Gee, I'm a pickle puss today. I guess it's cause I'm tired and sleepy and ruined my one and only best pair of undarned stockings yesterday at Church. Boy, that's enough to make a preacher cuss!! Only I didn't—didn't even think a cuss word, I just thought of 79¢ floating away. Oh, Anna Mae, I'm homesick for you and Daddy and warm weather. I just feel terrible inside today and I'm taking it all out on you.

March 27, 1940

Anna Mae, I'm in a predicament! I just have to blow off steam but please don't tell anybody about it. My daddy says that I can stay out here another year if I want to because Uncle said he would like it. If I stay, then daddy would go on living alone just as he has. But he wants to get married. He's so very lonely. If he gets married he wants me to come home and live cause then he'll have a home for me. I know I should go home and tell daddy to get married. And it would do me loads of good cause I've been so spoiled since my mother died. It would do me good to have to live with a family and Daddy is so lonely but Oh Anna Mae, can you imagine sharing a room with a little spoiled girl you hardly know and living with a boy that wouldn't even speak to you when you were introduced? He just looked away. And I'm afraid we'd be jealous of each other all the time cause every time Daddy would do something for me I can just see Betty go running up and saying I want it too, or I want to go too. Oh golly! I know it would be good for me and would take away a lot of my spoiledness and it would teach me to hold my temper and be braver about things. So I guess I'll write and tell Daddy that it's O.K. Anyway I've had a keen vacation for a year and it's certainly daddy's turn now. And they say God can make us be very brave.

Lois

Minstrel Wind

The wind is a wandering minstrel lad
And he sings to you and to me.
He sings of the far off rolling hills
And he sings of the roaring sea.
And if we would listen through all of our strife
He'd sing to us the mystery of life.

Gypsy Wind

Wind, wind heather gypsy
Whistling in my trees.
All the heart of me is tipsy
At the sound of thee.
Sweet with scent of clover,
Salt with taste of sea,
Wind, wind, wayman lover
Whispering in my trees.

New Providence, IA 1939-40. Written in my room in Roy and Edna's farmhouse on those windy fall days I had never before experienced, and which somehow gave me a high (no word for it then). It happens when the sky is an endlessly deep bowl of pure light blue, without a cloud, and the wind is high and the air is dry.

Lois:

In the Spring of 1940 my idyllic year in New Providence ended abruptly within a few days after the surprise 15th birthday party Aunt Edna gave me. Anne Elkinton, member of our Berkeley Friends Church, was driving back to California from the East and Dad must have arranged for her to pick me up. There was another woman in the car, I have no idea who. I sat in a corner of the back seat all the way home, stunned, numb, sometimes silently teary. I don't remember saying a word or hearing one, in an adolescent funk. It was a terrible jolt to leave so silently, suddenly, a place where I felt glimmerings of belonging, although I always knew it was a temporary time.

The birthday/farewell party was a huge ego boost, but I didn't get to stay and continue the friendships that seemed confirmed then.

Polly and I corresponded some, Aunt Edna and I exchanged letters a few times, but my tenuous ties with my wonderful year were weak, except for Don.

Don:

So we parted suddenly in June 1940.

On returning to Oakland from Iowa, Lois had two years of high school ahead before college. I entered William Penn College in the fall of 1940 and transferred to Iowa State College in the fall of 1941 to enroll in the electrical engineering school. I dated several girls during the next few years, but never lost contact with Lois as she finished high school and enrolled at Whittier College. I never found another girl who attracted me as much as the one I was writing to. We wrote many letters, back and forth, but I have no memory of what we told each other. I wonder if I made comments about the girls I was dating.

It was the era of the Big Bands—Tommy Dorsey, Louis Armstrong, Duke Ellington, Count Basie—and some of them made it to Iowa State College dances. It was a society in which I could never feel at ease. I took social dancing lessons for a time in an effort to feel more equal to the ones I wanted to associate with. But it didn't work. I was a farm boy with no sense of rhythm, and I couldn't make up for lost time. But I loved the music of the famous bands, and still do.

One girl and I settled in to pretty steady dating. We found each other through one of the church young people's program. She was a year older than I and soon became more serious than I was ready for. I even met her parents one time when they were visiting the campus. But she had another young man who was pushing for her serious attention. After Pearl Harbor I made a sudden decision to quit engineering school—even though I loved it—and return to Penn College where a program had been set up for conscientious objectors to be trained for relief work in China. This decision ended the relationship with her. I was relieved—I had cast my destiny more clearly with an effort to continue developing the relationship with Lois. That was by no means a "done deal," but at least I was no longer torn between two women. I felt good about the choice.

Lois:

Because I skipped second semester of 9th grade when I entered New Providence rural high school as a sophomore in the fall of 1939, I was one credit short for graduation. I was told this during the last semester of my junior year at University High in Oakland, spring 1941. I felt quite panicked at the news but was told I could take any night class to make it up. These were offered for adults and didn't even run the entire term. Technical High offered a crafts class.

After supper I liked the release of the one block walk to the College Street streetcar that rattled on to Broadway and part way down town to Tech Hi, a block long, two story white building with Greek pillars.

I was still living on memories and fantasies of Don, longing for the security and pleasures of New Providence days.

Was this the year or the next that Norman Katz, a boy from church who went to Berkeley High, became friendly? He was handsome, dark eyebrows, and a pleading look that demanded an unbearable amount of something I knew I didn't have. We were alone at times, but most "dates" were in the back seat of his parents' car as they drove us to a family picnic, a trip to Fleishacker Zoo in San Francisco, but usually to some church Christian Endeavor event.

He was an adept and fast groper for a novice and did get to the skin in spite of handicaps. I think I felt no strong emotions, although I learned a few more new things about human physical, sexual reactions—under control! We were probably educational for each other.

(Untitled)

Because she flaunts her loneliness,
Makes public how she needs her man,
Is it that she misses him much more than I do mine?

If I am still and do not express
This hollowness inside
Is it that I love him less?

It cannot be.
This pent up loss,
This dumb desire for meeting
Is not less
In spite of quietness.

I found this burned scrap that must have been in the garage fire. I wrote this in college, (1942-46) although I have no memory of writing it! Boyfriends and fiancées were in the war; Don was in Civilian Public Service (CPS) camps. When I returned to Whittier for my sophomore year in the fall of 1943 there were about a dozen men on campus. Lois, September 16, 2005.

CHAPTER 5

OUR DECADE OF THE FORTIES

Don:

We had parted so suddenly I was devastated by the loss. Summer farm work was in full swing and I went about it methodically and without my heart in it. My heart was two thousand miles away and I longed to bridge the gap. I felt, deep down, that I would eventually reach out to Lois and bring our lives together. How to accomplish this I had no idea. For the next four years our only contact was by mail, except for two visits each only a few days long.

It was easy to see that settling down on the farm would not bring us together, at least not fast enough to suit me. Electrical things had interested me for several years. I had acquired an Amateur Radio Operators (Ham) license during my junior year in high school and had a small transmitter in my room. It now occurred to me that a commercial license might give me entry to a West Coast job of some kind. I bought a text book and started studying.

By late summer college seemed possible. It didn't satisfy my short term goal, but was a realistic path toward a future. I entered William Penn College in the fall of 1940.

Lois:

There were two letters that probably represent two of the most massive impacts in my life, even up to the present almost sixty years later: the continuing relationship with Don, and Dad's marriage to Evelyn Cox. The Cox years, not more than two at the most, were really only a blip when seen from the present.

I remember working on the comic—I hoped it would be comic—word cut-out letter. I don't know how long I'd been home, but it seemed like a long time and I had not heard from Don. I felt strongly that a girl shouldn't be the initiator (of anything!) but I had to find out if he was going to communicate at all with me, and somewhere I got this idea for a joke sort of contact.

The second letter surprised me. I have no memory of writing it. I had been visiting Aunt Mabel in Marina, sixty miles south of San Francisco. She is the one who told me when mother died that I would miss her more and more as I grew older and that I was not one to wear my heart on my sleeve. We were sitting on my bed in the sleeping porch at the time and I was mute and remote. She was the only adult who spoke directly and seriously with me at that time about all that was happening around me.

My cousins James, Major and I had taken the wonderful camping trip to Yosemite in Jim's little blue roadster. We may have camped out for three nights at the most. I've marveled that a fifteen year old girl was allowed to go camping with fifteen and nineteen year old boy cousins. Uncle Karl, an austere, nineteenth century Christian missionary must have trusted his sons. Or maybe I seemed so immature, unattractive and unknowing that he, who fought the devil constantly, knew his sons would not be tempted. We made a dividing curtain in the tent. Aunt Mabel had given me the fabric and told me how it would get set up.

It was a wonderful time for me. We ate and hiked and talked long soulful talks with Jim while Major would play in the streams, throw rocks, climb boulders. We hiked up to the top of Half Dome, we hiked to Bridal Veil Falls. We must have brought all of our food. The guys built the fires and did the cooking.

Now I wonder if the trip was partly for me because of Dad's marriage and the Cox's moving into our house. I had no knowledge of this until I got home, and I believe if Aunt Mabel had known of it she would have told me in some way.

Don:

During the late summer of 1941, before entering Iowa State College in September, I had a major urge to see Lois. It had been a year, with many letters flying between us, and I was ready for a real visit.

It happened that our local minister's sister and her family were making the trip from their home in Kansas City to Oakland, Calif. I was invited to join them and would be there a week.

Hitch hiking in those days was common and relatively safe, so I packed a bag and hit the road for Kansas City. I got good rides into KC, but was left off a long way from the address I had for the meeting. "Thanks for the ride" I said, as I pulled my heavy suitcase from the back seat.

I had the address of my destination in my pocket, but was too thankful for the long ride to mention that I was miles from where I wanted to be. I walked for hours, but felt no burden since the goal was so attractive. I met the family in good time and the next morning we piled into their car and headed for my fairyland and the young goddess it held.

I don't remember a lot about that week, except one outstanding revelation. Lois was making breakfast for us one morning—I think we were alone — frying bacon and eggs. When the bacon came out of the pan she put it on a paper towel to absorb most of the grease. I had never heard of such a thing. My mother, the only cook I had to compare with, fed us all the grease available. It was a trivial thing, but I was impressed.

Lois was a wonderful cook, even though she never liked the job. Throughout our whole married life she was conscious of the advantage of a low fat, nutritious diet. She made excellent desserts, but not often—she would much rather read a book. I'm sure it was her thoughtful management that has kept me from an old age of blubber and paunchiness.

The trip home from that week was the saddest few days I have ever spent in my life. The departure from romantic California was almost unbearable. The family I was with seemed happy to be headed for home, but I was just the opposite. Yet my determination to bring our lives together had been strengthened no end.

Lois:

In the summer of 1941 Don came to visit. It seems there was nobody in the flat all day and we were left alone. I remember being embarrassed when he asked me to press his pants. We went on the streetcar down to the Oakland skating rink one afternoon. We went to San Francisco. Anna Mae and Alva went with us one evening to the park in San Francisco where a "rollo plane," a two seated rocket on the end of an arm that swung in great arcs and circles, ruined my evening. When I got off I vomited, but managed to avoid hitting anyone's shoes. I felt sick and weak for hours afterward. I couldn't even eat caramel corn! Another dent in the evening was the knowledge that Anna Mae and Alva were a married couple, living together, getting ready to fly to Honolulu. We weren't really just high school kids anymore.

A letter of December 1941 when I "get the job" brings back a wince of failure. A small restaurant on College Avenue a block away from home gave me the opportunity to learn to wait tables, a skill I felt necessary. Trying to fit in, to be aware of work to do, I began to clear a table when the only other waitress was busy. She came onto me, furious, and I realized finally that she was afraid I would take her tip. I may have lasted as long as a week. I was such a wilted wimp, never was acknowledged as a coworker by anyone. The guy finally told me not to come back and I left my first "job" defeated and unpaid.

December 7, 1941 I do remember. Dad and I came home from church to learn the news of Pearl Harbor. Evelyn and Richard were excited. It was probably the most conversational meal we ever had.

During the summer of 1942 I worked for the family of a colleague of Ralph, Teresa's husband. Perhaps he was a physicist, too. He was a dapper, small boned man with a strong European (German?) accent. His mother spoke little English, but his wife and two children, both preschool age spoke English fluently. They lived farther up the Berkeley Hills than Ralph and Teresa, in a luxurious house. For one who lived down in the "Flatland" of Oakland, all of the homes in the hills north of UC campus seemed rich to me.

I arrived at their house about 9:00 a.m. each morning after a streetcar and bus ride to within a block of their place. My first job was to wash all of the dishes and pots used in the previous twenty-four hours: yesterdays' lunch, dinner, snacks, and today's breakfast. Then I helped grandmother prepare lunch. Papa always appeared for lunch which was properly set in the dining room which had double doors open to a patio. Often lunch would be set up on the patio, but still using china dishes and full place settings. I helped with serving the meal and then ate mine in the kitchen. After lunch I helped clear, stack dishes, put food away, and then took the children to their room for naps. I read to them and we were good friends; they liked me. While they napped I did housecleaning for a couple of hours. There was a well organized schedule: change sheets and clean parents' room and bath, (I learned about stained sheets and bedside contraceptives here—she used a diaphragm), another day clean and mop the kitchen. My favorite day was cleaning the living room which filled the whole width of the house, with a grand piano in one end and oriental rugs on polished hardwood floors. When the kids woke up I watched them, sometimes also doing a dinner prep job in the kitchen and entertaining the kids. I walked down to the bus in late afternoon and was home about 5:00.

It was a fairly stress-free job. I knew they liked me, although it was always a formal, strictly employer/employee relationship. In late summer when I told the mother that I would be leaving to enter college in a few weeks she was shocked. I realized that she was going to lose a gem of a helper and that she had had no idea that I was qualified for a college education.

In 1942, my sister Naomi was teaching English in the Japanese detention camp in Poston, Arizona, and I was a freshman at Whittier College. I visited her there during Christmas vacation. It was certainly an education for me to visit a city of barracks closed in by high fences topped with barbed wire and manned by soldiers. Several families lived in a single building, with cloth hangings to separate rooms. There were communal dining halls for staff and prisoners. Naomi lived in a dormitory with other teachers.

The minute the sun went down the air turned icy, and by noon it was warm to sit in the sun against a sheltered building. It never got warm in the barracks beyond the area around the stoves.

Naomi taught high school and also adult classes. The kids were so eager and polite. Attention from non-military who got to know your name must have been a comfort. And the adults were keen to learn and loved any bit of humor. Most of the people had nothing to do. It was terrible for the old.

Posters and cartoons of the Japanese emperor-looking like a monster insect appeared, and I'm off to Whittier. I enter Earlham Hall as one of fourteen girls who will live in this house transformed into a dormitory. I live mostly in a fantasy world, waiting for letters from Don who is a real person.

I began my college career as a Home Economics major. I knew why. Naomi had completed a fifth, graduate year in English about four years before I entered Whittier. All the faculty still remembered her. "Oh, you're Naomi Wood's sister!" English/literature was my first choice of majors, but I could not dare to subject myself to comparison with her wit and brains.

To become qualified for the major I enrolled in organic chemistry, having not one iota of interest or knowledge in any kind of chemistry. I have no memory of such a class. I couldn't even do the math required, and when Don arrived in California in

February 1944 he pulled me through. The only possible explanation for a B grade is that I frequently worked for chemistry Professor Newsome's wife. They lived next door to Earlham Hall and I cleared, stacked and washed dishes far into the night after their dinner parties. They must have wanted to keep me on campus!

The course labeled Household Equipment finished home economics for me. I knew I could never take the study of the difference between tank and upright vacuum cleaners seriously. I knew I had some kind of mind and had to find some other niche for it.

The switch was to major in history, and of course get a teacher's certificate. Some of the brainier, more adventurous girls were working toward certification in physical therapy, a new field and sure to be a good one for being useful and for meeting men when the war was over. But I was traditional.

In the summer of '42 I had to earn some money. I came home to Teresa's house and got a job as a clerk in a leather goods/luggage store in Berkeley. High class, expensive. I was good, charming with just the right amount of genuine diffidence to please the customers. The manager liked me and I liked showing lovely things I wouldn't think of owning to people who did think of it. About two weeks later I got very sick. Teresa put me into the boys' room and a visiting MD diagnosed me as a measles patient. Sure enough, I was soon one living rash with burning lungs. For many days the world was a blur of distant noises and Teresa bringing me cool drinks in the darkened room. I never went back to my job.

In the meantime Dad developed the notion that he and I should visit Roy and Edna in Iowa. He hadn't been back since he left in 1919. Gas rationing determined that we would go by train. When we left Oakland I felt weak, a bit light headed, and had fading red areas on my face and chest, but I was excited about going back to New Providence. We sat up coach for two days and nights and I felt stronger each day. I was in a kind of cocoon of happiness feeling myself feeling well and anticipating seeing Don. The train was mostly a troop train, full of army guys, and MPs patrolling the cars constantly. I don't think I had one single encounter for even a minute with any male, or female, for that matter.

Don:

That summer of 1942 brought a little more togetherness. I picked Lois and her dad up at the train station in Marshalltown, Iowa, about twenty-five miles from home. We ate lunch in the famous Stone's restaurant near the tracks before the trip back to New Providence.

I wonder if her dad was looking at me as a possible future son-in-law. Our two Quaker families were quite compatible in many ways and it seemed like an ideal union to me. But I was not even remotely conscious of him as a future father-in-law, not because it wasn't possible, but because I was completely absorbed with his daughter.

The train they arrived on was mostly a cattle train with a few passenger cars added on. I remember Lois reporting a lot of jangling, hitching and back-and-forward motion in the middle of the night, in the Omaha train station, while they were trying to sleep. But she arrived in good spirits.

We made the most of the week together.

Lois:

Most of the memories of our visit are dim and blurred, mostly of Don picking me up at Aunt Edna's and our going off together for hours alone. We went fishing once. No fish, and I refused to bait with a worm. Cousins and friends from school were different, distant, as was I, of course. Even Polly was a disappointment.

I must have kept some old letters as symbols of my so many lost opportunities. One was my admission letter to Whittier, signed by O.B. Baldwin. He was a heavy-set, paunchy, double-chinned, soft spoken man, not a big wheel in the administration, I'm sure. Probably quite low in the faculty pecking order. But because Naomi had loved him and because he tells me that he hopes I'll be something like her, I could never say two words to him or look him in the eye. I knew I would be a disappointment compared to my sparkling sister.

In college, I did housework for Hocketts and cleaned up and did dishes for Newsomes for a dollar or so a time. I began to realize that while I didn't like the work, I liked the safe isolation and knowing I did well. So instead of trying out for drama parts I buried the longing by cleaning bathrooms and doing dishes for professors! How come nobody rescued me? Did nobody know I was dying?

When school resumed in the fall of 1943 there were only a dozen or so men on campus, ministerial deferments and 4-F's. For the next two years Whittier College was virtually a girls' college. There was an active anti-war Quaker group which I joined in a nominal way.

My sister, Naomi, in northern California, was very active in a group of conscientious objectors, political and religious. I had been exposed to this group through her while in high school, attending some conferences with her and going to work meetings where mailings were prepared and much serious conversation took place among people who seemed to me wise and sure of themselves. These people all seemed much older and more brilliant than I, had jobs, and worked for peace programs. I was a "little sister" on the fringes.

But I was anti-war, and didn't join groups on campus selling bonds, collecting for the USO, or Red Cross. I didn't know why I was anti-war. Yes, I did in fuzzy ways. The people I most admired were against wars. Killing is wrong. Jesus says so. Even the Old Testament Commandment says so, "Thou shalt not kill."

I went through a personal discipline phase, getting up early to pray, read and meditate in the attic of the dorm every day. I tried hard to make this an experience closer to God and goodness. Mostly I felt defeated.

Since many campus activities were war-related I didn't participate. I also locked myself out of the major social groups. I didn't participate in rush parties for four women's societies: the Metaphonians, the Athenians, the Palmers, and the Thalians. I blatantly lied and said I would not join on principle, but I was really scared to death that I wouldn't get rushed, maybe not even the Thalians, which was for the plain and dull ones.

Don:

The small town of New Providence, had one church which was ostensibly a Quaker church, but in fact it was more of a community church than denominational. The teacher of the young people's Sunday School class was a Quaker by birth and uniquely opinionated on theological subjects. Under his influence I was drawn inexorably into the traditional Quaker position on war. Other young men, under the same church influence, were not. Our home environments were probably quite different and of course of great influence on our lives. Also, this particular teacher, an English teacher in the local school, was not in tune with the general mood of this congregation at this time. War was brewing in Europe and tales of Nazi activities drifted into Iowa as everywhere else. There was a fairly strong contingent of German settlers in the community—some with a German accent. So it was important to these people to lean over backward to exhibit their "Americanism." Traditional Quaker attitudes toward war were swept into the background—the conscientious objector (CO) position was not honored.

I was a senior at William Penn College, Oskaloosa, Iowa, in the winter of 1943-44. My draft classification was 4-E—conscientious objector. I knew I would be drafted as soon as I graduated. I also knew that the policy of draft boards was to send those draftees classified as conscientious objectors to camps as close as possible to avoid transportation costs. Most COs drafted from Iowa at that time were sent to a land reclamation camp in South Dakota. I knew if I were sent to that camp, I would have almost no chance of seeing Lois until I was released from service. I decided to quit school, move to southern California, and get assigned from a draft board there in order to be sent to a camp in California.

Lois was a sophomore at Whittier College that year and my interest in keeping in touch with her was stronger than my interest in a college degree. So I dropped out of college and on a twenty-degrees-below-zero day in February, 1944, my dad put me on a bus bound for Whittier, California. I am certain my parents were disappointed. On the seven mile trip to the bus station, through blowing snow and drifted roads, my father, a traditional man of his culture, told me how important it was to have a woman who had never been "used" before marriage. He said also how important it was to have a woman who could keep house and get meals. I think he trusted Lois and me to order our lives together as he would approve. I listened to his advice. We didn't go as far as "having sex" before we were married, but certainly sex was part of our close relationship. In those days it was called "heavy petting." I suppose each generation defines its own "sexual relationship" to suit itself and to be different from an older generation. But I wonder how much generations really differ in the actual behavior of their hormone-driven young. In our case the model of our parents and their peers, and their unexpressed but clear expectations for our behavior protected us better than a chastity belt.

I arrived in warm weather and sunny skies.

It's hard to describe my emotions upon my arrival in southern California. The physical contrast alone from frozen snow and slick roads of forty-eight hours ago to palm trees and geraniums in bloom was overwhelming. And the powerful urge to be with the girl that I hadn't been able to give up was about to be realized. We had known each other only by mail for the past three years, so a brand new beginning was at hand. Lois had found a room for me at Mrs. Pearson's, a few blocks from the Whittier College campus. I quickly settled in and found a job at Philadelphia Quartz Company, a manufacturer of ingredients for soap and glass.

My assignment to "work of national importance" came in May. I was drafted from a board in Orange County, as expected, and assigned to a Forest Service camp at Coleville, CA. This particular Civilian Public Service (CPS) camp was administered by the Quakers with the work being directed by the Forest Service. Lois and I had been engaged for a couple of months and I was not many hours away. I looked forward to seeing her several times a year through furloughs and leaves.

My job that first summer was to help take supplies to a crew of CPS men who were building a Forest Service cabin at Pieute Meadows high in the Sierra Nevada Mountains. A Forest Service Ranger and I, each on a sure-footed horse, along with seven large mules, packed up the fifteen mile trail to the construction camp. We arrived at the corral at the trailhead in early morning, packed our mules with everything needed at the camp—bags of cement, lumber, food, medicines, and, of course, the mail for the men. Taking off in midmorning we arrived at our destination a couple thousand feet higher in late afternoon. On the trip up the mules were kept on a halter rope between us—one riding in front of the pack train and one in back. We stayed overnight, saddled up and rode back the next day. On the return trip we turned the mules loose and got them together at the corral.

Later that summer I transferred to the mapping crew in Reno. Our work there was to verify the Grazing Service maps with stereoscopic aerial photographs. But we were also an active fire suppression crew. Whenever a fire call came, ten to fifteen of us piled onto a stock truck and were taken to the fire. We were supposed to hit fires before they got big and into tree tops. As soon as we got to the fire we picked up an adz and an ax and strung out, about forty feet apart on the trail to make a fire break. We worked our forty-foot section, called out our number, and those ahead moved up. It was an efficient way to quickly establish a fire break for a ground fire.

My non-fire crew time in Reno was making maps for the Grazing Service. Maps had been made earlier of the back country, and our job was to bring them up-to-date. Some years before, the area had been photographed so we had aerial photographs of the country. The pictures were taken in sequence of parallel flights, so that with any two pictures we could get a stereoscopic view of the land. From these we could determine valleys, hills, tall trees, rock outcroppings and anything else of interest. We made maps from this three-dimensional view.

In October '44 another conscientious objector and I were issued a Forest Service pickup with camper and all the gear to stay in the back country for the month. We had cooking equipment, a tent, sleeping bags, lots of food and a chess set. We also had the stereoscopic photos and maps of the area. Our job, for that month, was to locate anything we could identify and get its exact location on the maps. We identified peaks, streams, valleys, abandoned mines, towns and anything else we could put on the map that would serve as a landmark. We were looking for the U.S. Geological Survey bench markers in order to get them on the maps. Sometimes they were a mile from where they should be. We learned that the way the western country was sometimes surveyed was to tie a rag onto the rim of a wagon wheel and count revolutions as you drove. So for a month we toured the country around the Mono Lake area—at that time, the source of some of the water for Los Angeles—on the eastern edge of Yosemite National Park. Our assignment was to bring the maps to completion as well as we could.

One afternoon, my work partner and I could see something up the mountainside from the valley we were in, but couldn't tell what it was. We decided to drive up on some abandoned roads and found an abandoned mine. We weren't able to even tell what kind of mine, but thought probably silver. We explored it some and got it placed on our map.

By that time it was late afternoon, so we decided to take a hike farther up the mountain toward a peak we could make out. We were pretty much above timberline so the terrain was loose shale rock. For each step forward we slid a half step back. We climbed for a couple of hours and got to a saddle in the rocks somewhat below the peak we had in mind. We had probably come up a thousand feet higher than the mine. We stopped to catch our breath, and sat down on the rocks without any communication between us. We could see out over the valley with the last rays of sun for fifty miles, and make out a town or two and a ranch or two where we had just been. We looked out for a few minutes, and then a snow storm blew in and closed our view. It was a light snow but swirled around us, and I remember the utter silence of the mountain side except for the swish of the falling snow. We sat for another fifteen minutes in complete silence and then got up and went back to our truck. It was the most acute spiritual experience of my life.

My partner at that time was an atheist—a clear and critical thinker. He had an active conscience toward injustice and I respected him for these qualities. He was troubled about being in CPS, and felt he should be doing more with his life than making maps for the Grazing Service. We didn't talk much of our religious feelings, but did spend hours around the campfire, between supper and bedtime, talking of the CPS experience and what it meant to us. Many evenings we played chess. Shortly after we got back from our month of mapping, he left CPS and joined the Medical Corps.

Lois:

Don arrived in Los Angeles in February dressed for Iowa where he had begun the trip during a cold snap winter storm. I was embarrassed by this pudgy little fellow getting off the bus. He would have been traveling at least 48 hours, and he was wearing long johns and two pairs of pants, and a heavy wool, bulky plaid jacket which was the usual outer coat at that time. No wonder that he looked out of place arriving in southern California during beach weather.

Old, burned letters indicate that the United States is in a war (Pearl Harbor, 12/42) and that I am rather aware of it. A letter about graduation and my inheritance and my "pacifism" in history class probably indicates more of my ignorant idealism than I wish.

Don was assigned to Coleville CPS forest unit and was in Reno by December. I visited him there and stayed with Dot and Bill Bruff and we spent the evenings walking and sitting on benches in a Reno park with temps in the freezing range. My ears ached a lot and took a long time to quit after we separated for the night.

But he was also in Berkeley at some point. We stayed at Teresa's, I was probably in the boys' room on a cot and he had the guest room. One night very late, we were lying on the floor in front of the fireplace, and Teresa came downstairs and shooed us off to bed.

A letter from Teresa is a rare opening of herself. It must have been written in the months before our wedding. I'm glad the remnant of her love poem is there. Years later she let me read some bitter ones she wrote about the "stuffed shirt" Ralph had become. Evidently he became increasingly possessive and jealous, and she once said she wished she had given him more to be jealous about. Her quiet demeanor and lovely smile may have attracted some of those intellectual scientists with their strident wives who came to parties at their house.

That spring (1944) Don and I became officially engaged during a day at the beach, which gave him a serious sunburn. The Associated Women Students had a barbaric custom at the annual spring banquet which required all engaged women to parade through a festooned archway and announce the name (and rank and service—this was war time) of one's fiancé. I dreaded this event. I had to buy some flimsy fabric and gather it onto a waist band for a formal. My dorm mates insisted that I go. Passing chocolates just in the dorm as the informal announcement was an easier time for me.

A long letter written in January 1945 refers to the education projects that Don had helped me build when he was in Berkeley during Christmas vacation. And obviously setting a date for a wedding which terrifies me is a large subject. I'm struck by my reluctance to commit to definite dates or plans that shows in the letters. I know I had (still have) a great problem with commitment to anything.

I did make dates, appointments. We went to a marriage quiz/info clinic for a session, the Paul Popenoe marriage counselors. I went at least twice to an MD for vaginal stretchings as a result of that clinic. I enquired about marriage licenses and syphilis tests, so I was not entirely childish. What amazes me is that I could still be so ignorant after reading so much.

I believe it was this same spring that Don came down to Whittier on leave from camp with an all-over case of poison oak. He was really sick, and no longer had a room to stay in so we rented a room in the Penn Hotel. I stole food from the Campus Inn and went to see him a few times a day. I don't believe he had any medication and we didn't realize how dangerous such a massive infection could be.

So I completed my sophomore year of college and went home to Berkeley for the summer. This time I took a job in a cannery. It was good pay and they were desperate for help. Some really heavy work, like unloading crates of fruit from trucks, was done by women. I learned much in that month, and have never been able to use fruit cocktail mix without a shudder since then. I would stand on a wet, perforated (to let the liquid juices and water fall to the wet, slimy floor below) metal platform about four steps above the floor, shoving pear halves into a slicer with no guard between hands and whirling blades. I was terrified. Sometimes (often) the cut pear cores had not fallen out and we were to gouge them out as the piles of fruit came tumbling past, and keep them directed into the narrow slicer chute. If you got behind, the pile in front of you overflowed. At break I sat in a huge bare room with a row of toilets and wash basins on one wall. Backless benches filled the rest of the space and women stretched out on these to rest. There was little conversation.

I've always been grateful for this taste of menial labor in the raw.

I was reprieved from this scary job by the explosion of two ships filled with ammunition in Port Chicago. Every piece of glass in the town was shattered. For the weeks needed to clean up, day camps were established to keep the children away from harm, and I was hired through contacts that Naomi had with the American Friends Service Committee (AFSC) to serve in a day camp for six-to- twelve-year-olds. About 100 kids tore out of the school buses each morning. Most considered this a vacation: time in a park with a swimming pool and crafts. We doled out food in various forms all day. Lunch was a real sit down meal at an area with a lot of picnic tables brought in for the crowd. Sergeants Collier and Charlie Gromack were the cooks. And they brought good food out of the tiny park shelter and food prep army wagon. At noon we all sang "Noontime is here/The board is spread/Thanks be to God/Who gives us bread."

An AFSC couple with small children were directors. The couple, the sergeants, and I stayed over nights. I had a cot and sleeping bag on the small platform built for a tent top, but the top was missing. The couple had a cabin with a tiny kitchen. The sergeants each had a small tent. Bathroom facilities were the public park. When I caught pink eye, which became a universal affliction, chipping the crust from my eyes enough for me to see my way to the bathroom was the uncomfortable beginning of each day. But the sergeants set me up with a small bucket of hot water from the kitchen every morning and that kindness changed my harsh views of the army!

Both men were delighted with this assignment. They were good with kids, constantly available, entertaining, joking around, as well as creating mountains of food. Collier was married to a woman in southern California that he often referred to with real affection. Gromack was married, too, but on the prowl, restless, bored after the buses left in the evening.

One night I was baby-sitting for the couple in the cabin and Gromack, terribly drunk, decided he needed a woman, and any woman would do. Unfortunately he was limited to me. He got angry and went into the kitchen and picked up a butcher knife lying beside a watermelon on the counter. I was sitting on the bed across from where the kids were sleeping. (These two beds filled most of the space.) He stood in the doorway muttering, cursing about uncooperative women, and loosely holding the knife. "Hey, Gromack, let's have a piece of watermelon!" I said.

I leaped up, grabbed the knife, passed him, and went into the kitchen before he put it together. I began to cut the melon, kicked myself afterward for not throwing the knife out the open window above the little sink. He could have easily overpowered me in a physical struggle. "Aaah, I don' wansher damn waater melon," he said, and he stomped the six steps across the room and out the door.

The next day Collier told me I should have run screaming for him. And leave the little kids there? He also said he'd been monitoring Gromack's drinking as much as he could, and wouldn't let this happen again. Gromack never referred to that night and neither did I. It could have ended so badly. I liked him, he was good for me to know, so different. He wrote me two or three letters from base after the summer was over. I hope I didn't write back.

I was wearing an engagement ring, the diamond from my mother, that summer. The evenings, after the buses left with the kids, were long. Sometimes I went to the pool alone and practiced diving. Sometimes I did so well, went so deep, I scraped the bottom, and took longer to come up than was comfortable. I knew I must stay within easy reach of the edge for I can't really swim. In retrospect, I don't know which adventures, alone in the water or with Gromack, were the most dangerous.

Fall of 1944, I began my junior year as a student at Whittier. Somehow I was elected as student body treasurer. The treasury was in debt. I felt responsible for it. Dear Dr. Cooper (English & Drama) said the income from a play would be given toward debt pay-off. I felt I had to sell every ticket myself. I spent hours going door to door (something I have never inflicted on myself again, not for any cause in the world will I go door to door) selling tickets to Whittier housewives.

I was cursed and overwhelmed with feelings of inadequacy. For money I cleaned an immaculate house once a week and helped with dinner parties at the home of the college comptroller, Howard Hockett. He had been a Penn College friend of dad's. I think he had something to do with the deal about our college tuitions and I felt demeaned when working in their house with no understanding of why.

Don and I wrote long letters to each other. He had transferred to a forest service camp in Reno and was doing interesting mapping work. He wanted to get married. A married college student seemed foreign to my traditional, conservative way of thinking. But he was my anchor, my life. We visited the Friends minister, Eli Wheeler, then living in Los Angeles, who had been pastor in New Providence when we were in high school. I had such a hard time making a commitment that we walked around several unnecessary blocks after getting off the bus before I steeled myself to go into their house and make plans for a wedding ceremony. I think we stayed overnight and his wife tried to have a conversation or two with me. I was impervious and numb.

So spring vacation, 1945, on Sunday, the eighteenth of March, we were married.

Don's parents rode a bus for forty-eight hours to see their first son married. My dad and two sisters came from northern California. I bought a new dress for under $15.00 at one of the Lerner dress shops in L.A. But I liked the dress and wore it for dress-up for some time to come. I also ordered napkins with our names and the date as well as announcements to send out which stated that I was the daughter of Mr. and Mrs. H. Ross Wood, which was not true. Dad had married Emily Hamilton a year or so before. I had spent some vacation time in the spare room of their apartment where the white hairs of her dog Snow covered every surface.

With a few CPS friends of Don's, his parents, my dorm mates, my dad, and my sisters, Naomi and Teresa, and with Eli Wheeler officiating, putting Paul's Christ and husband as head of the house, we did evidently become legally married.

I am forever grateful to my dorm mates who must have thought they were dealing with a retarded or demented girl. I didn't know how to do any wedding things, and I was reluctant to do anything beyond the stark necessities. They "did" the whole thing. I knew to do one thing right: We used the Friends marriage promise, which is a model for plain speaking: "In the presence of God and these friends I take thee, Don, to be my husband, promising to be a faithful and loving wife as long as we both shall live." I invented our own sentence for the exchange of rings. "As a symbol of the home we will build with our hearts and hands I give thee this ring."

I've sent years of silent thanks to the stranger on campus, a friend of a friend, who loaned us the use of her little house on Manhattan Beach. I had a terrible cold. Shades of childhood Sundays? Hay fever? Teresa kept me in bed all morning of the day. But when we finally boarded the bus, with enough luggage for a safari to Africa, to go to the beach, I think I was as happy and easy as I ever can be. And the days and nights together were mostly fun as well as educational for a couple of virgins. I got well from my cold.

So, I went back to school, somewhat embarrassed and shy about my new condition, and Don back to CPS.

In the summer of 1945 I lived in a nearly empty dorm and took classes. Don joined the sleep study at Cal Tech. When he was released from the study he rode out to Whittier on the bus, looking a bit hollow eyed. I illegally welcomed him into my room and we had a fine reunion after his few hours of sleep. It didn't take long for him to catch up on his usual sexed-up self. Sleep cannot be stored, nor does it take long to make up for a temporary lack of it.

On August 6, I was riding the bus to Long Beach. Suddenly, I don't know how the news spread, the bus erupted into yells and whooping screams. The soldiers and sailors jumped out of their seats, danced, jumped up and down in the aisle, grabbed at people in their seats, hugging and kissing us. The bombing of Hiroshima had become news, fires, city flattened, thousands dead, surrender soon. It was heart pounding, exciting to see such elation and yet I felt a reservation.

Before the fall semester began I moved several blocks off campus to live with Cousin Mattie Wood Gregg, because the school had a policy of no married students in dorms. Married students were almost unheard of then, but by the year after I graduated, 1947, the wonderful government education act for returned veterans would cause campuses all over the nation to provide housing for married students and their families.

My sister Naomi had lived with Cousin Mattie during her fifth year at Whittier, and they were fond of each other. I was never able to break through the formalities of both of us. I always felt aloof and, of course, felt a failure in my inability to match Naomi's gift for relationships. I kept Cousin Mattie's house clean. You could eat out of her toilet. She was demanding but kind. I think she liked Don more than me, but he was only there for occasional weekends. This was the year of pregnancy panics after every visit from Don.

During the winter of 1945-46 CPS men were allowed to join the United Nations Relief Administration (UNRA). This may also have been part of the Marshall Plan that helped restore Europe. War ships were modified into livestock freighters. Don took two trips before he was released from the draft, one with a load of horses to Trieste and one with a load of cattle to Danzig, Poland.

It was also the year of extreme student teaching stress. If someone had told me that I was not suited for classroom teaching, it might have saved me years of feeling a failure at what I was "supposed to do." My inabilities surely must have been obvious to my supervisors during those months.

Nevertheless, I applied for and was hired, sight unseen, by Haddonfield Friends School in New Jersey during the very last weeks of school. It was a big morale lift—I had a job, too, and a destination.

This was one of the few acts in my life that I initiated entirely on my own. Baltimore was the shipping base for Don and I wanted to have a place to be nearby. I knew even less about the culture of private schools than I did of public, and I knew nothing of eastern Quakers, whose lifestyles, manners, and views of the world were very different from those of the West Coast pastoral Friends. When I later came to Scattergood School I realized how ignorant I was about Quakers as well as teaching!

I didn't know where we would be or when Don would be released. I didn't know where to go. Home in Oakland had long ago disappeared. Dad was living with Emily and her dog Snow in her crowded apartment, and a few weeks of vacation time spent with them in the last year or two assured me that no home was there. I could have gone to Teresa's; she and Ralph were always welcoming, but I felt that would be a dead-end place.

No one in my family came to graduation. I hardly noticed because most of that year I lived in a kind of disconnected dream state, removed from any real relationship with anyone. I missed the daily contact with the girls in our small dorm. Practice teaching took up most of the days and there were few classes on campus. I was waiting for my "real" life to begin, when I would be a teacher and Don and I would have a life together.

The day after graduation I loaded my two suitcases of belongings into the overcrowded car of Jay Beede and his mother who were driving to Earlham, Iowa for Jay's wedding. They unloaded me at the farm of Don's parents in New Providence.

I think back to college days, grateful for the opportunities a college education has given me. I remember a few inspiring professors, and getting truly interested about readings or papers I had to write. But most of my college years are a blur of misery, and I think I was disturbed and abnormal much of the time. Either I was a good dissembler with everyone I associated with or everyone was singularly unaware that I was in such distress.

When Don came on leaves they were a kind of make believe temporary romance in a never-never land. I didn't begin to deal with a daily, repetitive routine kind of real life-together-marriage until we lived at Scattergood.

Don:

My parents were an integral part of our lives for as long as they lived. Without warning, I was suddenly discharged upon arrival back from a trip to Trieste with horses. So I caught up with my bride-of-one-year at my folks place in Iowa. After several months' separation, it was a glorious reunion.

My discharge changed Lois' plans for teaching at Haddonfield, of course. Breaking contracts seemed easy to do in those unsettling post war years, but it was, nevertheless not a thing we did thoughtlessly.

During the summer my dad had taught Lois to drive. Growing up in Oakland, and never needing to use a car, it had been a neglected skill which she gladly acquired on the farm. At first she spent time practicing clutching and shifting in the cow pasture. We had no automatic transmission vehicles in those days. After the pasture the road was next and finally at age twenty-one a brand new driver's license.

Our future was very much up in the air, but we felt as free as the wind to make decisions. I needed to finish college so we made plans to return to William Penn College in Oskaloosa, Iowa, that fall. But suddenly, out of the blue, a phone call came that there was an opening for a farm manager at Scattergood Friends School in West Branch, Iowa. I took the call and spoke briefly with the caller and thanked him, but our plans were already made.

The turndown was to be quite tenuous. We got to thinking and discussing. My dad wanted us to join him in the farm operation, but Lois had never lived on a farm except the one school year, many years ago. We were truly hesitant to commit ourselves to anything permanent or that would alter my folks' way of life in a profound way. So it finally dawned on us that the Scattergood offer for a year might be just the ticket to find out if I was a farmer, she a farm wife, and for both of us to size up farming as a permanent way of life.

We returned the call and made arrangements for an interview.

The school was first opened in 1890 under the auspices of the Iowa Yearly Meeting of Friends. But the Depression of the early twentieth century caught up with it and it closed its doors in 1932. The buildings were vacant for about ten years until the young people of the Yearly Meeting began to ask if they could have a Quaker high school in operation. The elders took it under advisement, and with much support and volunteer help to get the buildings back in shape it reopened in 1944 and graduated its first class in 1945.

In early August, 1946, we interviewed the director, and two local Quaker farmers who were actively involved in reopening the school. We all understood that I had no actual, practical experience at managing a farm, and didn't have a teaching certificate. Growing up on a farm was my only qualification. But the school year was about to begin. So, with no better prospect on the horizon and with their faith that things would work out, we were hired on the spot.

A few years before the school bought the farm, the large, old farmhouse had burned down. The farm family at that time had replaced it, probably in the late thirties, with a small Sears prefabricated house. That's what we moved into. We had no bathroom and only an outdoor toilet. It was primitive living and a brand new experience for us. The house was small with a kitchen, a living room and two small bedrooms. A coal fired furnace and a wood-fired cook stove in the kitchen were our heating equipment. Lois, having grown up with unvented gas heaters in her Oakland home, found the range in the kitchen a daunting, mysterious monster. But after a few bouts with smoke and soot and cleaning walls, she mastered it.

The farm buildings were about a half-mile, through the fields, from the school campus. In addition to the house, there was a large old barn with a haymow and stanchions for milking cows. There was a large lean-to shed attached to the south of the barn for bedding cattle in the winter. A one car garage, a concrete block milking parlor and an adjacent hen house were what we had to work with.

Setting up housekeeping here was our first time at really living together. We had been transients up to then, always living with someone else or temporarily here and temporarily there.

The first day of school, while the students were arriving, we sat under the maple trees and decided what each faculty member would teach. We had agreed to come for a year to see if we could handle it.

We stayed for ten.

Scattergood Farmhouse

CHAPTER 6

OUR PRISON EXPERIENCE

Don:

After World War II, when the peacetime draft act was passed in 1948, there were about 20 young Quaker men in Iowa who refused to register. This was a military act and we decided we could not participate. Even the act of registering was part of the military system, and to accept that was to accept part of the system.

At that time the usual sentence if convicted was 18 months. That was my sentence and I think most of the other men's, too. The standard practice was to serve one-third of a sentence then be released on good time, and be on probation for the rest of the sentence. We were all out after about six months.

But all this history should take a back seat to the question: why am I a conscientious objector.

When I was first involved, all COs I knew were religious men and women with Christian backgrounds who strongly believed and wanted to follow the non-violent teachings of Jesus. As time went on we found that there were other equally sincere people who had deeply-held reasons for being conscientious objectors. I now feel that the brotherhood of humankind is too large and precious to be relegated to any one religion or sect or society. All world religions, and many individuals who claim no religion, accept the brotherhood of all people. I believe strongly in the religious basis for pacifism, but at the same time I want to recognize that that may not be the only valid basis.

The Christian bases for pacifism are many and clear. Jesus was unequivocal in his directions to "love one another," "turn the other cheek," and "do good to those who despitefully use you." He said, "He who loves God, loves his brother." Adherence to these principals was more important to Him than saving his young life.

If I think of myself as part of the human family, how then can I destroy another member of the same family? The goal of war psychology is to dehumanize the enemy—reduce people to a universal name—"Huns," "dirty Japs," "the enemy," etc. Modern warfare even dehumanizes civilian people—they are known simply as "collateral damage" and forgotten. The military calls it "the price we must pay." As a human being and pacifist, I could not accept this terrible dehumanization and destruction of part of my family.

Most people, whether consciously religious or not, adhere to a set of principles of what is right, just, and loving. There is a report of Israeli soldiers refusing to carry out orders to demolish Palestinian homes. What was their motive? Were they following ancient ideals of loving one's enemy and being fair and just? Or were their actions based on purely contemporary experience of observing, and believing in certain standards of human behavior?

My experience began with a letter to Attorney General Tom Clark stating why I could not register for the military draft, and where I could be found if he wanted to contact me. That letter went out a few months before my twenty-sixth birthday. All men between the ages of twenty and twenty-six were required to register.

Well, he did choose to contact me. I got a call one clear October day from an FBI agent saying that he wanted to see me, and asked if I would be home that morning. With few options, I said I would.

It was a time of great apprehension for both Lois and me. I had never been accused of a crime before and we didn't know if he would arrive pointing a gun or with outstretched handcuffs. I didn't feel like a criminal, yet I was soon to be classified as such.

It was a busy fall time on the Scattergood School farm and I had in mind working while being interviewed. We had a chicken house that housed about 200 laying hens to provide eggs for the school diet. My bedding system was a common one of adding enough straw on a daily basis to keep the house dry and comfortable for the laying hens. Of course the layers of chicken droppings and straw got deeper and deeper as the season progressed. I cleaned it out only two or three times a year. He arrived on one of these days.

Chicken manure is a high nitrogen product and produces clouds of ammonia when exposed to air. When the agent arrived I had the manure spreader parked by the door and was happily involved in shoveling out the best fertilizer known to mankind. I was anxious to get everything above the smooth cement floor out and start a new layer of fresh straw before chore time in late afternoon. I greeted him at the door and invited him in. Breathing a mixture of air and ammonia was no problem for me, but he felt otherwise. After a few minutes of sputtered questions he came from behind his handkerchief and asked through watery eyes, "Could we please go inside?" I took pity on him, parked my pitchfork in the soon-to-be-removed floor covering, and with a feeling of smug superiority led him to the house—he could accuse me of a crime, but at least I could breathe under these conditions and he couldn't.

In the clean air of the kitchen, with Lois watching and our two-month-old son sleeping in his crib nearby, the agent and I made out a statement of my refusal to obey the law. He read it back to me, to be sure I understood it and that it was accurate, and I signed it. He tucked it in his official FBI briefcase and we shook hands in parting with no more emotion than if he had been a feed salesman. But Lois and I knew the dye had been cast and the ominous legal machinery would now begin to grind.

The boys' dorm director and I were on parallel legal paths. Both having refused to register we attended a double trial in Waterloo. Our carload to the trial included the school director, Leanore, Harold, my co-defendant, Lois, our by then seven-month old son David, and me. We were a quiet and anxious group. Leanore was losing her dorm director and farm manager, and Lois and David a spouse and father for an unknown period of time. Fairly recently a young Friend, and friend, former graduate of Scattergood, non-registrant, had been given the longest sentence on record by a judge in Kansas—five years. We were aware of this possibility.

The trial was without jury since there was no question of our guilt. Leanore spoke as a "Friend of the Court," with an appeal to the judge that we were vital to the operation of the school, not criminals, and should be dealt with in a lenient fashion—probation, instead of imprisonment was a possibility. The last few months had involved much discussion among staff and students of what our actions meant to all concerned. We were a group that knew our Quaker lineage had involved prison for many since the beginning of the sect. George Fox, the founder, born in 1624, said when refusing to join Cromwell's Army, "I live in the virtue of that power and light which takes away the occasion for all wars." Harold and I were not unusual.

We both received a sentence of eighteen months. The judge gave us the option of returning in a month, after "putting our affairs in order," or beginning our sentence now. Lois and I had already faced this, and we were ready. We chose the latter. After teary good-byes and a long tight hug with David in her arms, Harold and I followed the marshal to the Blackhawk County jail.

In a couple of weeks two federal marshals arrived to transport us to the Medical Center for Federal Prisoners in Springfield, MO. It was a minimum-security institution where federal prisoners from anywhere could be brought for medical care if needed. For ordinary travelers, the trip would have been considered uneventful, but not in our case.

The transport car was a standard four-door sedan with the marshals in the front seat and we three prisoners in the back. A young Tama Indian who had been convicted of selling alcohol on the reservation, a federal offense, had joined us. Someplace in the middle of Missouri, we stopped at a small-town restaurant for supper. We were not handcuffed or inhibited in any way so we were nondescript patrons of the restaurant. We ate our meal, the marshals paid the bill, and we stepped outside. To our surprise, the marshals were not with us. For twenty minutes we waited on the curb in front of our car for the drivers to show up. They finally did, and with apologies to us, but no explanation for their tardiness, we continued south.

When new prisoners arrive, the usual procedure is for them to be held for a few days in a "holding pen." This is for delousing, hair cutting, shaving, issuing of prison garb and whatever else is necessary to bring a man "up" to prison standards. We weren't allowed to talk to anyone, but discovered we could converse through the duct system and recognize voices of other COs who were a few days ahead of us. We spread the news.

Once the "holding pen" event was over we were assigned to a cot and nightstand in a room of a hundred others. The clientele already there were quick to point out that anyone who wouldn't fight would be in trouble with those "tough guys" in the exercise yard.

"Don't ever go out there, or they will kill you," was the prevailing advice.

We mulled it over, but decided we had to exercise, death or not. So began long conversations with men and their problems—law tangles, girlfriend problems, family problems, injustice of society and on and on. One man, in for life—a "lifer"— a professional bank robber, gave massages and lessons on the art of massage.

They couldn't understand a system that put men in prison for killing people and others in prison for refusing to do so. They were keenly aware of the irony and expressed it in crude and loud voices.

Most of the COs were assigned to work on the farm that was outside the prison walls and under the care of armed guards. They were different from the run-of-the-mill prisoners and soon established a reputation with the administration for work accomplishments that had never been seen before.

I found an opportunity to work in the electrical shop and do repairs in the several buildings within the walls. I was assigned to an older man who was the chief electrician—a short, stocky man of crude language and minimum ambition to accomplish anything. Mr. Guard and I toured the grounds with tools in hand to fill any work order he was given.

One such order was to repair a perimeter yard light that didn't seem to have any brightness. It was one of many high on the outside walls of all the brick two-story buildings. Mr. Guard helped me hoist the twenty-foot ladder to the base of the light, but had no intentions of hoisting his overweight frame more than one rung off the ground. I finished the repair as he instructed from the ground, and to this day don't know how I failed to insulate my repair properly, but as night fell it was abundantly obvious that something was awry. One whole string of perimeter lights came on with only a dull orange glow. In addition, I had left a sixteen-inch pipe wrench on a second story windowsill where I had been working.

The plan was obvious—a major breakout was in the making. All the guards were called back to duty for the night. The towers were doubly manned and the foot and motor guards were doubled. I slept soundly, oblivious to the emergency activity around us. The next morning, when I arrived at work, Mr. Guard admonished me mildly for the mistake I had made. I suspect he had been roundly chewed out, but he didn't pass the venom along to me in any way. I was amazed after learning how disrupted life had been for so many during that night.

Lois' life was drastically changed while I was gone. She and I had strong support from students and staff of Scattergood School. She and David moved from the farmhouse to a room in a small dorm and she was put in charge of some of the younger boys. A young Quaker farmer was brought in to manage while I was gone.

Lois took over my physics class even though the students knew far more physics than she. She mostly just monitored and saw that they assigned themselves work and carried it out. They were seniors and treated her gently and with respect, but still had to have some fun. During one experiment one of the boys with a magnet under the table manipulated her demonstration out of control. That boy was later elected president of one of the eastern Quaker colleges!

She made one trip to southern Missouri for a closely supervised visit. She and nine-month-old David were allowed into a small glass-and-wire partitioned room before I was ushered into a seat on the other side. What a glorious sight.

The one hour visit slipped by in seconds.

I've always contended that wives of social prisoners have a tougher time than the men. We were in a very secure place, with some choices to make as we chose—we could protest injustice or simply bide our time and get out at the earliest possible time. The wives were in the community which could have some ugly elements. Lois was fortunate. She was in a loving, close-knit society, and made only contacts she chose with the wider community.

My release came in August, 1949, six months after sentencing.

Ten years later, Lois' bravery showed up again. We were still at Scattergood Friends School in the same capacity we had from the beginning. But our family had grown to five children and our financial needs were strained by the salaries of a small private school. I looked into other teaching positions as a licensed and experienced physics teacher. I finally accepted a position as a teacher in the West Branch Public Schools, a 50 percent raise.

We were happy with the new prospects and knew it would take a lot of pressure off her in managing our family finances.

But the local American Legion Commander was not happy. As soon as he heard of the contract he appeared before the board to protest the hiring of a teacher with a prison record to teach in the public school. The board voted to rescind my contract.

I felt unwilling to push for a job where I might have a right to be legally, but be unaccepted socially. I was too unsure of what might lie ahead. I accepted the resignation. It was the weaker thing to do, but it was my choice.

Then everything broke loose. The resignation made state-wide headlines. Editorials and many letters-to-the-editor appeared. At the height of the publicity, Lois paid for ad space and wrote a letter of support for me, pointing out the injustice of a school board caving in to the protest of one powerful man. Did I give her enough thanks for her support?

In 1986 she compiled all the events surrounding the controversy. It was a book of copied editorials, letters, testimonials, reports—every bit of history she could find pertaining to the time. She found copies of FBI reports of interviews with neighbors in Springdale following my application for a pardon. She copied the pardon I received. It was a work of love dedicated to our children and me. In early 1987 she commented thus:

"I've been having fun compiling a book about Don's non-registration, school dismissal days. Nice way to do a book without having to write. It's going to be quite thick, an inch or more, spiral bound, with red divider pages and cover!"

Years later we were again embroiled in the responsibilities of the State toward people's lives and its authority to end life. Iowa had, since the days before statehood, vacillated many times between establishing a legal death penalty or not. In 1872 the Iowa Governor signed a bill abolishing capital punishment. In 1878 it was reinstated. With this action, Iowa became the first English speaking jurisdiction in the world to abolish capital punishment and then reinstate it. The 1878 law remained unchanged until repealed in 1965. Many reinstatement bills have been introduced and defeated since then.

In 1993 a joint House/Senate judiciary committee held hearings to listen to public thought on the subject of reinstating capital punishment. Sixty-three persons presented papers that night—five in support and all others against. Lois and I were two of those speaking against. Our arguments were very similar. In 1997 Lois spoke again before the same group considering the same legislation.

Lois:

"I am sorry to be here tonight for two reasons: First I'm sorry that legislators are spending time, money and energy on the possibility of any form of death penalty."

"Second, I'm sorry to be here because my husband and I are parents of a daughter who was murdered ten years ago in her Philadelphia apartment. I'm very uncomfortable using her death and our sorrow for a political/moral issue. But I've been told that being parents or survivors of a victim, and also being strong opponents of the death penalty, carries some weight. And I want to add what heft I can toward preventing a death penalty bill in Iowa. There are many survivors like us, most of them silent, who know in their bones or have learned from cruel experience that killing the offender does nothing to restore the lost one nor to ease the grief. Giving the State permission to continue the violence of the killer is not a healing process for the individual or society."

Don:

It was a bitter cold night when we drove to Des Moines to deliver our testimony. Each speaker had four minutes. She was nervous and frightened before the event, but satisfied when it was over that she had done the best she could for the cause we believed in.

Reinstatement that year failed.

The New Providence Farmhouse

Where Don grew up and where we lived
while we farmed with Don's folks for two crop seasons.

CHAPTER 7

RAISING OUR CHILDREN

Don:

After teaching and managing the Scattergood farm for four years, 1946 to 1950, my dad finally induced us to come farm with him. Mother and Dad had bought a house in Eldora six miles away. Brother Jerry and Myrtle farmed a few miles away in St. Anthony, close enough for farm work to be exchanged.

Dad's farm was on good fertile well-developed land. He had managed it with skill for the past twenty-five years and the mortgage was paid off. We had had a good time working together for two crop seasons. Our income was more, during those two years, than we had ever had before—we relished that. It meant a lot to Lois to relax a bit financially. If we stayed we could easily have made enough for our growing family and Dad and Mother to live on.

We rejoined the staff at Scattergood in the fall of 1953. Our decision to return was not based on family relations or income potential. It was based on the challenge the school job presented. We were invited, and felt truly needed, to help continue to develop an outstanding Quaker school with its unique farm involvement.

I sensed that our decision was a bitter disappointment to my dad as he had his heart set on one of his boys taking over the farm and he retiring. As Lois cleaned and packed I know my folks felt a deep sadness at seeing that beautiful house, with all its personal history for them, looking so empty again.

Leanore, director of the school, had urged us to come back, promising that the little pre-fab box of a farm house was to be enlarged and a farm income arrangement would provide us with an adequate salary. The house was about doubled in size, with a very nice kitchen and large living/dining room added. A new front entry-way with two large closets was a joy. A basement room and shower also were big improvements. I began working on these additions after corn picking was through in New Providence.

So during the fall and early winter of 1953 Lois lived in New Providence on the farm we were leaving and I lived in West Branch. She had the care of our three children. We wrote letters and made a few trips to see each other. Nothing lifted my spirits more than the arrival of that envelope in her characteristic sweeping handwriting. As I read, her presence engulfed me and I felt her breath on my neck.

Lois:

Thanksgiving Day 11-26-53

And I haven't really thought specifically of the reams of things I have to be thankful for. In fact, I've spent much energy being jealous over things some other people have. I've become very competitive minded and mercenary. Ugh. My outlook, my soul, has become wizened and unproductive like a dried apple.

11-30-53 10:00 p.m.

Washed. Cleaned basement & back porch. Lots of packing & sorting accomplished. Feel satisfied as this was one of the most dreaded jobs of moving.

A wonderful letter from Don today. I depend so much on him and on his love that I turn cold when really thinking what I might do without him, as Ruth is doing now without Carrol. Carrol Cook, neighboring farmer about our age with two little kids, died suddenly of a heart attack.

If I could make (let) each day be so good that we could say, no matter what happens, "we've had this and it was good," that would be an achievement. By good, I don't mean all must be sunshine & light, but that we'd be together in understanding my empathy. Don is much better at this than I, although he doesn't always express it.

I've wondered why if one believes in nothing after death one must also be accused of not believing in God. I have a great deal of learning to do to find a theology that I'm sure of.

12-2-53

The first time I've been in a beauty shop since that horrid $20 permanent (that was an expensive one then) soon after marriage when I was so tearfully disappointed and Cousin Mattie & Don both comforted and aided me.

Made gum drops, lollipops & Mexican wedding cakes this evening to store for Christmas, none very successful. I ought to stick to oatmeal cookies. My flights into the exotic nearly always end as belly flops.

Sat. 12-5-53

Ugh, a dreary day. Kids rather yowly. More rain, I hope Scattergood is getting some of this. A letter from Don today says the house is impossible to move into, but he wants us to come down to the apartment in the boys' dorm. I'm getting anxious, as he is, too, to get us together so guess we'll do it.

12-6-53 (Don's birthday, but I didn't mention it.)

Sunday School & church, wondering what it's all about as usual.

Going to get Don tomorrow, hoorah. If I can just remember the important things through this prolonged moving & building process we'll all be happier & healthier.

December, 1953

Davie has missed school all week with a cold & ear infection. Jannie & Martha have had their share, too, but not as bad. I've had it too.

My prayer is for patience & humor, far too short of both, for these hectic weeks of sick, irritable kids & of no place to put things or to belong. I dread the dorm session, but try to tell myself it may not be too bad.

Don:

We had finally moved from the family farm in New Providence to an apartment in the boys' dorm at Scattergood until our new house addition on the farm was finished enough to move into. Field work was done so I spent my days teaching, choring and working on the house. Lois was a full time mother with only voluntary responsibilities at school.

We moved to the partially completed farmhouse in the winter of 1954. Lois' insatiable bent for order made, for her, a major compromise—the cramped apartment or an unfinished house.

Lois:

12-14-53

Kids on the mend. It's been a strain of a week, all taking a turn at the doctor's & being sick & feverish. To top it all—this is it! We're having our first, and I hope our last, "mistake." I'm over two weeks late so I can't kid myself any longer. I'm glad in a way, but it is going to make a hard year harder, and will slow me up terrifically when there are so many extras to do. A case of loving not wisely but too well, I fear. A good joke—wish I weren't so civilized & took more of life more easily. If I could just learn to take each day and enjoy it the way it is.

Don is making his will today. Hope I have no need of it for about 80 years, but it does happen here sometimes. Jannie announced today that she likes "nose juice" to eat!

1-10-54

A month of flues, cold infections, and generally feeling below par. I've been low mentally, which is no help.

House going slowly, siding and inside insulation is about 2/3 on. A group from Whittier is coming again this week, which heartens me considerably.

Don back from the sale in New Providence and things look much brighter when he's here!

January, 1954

Typical conversations together:

"Well, we got everything sold—all the machinery and livestock went. Sometimes some things don't get a bid. So that's good. It was a good day and a large turnout. Bidding was active, so prices were a little higher than I had expected. I think Dad was satisfied, too," Don reported.

"Thus ends a chapter in our lives, Don," Lois said. "That bridge is now burned. I hope your folks aren't too devastated."

"It's hard to tell how they feel—they keep it so well hidden. We must keep in close touch with them. Are you going to survive a few months in the boys' dorm while I finish the house?" I asked.

"I will, but I'm ready to move any time," she said.

"I'm going to get an appointment with Dr. Comly as soon as I can. I'm going to ask him if he can help mixed up mammas as well as small children," she added.

Don:

May, 1954

Our marriage came with the usual friction of everyday living, and renovating a house while farming, raising children and working made for more opportunities than most.

Typical conversations together:

"Loie, come here a second. How do you expect me to put this door on? Frames are square you know, and a door that's not, won't fit," I said.

"Well, I thought the screen would square it when I stapled it on, but I guess it didn't."

"It sure didn't. Oh, well, it'll only take an hour or so to take the screen off and put it on square," I exaggerated, not really feeling angry with her, but wanting to exhibit superiority.

"Did you get the bed sawed off like you wanted?" I asked with a change of subject.

"Not quite. The blade broke on the last post," she answered.

"I've got new blades. I'll put one in," I said. "And by the way, you know that hay rake I bought at the sale yesterday? Well, it's a three bar instead of a four bar! I can't believe it. I looked it over so carefully, but missed the obvious. How could I do such a stupid thing?"

"But it'll rake hay won't it?" she asked.

"Sure, but the four bars are so much smoother and don't knock off leaves as easily." I explained.

"Kind of like putting a screen in crooked, Huh?" She got the last word.

Lois:

Mon. 5-24-54

Davie picked up Hal's light meter Sat. & Don spent most Sunday afternoon tramping around with him trying to find it. For a long time Davie wouldn't admit to even having it. Today Lawrence found it under the old watering tank after being told it was in the old truck. This was just a few minutes after I'd been out with Don looking in the truck & water tank. I don't know how to handle such 5 1/2 year old duplicity. He's vowed all along he didn't know where he left it.

5-25

Arnie Hoge is working on forms for front walk. Will be working for Scatt all this week. Don is planting (male corn) today.

We had dinner & a show "out" last night, nice to get away, but especially nice to be remembered specially.

Davie's last day of school today. Saw the circus program. I just feel sick when seeing that class, absolutely no creativeness. Clay plaques of hand prints were given by children to parents, but writing, painting, even shaping of plaque were done by the teacher. Do I have a responsibility to try to reach her? Or the superintendent? Or the board? How?

5-29

Scattergood Graduation Day—for me, too. A feeling of belonging & security, the lack of which I usually suffer during these affairs, sustained & happified me all day. Bible School committee meeting this afternoon. Kids were good & played at school till Jannie got stuck on top of slide & wouldn't come down either way. Jane V. rescued her for me. People poured in from 3:30 on to see our "new house."

Sun. 6-6-54

Day of rest at home while Don & kids at meeting. Dreading another week of Bible School. Kids demand so much, give so little in immediate return. I long for more adult companionship & wonder how we can face another baby.

Don:

We were still working on the Scattergood farmhouse we had moved into. The structure was complete but the interior and furnishings were not. I had built mahogany plywood valences for the windows and Lois was making curtains to fit. We had worked within the budget enough to buy some used furniture which Lois was doing as she found time. Spanish teacher, Agard, was also a skilled artisan, and taught me to lay roll flooring with invisible seams. We enjoyed our homemade surroundings. The school staff exchanged baby-sitting needs for routine doctor appointments, so that made town trips much easier.

Lois:

Wed. 6-30-1954

Six weeks to go. Wish I felt more enthusiastic about this new arrival; probably I will when it's here. Martha walked about 18 feet by herself today, and has taken several little trips. She feels very proud and will, in a few days, really launch out on her own, I do believe. She's a cute little dickens even if she is a slow poke.

Got the front room woodwork sanded and stained today, finished at 11:30 p.m. Two coats of lacquer & it's finally done! Agard comes tomorrow & I have great hopes for some finishing work, but he's very slow.

7-1-1954

What a difference this heat makes to me; felt so good yesterday when it was cool, but today I wilt & drag again.

I've been very impatient and unloving with Davie & Jannie for several days. D. is so jealous of J.—always something to bicker about.

Tues. 7-13-54

Big excitement. Don & Roy just drove in with a 4 1/2 foot combine they bought today. Thirteen years old & no guarantee. $100. Hope it works fine.

Heat wave again, whew, these days get me! The folks and Jerry and Myrtle & boys were all down Sunday. And we had the house & grounds looking better than I'd hoped for. With Agard working here since July 1, we've made some real strides on the house. All the windows are completed & have screens now. The roof boxing is all on and painted with one coat. The front room woodwork is completed (a project I got mighty weary of, but it looks satiny and satisfying now that it's all done).

Sunday night when getting Martha ready for bed she was crying & suddenly wasn't breathing. Her lips were turning bluish & I grabbed her up, her eyes rolling & head flopping. I yelled bloody murder for Don who was putting the other two in bed & when he got to us I had M upside down patting her back. He picked her up & she was all right then, breathing very fast & shallowly & content to sit very still. She has seemed fine ever since, but I couldn't get unwound to sleep (it was so hot, too) till after midnight, kept wanting to check her breathing.

Three weeks from today our fourth (and last!?) is due. I'm awfully sore & stiff but otherwise fine. Doing better emotionally than with Martha, I think. Things are getting into fairly good order and that certainly helps me feel better.

Sunday 7-25-1954

I had the detached attitude that seems to accompany labor. Went to Sunday School & Meeting, got dinner & did dishes. Don put kids to nap & we napped. Don amorous & allowed for first time in weeks. He's been an awfully patient man. Rested & read, couldn't sleep. Began trips to bathroom about 3:30. Still cramping lightly about 7:00 and began to think yup, this is it. Don took kids to Sara at school. We came in to hospital in the pickup (Hamptons had our car), arrived about 8:30. Pains very mild & far between while being enemaed and prepared. Read from 9:30 to about 11:00 with interruptions by nurses checking dilation & asking me if I felt anything. Getting discouraged—then one good pain. Got better ones till 11:30. Went into delivery room then, strapped in & gassed—too much—lost track for awhile. Remember thinking once "This is having a baby," during a splitting pain. Felt the crowning & the episiotomy cut and the release as the head came through. Baby cried, and then shoulder push & through. Liked that it cried so soon. Disappointed that it was girl for Don & Dave & some for me. Yet, already, on fifth day after, can imagine nothing else—she's ours. Refused ether for stitches. Doctor said, "Give her nitrous oxide, there are very few." I counted only three clampings or whatever they do and I'm very mobile.

Talked to Don on phone on way out of delivery room. He'd gone home about 10:00. He came in about 6:00 the next morning to see me; that was nice.

Tempus has fugited and we are now six. Ruth Edna arrived 7-25 at 11:55 p.m. A wee 5 lb., 14 oz mite, but very pretty (I think), fine featured. She seemed so little, I was really frightened of her at first. The other three went to Mother's & Myrtle's for two weeks. The week at home without them was so quiet & peaceful! I gave up nursing her as she wasn't gaining fast enough, even when that was all I had to do. I haven't regretted it, except for a nostalgic knowing that it's the better way, basically. I think she is being accepted very well, no major upheaval that I can tell. Martha keeps busy in her new found walking ability, and is the worst ever for getting into things. Drives me stark raving mad in the kitchen at times.

Tues. 8-31-54

Davie started school yesterday and seems glad & proud to be a first grader. I'm finding out that mothering four is a full time job leaving no time for me. I don't mind when I can keep a perspective & some serenity, but it's awfully frustrating when I get too eager to finish responsibilities & do something of my choice, because there is no finish.

10-30-54

Don has been pouring cement till it runs out of his ears; his hands feel like gravel, too. He's poured an 18 x 40 ft. feeding floor, 3 10 x 12 slabs for houses (hog), built two steel corn cribs (on concrete) and a 20 x 12 ft. floor for the farm shop.

Ruthie weighed 9 lb., 14 oz on her third month birthday. She's getting quite social & awfully cute. She's so good; I enjoy her little babies more than I did the others, partly 'cause she's the last (?!) perhaps.

Don is all ready to start corn-picking Monday, picked one load today. 60 acres with a one-row picker, an old beat up one, here's hoping it keeps plugging.

c.1955

Naomi was born July, 15, 1955

LIFE AT SCATTERGOOD

On the way to Meeting

Science Class

Farming

Feeding the Holsteins

"How would you like to be fifty and a thousand years old? Then you'd be big as a giant." Asked by Janet on my thirtieth birthday. Growth and age synonymous to child.

8/25/55

Oh, the horrible frustration of trying to do anything in a day. I lose all sense of humor, the children act (and feel) ugly and unloved, and so do I. My prayer for the year should be to lose all desire for efficiency and outward order and neatness. Let me suffer messes patiently and develop an inward peace, which transcends the outer chaos of five children. Let me look at them and see their needs, listen and hear.

A report should be written expressing the inconsistencies of American home magazines which advocate beauty, cleanliness, order, etc. and also the "happy family." Is there really possible such a combination or are there not enough hours in a day and feet/pounds of energy per wife to truly accomplish both? For me, the striving for both almost makes me schizophrenic.

Don:

In spite of Lois' misgivings, we were a "happy family." She took on the bulk of childcare, so her different take was understandable. She was intimately connected to the kids for many more hours a day than I. When I came in for the evening I was often able to shift the burden off her shoulders. I played "mousetrap" with the kids. I would lie on the floor and "trap" them with my legs if they got too close. I released them just before the distress point set in. It was hilarious for them and took little energy for me—after all, I was lying on the floor! They could play endlessly so only the signal for supper ended the play.

I had access to a good electric welder. Even though far from professional looking I learned to make a safe and sound welded seam. With this skill I could keep the farm machinery in working order.

From scraps of old pipe and angle iron I welded together an elegant swing-set for the kids. One end was on an "A" frame and the other in a hole in the trunk of the big maple tree just outside the kitchen window. It was safe and visible and they used it for many years.

Lois and I lived during the Great Depression. Even though our growing-up circumstances were very different we learned the same lessons. Instead of buying luxuries, or even necessities, we made them. She was a skilled seamstress and made many of the kids' clothes and household furnishings and repaired the things we wore. My favorite pet peeve was her unwillingness to pay attention to the color of the thread with which she darned my socks—white socks with black yarn and dark socks with white. But I was so thankful for socks with toes and heels that I didn't complain. Our girls grew up with hand-me-down clothes from loving friends with daughters slightly older than ours.

I often felt thankful for a large family to take care of. I had a legitimate reason to do creative work. The family needed physical things—larger house, toys, valences, and on and on. I enjoyed using the skills I had to bring these improvements into being. I took pride in the things I built, as Lois did in the things she made.

Lois:
8/31/55

Weary—mostly in the head from the old frustrations. (I hate that word, must find a substitute.) But also weary in the middle from a flu bug that seemed to hit us yesterday. Jannie's teacher thought hers was first day excitement, quite understandably. Don has it the hardest, I think.

Changed sleeping quarters for everyone on Mon. and I'm still trying to sort & arrange clothes. My innards yearn so for absolute neatness and order that I would be happy to be a nun (in that respect only), for surely nuns have only the barest essentials of clothing.

Now, I am enjoying these minutes of sitting & writing. And I enjoyed sitting in the sun feeding Naomi her bottle & reading & visiting with Martha; I forgot to feel the pushing toward the next job. And yet part of the pleasure was because of accomplishing several things at once—feeding, sunbathing and attention to kids. It would be better to enjoy the moment for its own sake. Don has a terrible list of things he wants to do this fall; I wonder if he feels the push as much as I do. If so, he controls it better than I, doesn't let it anger him so he takes it out on the kids as I do.

I dread the winter—always struggling against heaps of winter clothes, wet ones, too, and kids' playing messes and trying to keep warm, and laundry drying slowly in the dirty basement, always overlapping, past, present and future laundries. I'm anxious to organize and simplify as much as possible and then I must let be what is inevitable and enjoy a cluttered and cooped life.

Wondering if it isn't partly a matter of self-discipline, which determines whether or not one goes crazy, or becomes "mentally ill." I have many elements of craziness in me now, I think—extreme irritability, depression, lack of drive and unable to get a job done with dispatch, fear so bad that there are physical aspects of it. Now, if I could, I would go off by myself & think & mull over the problem with no interruptions & as there is no answer possible—at least not until the problem is known—I think I would go insane, lose all contact with reality. As it is I'm forced to carry out responsibilities and so must hang on to a semblance of social normality, so it's circumstances, not my discipline, which keep me sane, if I am.

These last six weeks since Naomi's birth have been really euphoric ones. It's felt so good to feel good, to feel myself getting stronger and trimmer. The only real problems were the constant one of my own personal desires for outward order, etc. in opposition to the nature of children and the one of getting closer to the kids (really all one problem?) It seems impossible that this new specter of a No. 6 can loom so horrendous.

10-5-55

Well, the nightmare of over three weeks wondering if I were pregnant is over, and I'm glad. We really had a round of it. A doctor at the clinic where I went to see about sterility possibilities told me I had "signs" of pregnancy. That was a terrible day. We were both about the most anguished we'd ever been. Don admits & so do I that pride was an element in the pain, but also the physical & financial burden of another one (especially only ten months younger than Naomi) seemed, and seems, almost insurmountable. Don saw Dr. Conly ($15 worth) the next day and he could offer no help unless I'd get a good case of depression, the kind diagnosable as mental illness, not just a heartsick discouragement. Dr. Eikleberry still held out hope & gave us Dr. Sautter's name. He made it more clear than anyone else how difficult it is to avoid being maternal. And if pregnancy is real, nothing can be done legally or safely unless one is crazy or half dead from TB, heart trouble, toxemia, etc. After all these sessions what should happen but a beautiful menstrual flow. Now our confidence should be strengthened, but we're scared into celibacy—technically, at least. And the old problem of whether to become barren or not remains with us:

Don

Pro   1. Easy, office procedure

       2. Can be secret more easily

       3. Doesn't fear regret or resentment later, he says.

Con   1. Doesn't know later reactions possible

       2. Dr. said "hard on ego for men"

       3. Limits future wives

Lois

Pro   1. Rather be "done" than have a "done" husband?

       2. Become sterile many years sooner than Don anyway.

Con   1. Operation and hospitalization

       2. Fear personal reaction & fear Don's reaction to a barren wife. Think I can accept & adjust but sometimes wonder.

Us—Pro and Con

       Relieve forever the tension of possible unwanted pregnancies. But is this very tension one of the appealing things about sex?

       Know better now than ever could have before, that there is real suffering in having more children than one feels able to handle. But who knows what we will want or need tomorrow (or in ten years)?

Don:

    We had carried on conversations for years about sterilization. I argued for a vasectomy, but she insisted she didn't want a sterile husband. She was thirty now, we had five beautiful, healthy children, so freedom from pregnancy fears seemed, to me, like a good addition to our lives. The existing equipment available—diaphragms, condoms and several other devices were not one-hundred percent protection. Close friends called their second child their "IUD Baby." Their intrauterine device had failed!

    We could not come to a meeting of the minds, so continued, as we were, for a few more years—seven to be precise.

Lois:

10-7-55

    Oppressed & impressed with the shortness of life. Teach kids, learn self, to enjoy other people & their queerities and smallnesses, then able to see greatnesses, too, & not be upset by differences.

10-16-55

    Here we go again—two weeks before time for that beautiful flow I'm worried, although logically there just can't be a chance in a million that a sperm got through. In two weeks my libido can forget the terror—just in time to beget another terror! I'd like to know how universal this fear is. I've never had it before, but I feel a 6th child would be very bad for all of us. To me it would be the end; life would change from a busy, but happy and usually manageable one, to a dreary drudge. I've so enjoyed the last couple of months, except for the stomach shrinking fear that attacks. The children have been such fun to watch and work with when I feel so well & I have keener appreciation of them than I did.

    A recorder group has started at school. Bought a recorder & want very much to join, but very difficult to jibe with their practice hours. It's a nice little instrument, so simple, I think I could learn to play it, but it needs a group to sound best.

    I'm also hungry for a good book.

    Four sleeping bags are about accomplished, only the snaps on one double one left. Don helps put those on. I'm inordinately proud of these bags, think they're about the best do-it-yourself project I've ever done.

Don:

    We loved to camp, and sleeping bags compared to loose bedding were a real luxury. New ones were out of our financial reach so Lois plunged into the homemade project. She planned carefully and bought yards of denim and soft cotton batting. She bought snaps for closure and started construction. She quilted the finished bags so the batting wouldn't bunch up as we used them. They were our camping standby for many years. The three older kids claimed possession of the singles and we had the double.

Lois:

11-7-55

Now here's a problem—whether to use this book as an outlet for thoughts and feelings, not bothering too much about the language and composition, or whether to think of the literary aspect (ahem), too. The latter does slow the former. I shall have to muddle through to a policy, I guess. One thing I do know: an important reason for this book is to be as honest as I possibly can, and that is hard, especially since I feel self-conscious about my writing anything. Also, seemingly, what is true for me one day is not necessarily so the next.

Elfrida Vipont Foulds, author, singer, historian, and parent is visiting at school. At a tea this afternoon she talked about writing; it was interesting. She's charming and cultivated, but in not too canned a way, and I liked her. I returned home swirling with ideas as I usually do. That's my chief trouble; I never get beyond the swirling to the slow plodding that accomplishes. I want to make music on the guitar, piano, recorder, but I never practice. I want to be a teller of tales, especially Bible stories, but I never learn any. I want to write, but I don't even know what I want to write about. I want to be a social butterfly, but I never open my head in a crowd. I want to be a really good & wise parent and wife, and here I do practice, but what blotches I make. And one of the worst blotches is that of feeling that being a parent frustrates the other creative desires. But I'm getting better accepting the fact that for years ahead, being a parent is my most important job, nothing must let me forget that. And I keep hoping that when those years are over I will have something to write about.

I must confess here a most ridiculous sin. Sara B. is going to have a baby next Spring—and I'm jealous of her! Don would be bewildered if he knew, bewildered, amused and disgusted. And so am I. Surely with our five I can't want another one now. No—I know I don't. I think I'm jealous because she's 37 or so and having one, and I've had all we should have by 30. So at 37 for me, when I'm feeling old, ugly & less needed, I won't be able to renew my youth with a new infant, and Sigrid Undset is right when she has Kristin Lavransdatter say that a woman is young so long as she holds a child in her arms. I was stupid and slow learning to enjoy babies and the last two have been so much fun in spite of increased duties and family problems.

11-9-55

What is this inner sickness that always leaves me feeling so inadequate, valueless and depressed after hearing an inspiring person? Isn't an inspirer supposed to elevate, to add richness to life? Then why do I feel trodden and poorer after such experiences? Am I so weak & spiritually poor that challenges can only oppress me?

I'm obsessed lately with how to make my life do something. I want to do something worthwhile with it. Or is it only a disguised desire for publicity & praise? I know that what I'm doing, the daily round with the children, is the most important (really) and basic thing I can ever do, and I do find satisfaction & joy in it—not enough though. But also there is so much sense of failure in it that it seems another job might not (?) have. And I worry about what I'll do after there are no babies. In ten years I'll be forty and Naomi will be ten. Will there still be only meals, washings, mending & sewing to consume the whole day? Surely there will be time for something else. But how does one get started into other things if having lived in a vacuum (that's not a good term for describing life with five small children—I always think of a vacuum as totally soundless!) previously.

11-14-55

A kitchen cluttered with the remains of the day signifies the condition of mind in its mistress. The table is not quite cleared, bread, 2 slices, 3 various sized pieces of pie, a few paper napkins sagging in their holder, and a plate of butter which has been hacked & dug from all angles add up to a kind of forlornness which the salt & pepper shakers cannot dispel, in spite of their blue plastic sentinal-ship over the scene. The sink and counter are as bad; clean dishes are stacked without order in the drainer, and those that couldn't be forced in are left in the rinse pan. A few dirty dishes remain on the other side of the sink, along with a pan heaped full with a volcanic shaped mountain of garbage. Wet diapers, baby's shoes and dirty overalls, lunch boxes, baby bottles, a kettle lid and other sundries lie haphazardly on remaining counter space. To top it all, the floor and stove are sticky and dirty.

Just such stickiness & disorder dwell in the housekeeper. A mind full of jumbled, unrelated desires and ideas.

How we would love the trip to Washington, but where can we leave five children? We need a vacation—just us. Why do I resent time spent with the children with one part of me when another part realizes how important it is?

Thanksgiving Day 1955

Oh God, I thank thee for our children, but help me to bear them. I seem to be steeping in a solution of defeat and, I suppose, self pity. Martha mumps & cold, all the others home with colds, very interrupted nights, might account for some of it, but not all. It is my own sickness that drags me down. I'm most certainly not living in a state of grace. How well Anne Lindbergh says it when she says one can hardly tie a shoelace when "out of grace," and all tasks seem borne ahead of one, & lightly, when "in grace."

Ruthie has a bottom in need, as always.

12-5-55

Janet on hearing that tomorrow her daddy will be 33 said, "That old?! Well, he's still a good daddy even if he is that many years."

1-8-56

Before I forget it I want to record that we had a nice Christmas and holiday time. It felt so good to be unpregnant & unnauseated! And I feel I did a better job with the kids than before, time with them for reading & singing & talking.

Since Christmas it has been a round of colds & bad ears. Jan will go back to school tomorrow, and Martha is at last much better after five shots in the bottom, a professional ear cleaning job, and some oral medicine. Naomi is having shots now (penicillin) but seems to be coming along better. Ruthie got over hers fairly quickly, too, but today she has given us a worm again! Always something! Davie has been sick with jealousy & I suppose insecurity these last weeks. That's the illness that really worries me!

I think I'm growing some these months. I'm tied down but not too resentful, even enjoy watching the interesting little creatures even though I get bone weary from their demands by day's end. It's almost a non-regretful nostalgia I feel about going out & doing anything. I can see why conscientious mothers get like Mother Laughlin, absolutely no other interests. I hope not to get that bad, but I certainly have too little energy, and interest in anything else. A bad sign.

We want life to run smoothly with no conflicts, but as soon as it does we become bored & frightened. What in the heck is this cycle we go through & cling to so tenaciously?

1-19-56

Nothing is so tiring as fretting over how fatiguing the inconveniences of your household equipment are. Thought inspired after listening to one of those how-to-have-a-perfect-household lessons. Why don't they ever give us lessons in the really important aspects of homemaking—like how to be as sexy as you'd like to be after a day with five children draining you.

2-12-56

A thought for Lincoln who will always shine for integrity.

Life has been very enjoyable and intense lately, as Pepys would say, "Please God it may continue so." Part of this is due to the reading of the Kinsey book—a truly inspiring hunk of writing & statistics. Must spend an evening catching up some of the most important, for us, elements from it. For now, only a hurrah for sex, and a gratefulness that we seem to be succeeding in keeping sex and reproduction separated. Don & I have had some good airings of thoughts lately, which increase my love & respect for him.

Today at 5:00 he and three friends left in Roy's car to go to Washington for a week long seminar on the Ag problem. They should be back in about 10-11 days. It's going to be a long pull here, but I'm awfully glad he could go.

Early January found all kids with colds & bad ears, worms & a bladder infection for me. So, with polio shots, too, we have already spent as much as in last year for doctor and medicine bills. And last year we got a baby out of it!

I had an overnight vacation in IC a few weeks ago, very satisfactory and fun to spend a night alone in a hotel & have a whole day to use as I pleased. Browsed in library, did errands, browsed patterns & materials, visited a court session, and saw a movie, came home refreshed & eager to see how the family fared without me—they did fine.

Had a nice visit with Dr. Taylor about kids (wetting problem) & family life in general. Always so good to see him because he's a good listener or counselor—just listens & accepts—a goal for a mother of 5 to reach for! And a wife of one!

5-6-56

Why am I gloomy so much of the time? In high school & sooner, my trademark was being the clown. Not so much so in college, and now I've become absolutely humorless, especially in dealing with kids. Where along the line did I become so "sot" & inhibited? Been reading a diary, *Growing Pains*, by Wanda Gag. She was, is, a remarkable girl. At fifteen & sixteen she accomplished more per day and against greater odds than I do now. She made a point of not writing in detail the sad things—stressing the glad—a point I might do well to consider. I've considered writing the bad thoughts as sort of therapy, but it may be just a bad habit. Also I fear my moods & fits of depression & joy are so like hers at half my age, that I must wonder whether I'm still adolescent emotionally.

Why I hate my children is because they so strongly point out all my deficiencies, and in my copelessness I get to not liking them. This reason is a more important one than that of their constant messes & work causing. It's the emotional sides of all of us that wears me out!

Don got my engagement ring fixed for an anniversary surprise. I'm really pleased! It's bright & I love to look at it when I'm working.

I've been a terrible wife for months, two anyway. All libido seems gone or dormant. I get just plain hungry for sleep & wish he'd leave me alone. Sleepy nearly all the time, so suppose its mental hygiene rather than physical that is bad.

5-7-56

A good day—peaceful & constructive. What a lovely change. That wonderful Don talked to me last night in bed, and let me talk to him, which always helps so much. Full of plans today for a good summer for the kids & us. Do wish I could carry out some of them to the point of achievement, and do wish I could keep alive my ideal of a cheery mother who can cope with whines, etc. without letting them penetrate the skin. Baruchs advice: Look & see. Listen & hear. Your children (& husband) have been with me today.

One thing I miss is someone to talk ideas with. I notice it so much in Wanda Gag's book—always talking ideas with friends. That's a great lack, no one ever does around here, except Leanore. And the worst is I don't either because I'm never unselfconscious enough to let an idea out when with casual friends. And non-use causes death, or at least sterility.

Fri. 5-11-56 9:00 a.m.

Ha—the three littlest ones in bed, Martha & Ruthie for punishment, or just to get them off my skirts really. Naomi because she's sleepy. Martha wanted R to go outside with her & R. didn't want to. My diplomacy did no good & soon both were hanging on me while doing dishes & I disintegrated (as so often) & swooped 'em both to bed & they went to sleep. Don would have been more patient for a longer time, and taken them in his arms & the whole affair would have been a scar-less one. As it is, no telling what kinks it's developing in them when added to all the other indignities they suffer from me.

But perhaps there's some good from the incident. While feeling bad & guilty about it & knowing how Don would disapprove, the thought came that this is what I might write about—family relationships in the raw of a very ordinary family. You see, I've been wanting to write—or do something creative (besides bear children) for a long time. I used to think I had a small talent for writing. If I did, it has atrophied from non-use, and when I would think, "All right, write something," there I sat, high & dry without a thought. But maybe, if I write a developmental account of our family relationships, as I see them, which will be only one seventh of the picture, (less than that if we account for all the possible inter-relationships), in a few years I may have some material to work with in writing something—for publication. I may as well say it. I'd like to have something published. Fame seeker? Maybe. But I think it would be fun. I think it would be fun to get money for something I did, too.

This changes my concept of a diary—or rather gives me one when before I didn't have a conscious one—from merely an expression of personal feelings & happenings. I'll probably still do that but I must remember that the interrelationship aspect gives much more purpose to my writing. Of course, a wife of one and mother of five doesn't have much but family relations to write about! Would that I could become an expert on them, not only of the head but of the heart, which is where families really grow. Or is that true? A good head & a cold heart leave a child cold & stunted, I'm convinced. But do a brainless head & a warm heart equip him for life? Or can there be a loving heart without intelligence any way? Is it really loving if it's applied without thought as to needs, means, etc?

I wanted to put down that I've been tremendously impressed with Wanda Gag's diary of her adolescent years and with how much she had to write about, and with how much she learned. In no way do I compare with her intensity about life and art, but in a way I feel under strain that she might not have had because in learning her art she could apply her knowledge to subsequent experiences, but in learning the art of parenthood time will run out soon and leave no subject for application of the knowledge. Davie at almost 8 is already about one half gone if he goes to a boarding school for high school.

Even worse than lack of wisdom is lack of will to do when you do know what you should do!

Enough. I feel ever so much better for having written and for having something to write about. From now on no search for material should be fruitless with 42 entanglements possible in our group!! I'd better think of a clear way to write these relationships.

Thurs. 5-17-56 p.m.

This morning I cut Dave's hair. He hates it & cried immediately on being told this was the day. We are always in such terrible battles as we wage sometimes.

Why does he get so upset at an impending haircut? And why don't I be more patient and certainly not resort to socking back like a child? Next time I'm going to give him a choice of day and time & see if that will help. I sent a little note in his lunch pail reminding him I loved him and was sorry. We'd pretty much made up before he left but I thought an added encouragement at school might help him. He does get rough treatment, always being scolded for being himself—or at least being disapproved of. I'm the worst offender at this, but I think Don expects too much in the way of manners, etc, too, sometimes. The worst is that he's always faced disapproval ever since Janet was born (no wonder he resents her sometimes.) and we are more tolerant of the shortcomings, messes, etc. of the others. I think now, with me, it's largely habit that makes me snap at him when I know better. I must help him like himself and gain confidence this summer. Too much I destroy his self-valuing.

Tonight, when arriving home from school his first words were, "Janet is the leader of her dance," said in very pleasant tones. In fact most of the evening he was very pleasant.

5-28-56 3:30 p.m.

Do other mothers sometimes look at their children and think how much they hate them? Why can't I be simple & loving instead of so tight inside and so full of conflict? Don thinks I should be very happy, and so do I, but I'm too knotted (a real physical feeling) to be so. How I'd love to relax & let the roars and the jobs & the messes just roll on & pile up and not care.

This, the first day of summer vacation, has me wondering whether we'll make it. Oh, how I hate kids wanting food all day, wanting to "do something," and clinging to me. Neil here in the a.m. for the next two weeks during Bible School makes the day more of a wear; he does miss his mamma.

How do people learn to do what they can & not care about what they can't. It's the caring that hurts.

7-4-56

I must write, have waited too long & have become so full I'm empty. It is being a good summer. Al & Paul fit in very well. I admire their adaptability and ease in living with others.

Don:

Paul and Allan lived with us as farm help for the summer. Their room was in the basement, musty and damp, but they never complained. This was the summer following their sophomore year at Scattergood.

We had a good dairy herd of about ten cows and were selling grade "A" milk from our refrigerated bulk tank. I was interested this summer in trying a new pasture management system. In traditional pasturing, the cows tramp down a large portion of what they could be eating. To avoid this I planned to keep the cows confined to the lot and cut alfalfa silage each morning, rain or shine. We had a new, somewhat experimental, John Deere silage cutter. It had some auger problems in handling very wet, green grasses. Had the chopper worked well it would have been a good summer, but it turned out to be very labor intensive.

The boys were wonderful help—both good with machinery and patient with cattle. But we couldn't avoid a seventy-hour work week for all of us. It was too much for young boys, even though willing, but I felt trapped in a system I couldn't avoid. In future summers the cattle went out to pasture damaging foot prints or not!

Lois:

I should say it's being a good summer for me in these ways: relationship with kids has been fun usually, am enjoying them as they are; have made progress in living each day at a time and enjoying it as it is with things undone as well as done; have felt good physically—sometimes bursting with life & energy that seems not used, which is strange, since we work from 5:00 a.m. till 9:00 p.m. It's evidently an emotional energy.

On the more negative side of the ledger: Don's health is not the best. He's had a couple of fever attacks, but brucellosis test was negative, also a sed rate test. Due to take some more tests soon. Also work has gone slowly this summer. Silo filling is going better, but also slowly. Of course, I get weary of feeding hungry people.

We had two nice cherry picking sessions & I have 16 potential pies jarred away now. Strawberries were almost nil due to the dryness. Peas also did very poorly. But I've been proud of our garden and the way I've managed to keep it up this year. Have been struggling to get some Hollyhocks started along some fence rows, but grasshoppers, very bad this year, are finding them.

7-25-56 Ruthie 2 years old

It's been a happy summer on the whole, much more so than I had expected. The outbursts of hates I had of the summer to Don earlier, must have "let the poison out."

Sometimes happiness is so great and such a delicate thing one hesitates to examine it closely, rather choosing to accept it gratefully, knowing it's temporary. But why is it temporary? Today—did dishes, fed ten at noon. Did dishes again, ironed a huge basketful, picked over an hour for about 6 quarts of beans, got a picnic supper very quickly and easily from scraps & supplies. There's a real reason for happiness—a meal that makes itself. After supper we played hide & seek, tag & leap frog. Now what is so different in that from another less happy day? For one thing it follows two terrible days, and there's another subject worth investigating for whys! Why these undulations? Is that the term used in the *Screwtape Letters*? For another thing, it follows a very satisfying night of love & sharing of thoughts. Another constituent was physical activity. How good it is to run fast & to feel unencumbered & free all through my body. Stimulating conversation at mealtime means much to me, too.

11-10-1956 8:50

Sometimes this journal seems to be a record of only the miserable hours; when I'm happy and busy it gets forgotten. And I have been happy & busy for many weeks—even months. An important event of about a month ago was a talk with Don (which brought about the end of a depression for both of us) in which we discussed giving of ourselves to each other & family, and Don pointed out so simply such a simple fact that I had never been able to really grasp before: Is it possible for a person to have no respect for himself & then get to feeling sorry for himself which leads to resentment and anger over every trifle? That has helped me no end ever since and I'm working on being worthy of my respect. In short, I've become such a whirlwind of efficiency that there is danger in my being lost in "creaturely activity." But it is so good to feel well & strong & to be doing things, & have always lots of things more wanting doing. That used to bother me, make me uneasy, to have many things to do.

And I still get too eager to "finish-period" a job, but I'm learning that having things you want to do is making life full. I hope my interests change as my power for activity lessens, so that I not be left empty.

One reason for my contentment is another person's tragedy. That sounds terrible, but it's true. I've become important and "in" (must read *The Outsiders*— sounds scholarly beyond me but too much I've felt that way) by caring for Carolyn (6 1/2 months) while Sara goes in to the hospital to see Paul, just Jannie's age. Jannie is sitting up with me now coloring, a privileged character to be the only one up. We're such a lucky family; I don't know any seven people who have more to be thankful for than we have. Paul has leukemia and only a few more months to live. There are medicines to help hide the symptoms for 2 or 3 months, then nothing more can be done but to make the end as comfortable and painless as possible.

Sunday 12-9-56

My emotional pull over Sundays must be lessening, and that's good. This a.m. Davie & I had a terrible row and one time I would have felt especially terrible because such a thing happened on Sunday. Now I don't care what day it is. It was a terrible thing, but Sunday makes it no worse, nor any better. Dave's been so irritable & irritating for weeks. This morning's mess was just another straw on a whole stack of straws & I'm the one that blew. Afterward we rocked & I didn't say a word, except to explain that the straw I blew over was a misunderstanding on my part. I wasn't very contrite. He never said anything either, but I finally did get his hands down from where he'd locked them against his ears (expecting a sermon?) and he did relax some finally. I've got to get on this & do something—our relationship is not good. Do wish I knew more of my mother's relationship with Kersey in his first ten years. Certainly I didn't pick up a good pattern to follow from them when he was fifteen & beyond, so I suppose it must have deteriorated before then.

Thursday was Don's 34th birthday & I had a surprise party for him. The kids did amazingly well keeping the secret & he really was surprised up to the last minute, although so many breaks had been made by then I couldn't see how he could be. We played Clue & visited. I think people had a nice time.

1-23-57

Things have been popping inwardly for us. The lack of salary here had reached a crisis with us. Also Don's restlessness with farming. We asked for a raise and got it, and we are officially no longer farm manager. In fact, we are and will be till a new one is found. Don will become teacher and student, for he is very eager to go back to school and earn an MS in physics. It means continued scrounging, maybe more, if that's possible, but I'm willing (praying to be willing, and gladly willing) for it. He needs a chance to try a new thing. So we're full of plans & dreams of near future changes, not all of them pleasant or comfortable, but they do add richness to life.

Am filled with *Precious Bane*. What a woman she would have been to visit with. "He was ever a strong man, which is almost the same as, to say, a man with little time for kindness. For if you stop to be kind, you must swerve often from your path. So when folk tell me of this great man or that, I think to myself, who was stinted of joy for his glory? How many old folk and children did his wheels go over? What bridal lacked his song, and what mourner his tears, that he found time to climb so high?"

Wed. 2-20-57

A brief report to myself about our changed life. It may be very significant, although so far we roll along about the same. It all came about because we have not been making a living here and now we've used all our savings from New Providence days. I could get very eloquent about how shabby our household effects are—none of which were ever new—and about how few things we have and about the increase in needs that is bound to come in the next twenty years. Don asked for a $100 raise, half hoping (I did anyway) not to get it, which would have made the problem simpler in many ways. Well, he's not expendable and things have been changed to keep him here on staff salary which turns him into a teacher rather than a farmer. So far, no new farm manager has been found so he's both. Also, he's taking a course at SUI to renew his teacher's certificate, and dreaming toward an MS degree. Many obstacles in the way of that, but it's not impossible if his wife is willing & able to happily scrounge for five more years.

Don:

I loved the life at Scattergood but I gradually came to realize that our family had outgrown the ability of the school to afford us. During a visit of Lois' sister and family, my brother-in-law asked if I had ever considered going back to school. It was an innocuous remark, but I couldn't forget it. He had a PhD in physics. Was I that kind of material? I knew I was starting too late, and with too many responsibilities for such an ideal, but perhaps some engineering education was possible.

Typical conversations together:

"Loie, when you go to town this week, would you please pick up a good used calculus book for me? No, on second thought, I better get it. You wouldn't know a calculus book from a music book," I said. "If I worked the problems in it, maybe I would be ready for engineering school this fall."

"Are you kidding?" Lois said. "Have you lost your mind? It's been ten years since you've been in engineering school. You can't recover lost years that easily."

"Do you think it's worth a try? It might do great things for us. Maybe I could find an engineering job without our even moving. I really loved the electrical engineering courses I was in before the war."

"I know you did. But it's a big deal now. You're not single you know," she reminded me.

"You're right. It is a big undertaking for both of us. Especially you, I think."

I did buy a calculus book that summer and worked most of the problems, and felt ready to tackle graduate engineering that fall. It took the full five years, as Lois had suspected.

Lois:

2-24-57

Life is so full of the bitter & the sweet, and they interchange so rapidly and so often in one day that it's no wonder this constant response makes me "tired."

The other day I was having what seemed like profound thoughts on the subject of time & thought use. It seemed that those who didn't have to do without so many things they'd like (we don't lack any real needs for life, I must admit, but I do sometimes think we do lack playthings for the kids) and who didn't have to spend so much time planning how they could get a hairdo repaired (once a year I get a yen to have a professional hairdo & it's creeping up on me now) or new shoes (none for four years has given me a great interest footward), etc., but could just go out and satisfy those desires, would then have more time & energy left to think on noble things & do noble acts. Now I'm not so sure.

It's more a matter of habit, for everyone always has picayune troubles he could dwell on if he lets himself. I'm far too prone to fancy myself more abused than others. Self pity is terribly damaging and damning, and so hard to lose, even though I realize I'm wallowing in it.

3-18-57

One dozen years of marriage from today at 3:00 and they have been good. What else can one say? My very life hinges on Don. It occurred to me this morning in thinking over the depression that hit me so hard yesterday, and Don's treatment of it, that it may be that I'd be in a mental ward somewhere by now if it were not for him. What is neurosis? Am I neurotic? Why do I fall into these chasms of despair when my life is illuminated so brightly with all the important things necessary to happiness? It also occurs to me that when Don was in talking over our family, when Davie was in the clinic, and again when we feared a 6th one, that he might have been told I was unstable or some such thing—or is he just naturally wise and all loving, so he is enabled to give & give & give with such patient tenderness when I am in such need of it and yet in such an unlikable disposition? When I am frozen & hard inside & have nothing for anyone but black looks and curt words, Don holds me, and what a help to be physically close, & talks to me with never a word of condemnation! Now this amazes me because I do know how unlovely I am in this condition, and I do know how I feel when I see someone else in a like condition. I feel no sympathy for him, only scorn & disgust that he should think he has it so hard. You might think one who has this affliction would be more understanding of another who does, but this seems not to be the case. Oh, will I ever grow up to where I can be more reasonable, more loving & understanding of others? Surely since marriage my environment has been such as would develop this if ever it can be learned.

A related question I wish I could answer is why Sundays are such a hated day. Is it spiritual lack that catches up with me? Is it something about childhood Sundays that sours still? Is it frustration because there never seems time for any personal catching up on a so-called holiday? If I could understand Sundays and abolish the tension that often begins on Saturday, life would be easier.

Two little girls are fighting over my lap.

Sat. 3/23/57 10:15 p.m.

Once today it seemed I had almost grasped a truth, but now that I come to write it, all I can express is that the reason I'm so unfree and apprehensive is because I'm afraid I won't be able to do well—at anything, whether raising children or raising Cain. This doesn't seem to be a very definitive truth, and it leads to that old unanswerable question, "Why?" Afraid—wanting success, wanting praise and recognition. These are my worst enemies. Is there help for such muddled wills as mine if one can "lean on the everlasting arms"? Is it a matter of terms I don't understand, or how does one reconcile "leaning" and using one's own brain.

Sat. 4-6-57 9:45 p.m.

Don has gone on the Wisconsin trip & I'm home. Not even feeling very sorry for myself. It's good to realize growth sometimes, or am I being so "mature" about this disappointment because I didn't really want to go so terribly much anyway? When two kids got sick, that solved the problem.

Dave has been harboring an infection in the sinus for a long time & now the doctor is treating it quite seriously. She's wary of streptococcus germs, says they're especially vicious this year. Dave's been running a temp well over a week now. And Naomi's been on the tear with throat & fever the last couple of days. Temp of 104.2 all one night & cried.

Am full to overflowing with *Measure of Man*. Don't understand or appreciate all of his references to philosophy and science, but even so, get enough to be thrilled (gacky word) by his ideas and by such a mind as his. Have been impressed lately by the repetition of almost identical themes from my reading— *The Organization Man*.

Sunday 4-7-57

One o'clock & five little ones tucked in for naps; the peace is utter & unbelievable. Can I use it profitably?

Still don't know what dialectic materialism means. Must seek a better dictionary than Webster's Collegiate, but I doubt if even an unabridged explains it too well.

I have been a spiritual materialist in recent years, believing that when you're dead, you're as dead as you look, and that any immortality is your influence, impact on those around you, and of course, any hereditary factors you passed on. This idea was developed partly, I know, to counteract Heaven. The very word has been unpleasant to me for years. "The kingdom of heaven is within you," is or can be the only description of heaven that is palatable or meaningful, and that seems independent of immortality. Also, I like my body, its feelings and its uses and the thought of a life without physical pleasures leaves me cold.

I have been largely a mechanistic determinist (feel like a college froshie using all these multi-syllable words!), having been largely educated in school & by personal reading, to accept a lot of the behaviorist psychology which spends more time pointing out man's similarities to animals, than in pointing out his differences, and which blames a lot of the end results (personality & society wise) on unremembered traumas which cannot be controlled.

Bach's *Will to Believe* smacks of popular religious books in its conversational tone & chatty illustrations, but a good half of it discusses life after death with no Heaven marked out like Salt Lake City. It's not hard for me to see his point that the will to believe in everlasting life is worth having because it's a positive approach, increasing regard for individuals & recognition that life and death are a unity. He spouts no punishment or reward system & I assume he thinks you go through the door marked end on one side & beginning on the other with pretty much what you have made for yourself, and what more fitting punishment is there? But a determinist cannot believe this because he doesn't have much responsibility for what he is, he's a victim rather than a chooser.

And that's what Krutch's *Measure of Man* is all about. This is the book that has me agog; it is truth-Truth-I do believe. We do choose, we must choose, and we are responsible for our choices, and there are absolute values to live by. These ring out as great comforts to me although I feel sort of medieval accepting them so earnestly.

Other stimuli have been battering my consciousness, too. Reading some material on mongoloids has changed my thinking about defectives. Or has it? At any rate I at least see another viewpoint which says they are valuable in their own way; they can even add to society by teaching us who are hard hearted & hard headed, to love. I can not yet see beauty in a little Mongol face, but I haven't become the parent of one. Having a Mongol in the family, having Paul dying of leukemia, reading *The Story of Gabrielle*, the story of a 9-10 yr. old girl's sickness & death with cancer, makes me realize as I never have before, that bodies are not always a joy, that they can be almost unendurable, thus a life without such a hindrance must seem very appealing. Is that why older people become more religious than the young?

Mon. 4-8-1957

What is this inner excitement & wanting & wanting so that I can't do, or don't do, the work that needs doing? I've read the "Progressive" all a.m. Don subscribed to it for a year at this conference. I'm no brain—all emotion—reading controversial articles, especially in political fields, leaves me a jumble of ideas, but making a choice as to which is right or true is impossible.

Don came home last p.m. about 7:00 and that was a good & fun evening, but today I feel more stimulated than satisfied, partly sexual, but not all. I'd like to have people to talk & talk & talk to in an unrestrained way, who would like me even if they disapproved of what I say. Frustrated verbal exhibitionist?

Picked up *All the King's Men* and scanned a few minutes the other day in the library. Read the part about his marriage to a Lois. How she was all body and no mind, or at least not his kind of mind, and how they were perfectly adjusted sexually but with no other ties, and how corrupt & horrible their relationship became. Of course I can't accept the idea of superficial perfection in any phase of a relationship, even if it were possible to have a satisfactory part of life together when all other aspects were lacking or miserable, which I cannot accept either. Surely perfection is a thing of a moment only; the very fact of its existence seems to drive us into wanting more & then it's no longer perfect.

Naomi has spilled the bubble soap, a whole 10 cents worth, dumped out most of a salt cellar, and the house is a heap. I can hardly bear the thought of cleaning, partly because I feel so unsettled. Why clean a house that always increases one's affection for it, & then suffer the pangs of moving out of it?

Oh, why doesn't something terrific happen to use up this restlessness? I feel like Jannie, would like to "marry the whole world."

Spring work has started, disking for oats planting today. Coldness remains, but it will leave suddenly and then we'll be in that beautiful, balmy time where everyone seems to be so happy & glad, & I am too. Yet there is always a sadness, a sense of inadequacy that depresses me in Spring, which makes the cheery attitude of others hard to bear. Do they really feel so openly happy? I like rainy days & gloomy cloudy ones. They don't make me feel gloomy. I like to be snug & comfortable inside in this kind of weather must be added for truth. I'm not a nature lover; I like to escape it in spite of sentimentalizing over it & thinking it's important to know in forming a sense of values. Oh nuts. Oh, life. I love it and want more of it.

But I'm young, healthy, sexy, & very fortunate in husband, children, social strata.

Friday 5-3-1957

What a terror I was tonight & kids were so good & patient with me. That makes it all the more shaming, of course. I'll bet we have about three wet beds tomorrow.

Made & hung Maybaskets, about 18 of them! That was hard on my weary patience. I feel terribly taut & snappy lately. Why?

Moving? Yes, partly. It does hurt to leave where we've put in so much of our lives and labor. Leanore? Yes. Why does a woman I don't see more than once a week & don't talk to that much bother me so? She does matter to me, terribly & I do feel very resentful and estranged with her. A girl spoke in meeting last Sunday saying we are as far from God as we are from the person who's most separated from us by barriers such as I feel exist between L. & me. Although she is probably unaware of all this. Yet, sometimes I think if one knows the other must know, very unscientific, I'm sure.

Sunday 5-5-1957

A good day—in love with the world & even with my children! Walked to Coppocks & back with them. Nice visit. One of those "in grace" days & I thank God for them, really do!

Sunday 5-12-1957

Mother's Day. Have received 2 paper plates with flowers pasted in the middle, a melted crayon picture & a pasted picture & a copy of the monstrous MOTHER spells Mother thing. Listening to the radio a few minutes convinced me that all mothers are very old, very religious and constantly praying (usually out loud), and never have a thought for anything but the welfare of their children and to this end gladly make sacrifices. Hmmmm.

Am using up all my diary paper writing & reorganizing my part in the AAUW program tomorrow night. I'm a terrible egotist, too concerned over the effect I'll make. Why don't I just relax, give what I can & to heck with the rest?! OK, I will.

6-15-57

Delusions of grandeur. Ambitious beyond my abilities. This is disgustingly true of me. Lately I've been preoccupied with going back to school (a la correspondence courses at first) to get an Iowa secondary credential. Again come my dreams of doing something other than meals, mess, mopping & moping. And of course my reason tells me if I am mopey now I'll probably be mopey at any job. One reason I want so much to get away from mothering is that I feel so terribly inadequate and inept at it. If only one could feel a sense of accomplishment, of doneness once in a while, then one could feel successful. But there is rarely, almost never, such a feeling. Mistakes and good things pile up on each other day after day till the teetery, uneven wall of all our interwoven lives ought to totter & fall, but it never does. Suppose when a child at last pulls his skein from the pile to form a new one of his own you can see what you've made—a person or a brat. But for so long it's all such a matter of faith & hope & knowing how weak the foundation is.

I have the mind of a clerk—would like to file away the day's assignment & see it done and stay done till the next job. All real jobs, teaching, politics and human relations jobs are the tough kind. Being a parent is one of the toughest & I suppose most rewarding in the long run if one succeeds in any measure. But I want my satisfactions & rewards now. But I don't work at it hard enough, or try hard enough to appreciate the rewards now. I suppose rewards are always based on state of mind, & if you don't train yourself to enjoy them you never can enjoy the most fabulous happenings.

God, give me a—no, God doesn't give

God help me to be willing to seek, not content to sit & receive. And help me to learn to give myself.

We've moved two loads of miscellany over to our new house. I don't think it will be too bad there. If only I could feel settled inside, outside settledness wouldn't be such a worrisome thing.

Don:

This move was from the Scattergood farmhouse to the house on the Coppock farm. Scattergood had bought the 80-acre farm with a good four-bedroom house and some old outbuildings. It was a move of about a mile, so things went over in many small loads. We lived there about two years.

My status had changed to part-time teacher and to help break in the new farm manager. I had taken a part-time job in Iowa City as I entered graduate school. My afternoons were free for work and study. But this arrangement didn't last long. I found a second half-time job at the University of Iowa Hospital and dropped the work at Scattergood. So now we were back on an improved full time salary with evenings free for family and study. A few years of long hours were ahead of us.

As we disassociated ourselves from the school it became necessary to vacate their property in favor of resident staff. We considered many options. With financial help from friends and my folks it became possible to buy our first home. The Springdale community, three miles away, appeared to be a good place to raise our kids. The deal was completed and we moved, in 1959, to what was to be our home for the next forty-eight years.

Lois:

Mon. 7-22-1957 4:30 p.m.

Am reading an anthology of Rufus Jones' writings, edited by Harry Emerson Fosdick, names I've heard my mother admire, I'm sure. Have wasted the whole day being moody & distant from Don to hurt him.

We're anxiously awaiting the arrival of the prospective new farm manager & his wife who have left their two children in California to come & look over the job. I'm going to try hard to like them, and it will be hard because I'll have a displaced, loss of prestige feeling when we move over to the other place and are no longer "manager." Don & Leanore were talking last night about arrangements. He will probably work from 7:00 till noon for school and have afternoons & nights for SUI. At this point I feel depressed & out of the whole deal. If I can't give myself willingly & happily for this year it will be lost for all of us. No matter how lost or scared I am, if I can only remember that my most important job is to help good kids grow, that should keep me going. Brother Lawrence said that the way he found best to be with God was to go about his appointed tasks as they came. Such simplicity is the answer; I'm convinced, to a serene & happy life. But my habits are so wrong.

Tues. 7-23-57

Am always haunted by the guilty feeling of being not good enough. This makes me sad & angry, and I become truly no good by letting the symptoms of sadness & anger show. If I can put on a front will this reduce the basic cause? Where does the living God fit into this? My will alone cannot make me seem happy & pleasant if I'm not. How does one open to receive and give?

Don:

Lois was a very private person. Her journals revealed much more of her personality and inner problems and insights than our actual shared thoughts did. Our daily give-and-take was about our immediate lives, the kids and the needs of all of us. We did, occasionally, discuss our thoughts on the nature of God. We agreed on rejecting a belief in an anthropomorphic God. We agreed on rejecting a belief in "a better place" after death. These rejections of conventional religious thought were private—we assumed we were very much alone in some Quaker Meeting circles. It was important to us not to shake anyone else's faith in a different belief. We also agreed that there was a lot that we didn't understand and many questions that we had no answers for.

I graduated from engineering school in 1962, the same month our sixth child was born.

Lois, 1962

CAPTER 8

LOIS STRUGGLES WITH TIME, WRITING, AND READING

Lois:

2-12-60

I have not the courage of an ass. For 25 minutes I lay there thinking about getting up and of all the difficulties involved: I would bother Don, lack of sleep (rest) for me, the uselessness of it, etc. Mental energy, that is the secret and that's what I lack, I fear. But here I am up at least one time, and the world still seems to go around. It's terrible to be so bound by narrow habit. When Don got up regularly at 5:00, I did too, if I were to help him. Now to rise at six seems a major problem. Having done even this much is a victory of sorts. The next exercise, to write at the appointed times during the day is even harder. We will see what we see.

Snow vacation is upon us. For two days I have felt as buried under kids, their noise & needs, as the fences are buried under drifts. Really, what buries me is internal feelings of inadequacy and lack of willingness to give myself over to the kids. If I could find a creative outlet and if I could use it effectively, perhaps I would be less stingy with myself toward the family. Always I have assumed that my non-giving is a sign of inner weakness & turmoil, and it is, but it just occurs to me that possibly the turmoil is because of dissatisfaction or hunger for a personal need. If this should be so, if the need should be to write, what a rosy outlook occurs. I could become more independent emotionally, and more possible all around.

There. Only 15 minutes. I could have had 40 if I had gotten up when I woke up.

2-16-60

"Seven at one blow"—seven chickens in the jars give us some more meat again. Don did all the plucking & cleaned 4 of them. That was wonderful & even if he hadn't helped, it's wonderful to have a friend with you in such a stinking job.

The more I read about writers, about being a writer and writing, the less sure I become that I am or ever could be an author of anything more printable than this. But I am going to try to follow these exercises for some weeks without worrying about more. Already, I do appreciate more what writers do.

Ever so often, there is consciousness of wanting or needing to be writing when I am having to do other things. This is probably just an affectation of Lois the Lofty, but I wish I could know for certain if it is a real need & desire or fluff of self-esteem. Since I have no work in progress, just the act of sitting and maneuvering a pencil must appeal to Lois the Dull as important. Also I am aware of a lack of originality & freshness in my imagination—maybe lack of imagination better describes it.

2-18-60 5:25 a.m.

Write, write, write—but what? My unconscious is dormant. I do begin to see more & more the time one who wants to write consumes. And how does a housewife possibly combine two such time consuming tasks, given only 24 hour days? "Mental energy," the SUI teacher calls it. Yes, and mental ability—even if I had the one do I have the other? Keep calm & don't strain after anything. That is the only possible solution.

My ring has a blue point in one corner, and a white fire spot toward the center if I angle my hand just right as it lies on the paper.

My hands grow more & more like my dad's, fairly long and fairly broad, with a disgusting way of moving the fingers in a kind of stiff oneness. Perhaps it isn't disgusting to others. I can remember when it was pleasant to put my hand in dad's, a memory of walking down a street this way seems real. Did I used to walk the block to meet him at the streetcar on the corner of College & Alcatraz? Would I have been about 9 or 10, Janie's age, and in love with him as she is with Don, falling into his lap or on his chest in frequent spurts of passion? What happened between those years & the one where I could not bear his slightest touch? Was I unable to accept a rival other than mother? I sensed something sensual in those hands, the giggle, how else describe that tenor heh heh, heh? It certainly denoted sexiness to me. More than to him?

Still quite dark out. A bright half ball in the southern sky and a lone star in the SE make the snow light.

2-19-60 6:05 a.m.

If I would follow my first impulses, I'd get more sleep. Up at 3:30 with coldness and full bladder. Found the furnace had stopped working. Don up and to the rescue. Brief time to cure. Couldn't get feet warm or brain stilled. Had slight desire, no initiative. Time passed. Don turned to cup me & we had lovely lingering time. Ah—and feet warmed up, too, but no peace in brain. What time is it? Should I soon get up for writing? No—sleep a good nap & will wake at usual time. Naomi is such a good girl in the mornings. I don't give her enough attention. Narrow, protruding arch of upper teeth. Will it cause ugliness in that face?

I'm not writing fast & uncritically enough. Have been quite happy & healthy—asking, is this it? Will learning to write, trying to, fill the hungry spot I've known so long? How will I fare in the next depressing period? Will I slough through it? Am I gypping the kids?

2-22-60

Don & Davie did buy a Guernsey, to calve in two weeks. 4H project for Dave, & work for mom, but I kind of look forward to it.

Don:

The local school supported an excellent 4-H program. It was not part of the curriculum but we did meet in the public school building for evening meetings. Kids chose from a list of possible farm animals to care for—beef cattle, dairy cattle, hogs, chickens and rabbits were all available. Each student bought his own animal and cared for it throughout the project.

Dave wanted to join 4-H and we encouraged him. We considered which class of livestock was best. Our fences were not good enough for a hog, but would easily confine a cow. A dairy cow, rather than a beef calf, would give the family a steady supply of milk. Our old barn was adequate shelter for a milk cow, with space to store hay for the winter. We found a Guernsey cow at a reasonable price. The farmer would deliver her, so we settled the deal. We bought straw for bedding and hay for feed. The barn came to life. Each morning and evening meant feeding, cleaning the stall, and milking. Dave learned to care for his cow and keep records on her feed and care. We all enjoyed the project.

Lois:

Tried to toboggan yesterday at Milletts. Snow fell Sat p.m. & all night till Sunday noon, dry, powdery stuff. Then wind came up and blew it, hope it hasn't drifted enough to cancel schools. It was wild out on the hillside, blew into the face & froze there. And walking in knee high drifts up hill or down is slow & hard work. Felt good to go in & get warm & dry. Watched Olympic ski jumpers on TV. I like Milletts. Hope they like us and don't think we're just a queer nuisance.

2-23-60 6:15 a.m.

Nothing—wasted day yesterday. Used up all my energy hating me & the kids, feeling hopeless. Snow vacation. Don so kind, loving. How can he be so & give so much when I give so little? Too neat. Davie too. Must learn to continue living, functioning in a clutter. Why does clutter upset? Cause of clutter? Shakes something internal! Fear to lose control over my own world?

Children—always forget to appreciate their inner world—impose on me and my desires. Pick up, pick up, pick up constantly. How do they grow & thrive? Do they? Are they being crippled? How I weary of their silliness. Is it an escape from my dour climate?

Write, write write. Forgot a conversation between Naomi & Ruth that was delightful. It's their tones & inflections which are so pleasing as much as what they say anyway, & I don't see how to write that down.

2-24-60 5:30 a.m.

Come on brain, write write write. More snow, don't know how much. School vacation? Oh, no! Went to Homemakers' meeting yesterday afternoon. Penelopy with a pronounced widows hump, and a mind dwelling in green pastures of the common. Every time she opens her mouth, which is often, she utters a commonplace, redundant bit of wisdom, but embellishes it, labors over it, with puckers of thought & changes of vocabulary as if it were a rare bit of wisdom.

Oh, Lois, and who repeats sometimes thinking your listeners might not understand your erudite remarks?! Ouch. Could I be as hopelessly dull and deadening as Ethel Pent, short, square & fifty +, with a bright scar of lipstick and lopsided glasses on her wrinkly face. Also has nice hands, well preserved for a farm wife, which are carefully manicured with bright red. Earrings & necklace on the short fat neck, and big rings. All of this jewelry of the rhinestone type gives her a flash. Such women do not increase attractiveness with age. My heart aches for her—and for future me. What does a woman do at this stage in life when the conventional brighteners make her look gaudy and cheap, and her insides are quivering with endocrine change and the dread of being old. Grow old gracefully, accept limitations, develop dignity. Ha! These are good ideas, but they are imposed on a culture which does not develop or encourage or accept growing old. Only the wisest can really do these things. Slow today.

Slept all night till 5:30. What a lush reward for ill temper.

2-27-60 4:10 a.m.

Ha—is it the encouraging return of lessons 2&3 that has me up before dawn again? Or is it physiological? I went to the toilet to find myself overflowing with menstrual mess. I should have known because I am certain now that there is a most uncomfortable tension that develops a few days before it starts and on the day it begins. I almost visibly begin to unwind, the world is tolerable again. But does this account for the whole horror of a week I've struggled with beginning last Saturday? Does my functioning femininity have the ability, the right, to knock out one fourth of my life? Or does it become an excuse for less showy functions & malfunctions of the mind?

2-28-60

Are we back where we were before nine months of twice weekly visits with Counselor? Surely this cannot be. Is it only a matter of self-discipline? Is it a matter of understanding why self craves so much attention & sympathy?

Why am I so reluctant to take part in community affairs? Of course the urge to withdraw I've felt so strongly recently is withdrawing from life, not just community responsibilities, & this is direct path to death, I know.

And I've got to quit acting or rather feeling as if I'm a writer, with things more important to do than being with kids. In the first place it's a delusion. I've written nothing. And in the second place, kids and husband have to be first. Have I physical & mental energy enough to keep aware of them and their needs, try to meet their needs (fail miserably, usually), maintain a lack of strain (certainly haven't this last week) & still learn to write? Is such a difficult combination worth trying for?

Cow comes today noon. Davie so excited with his check book and money in the bank to write checks on. He's learning a lot by leaps & bounds, already knows more about handling money than I did after college. Don is a wonderful father & husband? Yes—for a wife less insatiable in her needs.

Since our wild week (seemed wild to me, which is, I suppose, a sign of my conservatism) we have had a week bare of passion on my part. Don tried, was determined to seduce me, but this inner flatness & fatigue, constant sleepiness & laziness, & lack of interest in anything, sexual or non, made me beg him to quit breaking his heart in the effort & just satisfy himself. From the purely physical aspect, this is a most pleasurable experience for him. For me it accumulates a little resentment after a time, yet I don't blame anyone but me for my apathy.

Last night I played Concentration with the three little girls, but it was not a howling success. Their horsing around irritated me and I showed it. Then I started baths, which I always hate. Naomi wouldn't take off her shirt—of course I'm always pushing & nagging, "Come on, let's hurry, etc., etc." I spanked her bottom hard and she howled. Don came in & said he'd bathe 'em & I tensed my jaws & locked my lips (a sign of disgust, despair and defeat I find myself using too frequently) and retreated to the dishes. I get along better with inanimate objects! In two minutes, Naomi was having the time of her life. Baths are fun for Don and those he bathes. Should a mother be so unable to enjoy the things a mother should & must do? Of course not.

Time—when time pushes me, instead of using time I am off my rocker. Why is time so significant to one who wastes so much of it?

3-22-60 Thoughts while doing dishes.

Looked at a new McCall's today. Bought it to see what women are wearing this year and to make me feel like a woman after three days of chewing, picking nails & fingers into painful sores, but not so painful as the inner tension & sense of futility. It is a beautiful magazine. That is, if a mag can be beautiful, it is. Each page a work of art or superlative craftsmanship. And I, the reader, am welcomed and embraced on every page. I am interested in the pleasant things going on in the world, such as new products for household or beauty care, new clothes, clever ways to cook chicken, famous personalities, etc. I loved looking at the pretty patterns, 14 pages of them, modeled with stellar personalities. The advertisements, colors & designs are pleasingly startling, and I ache to be a consumer of these glistening kitchen appliances, of those lustrous bedroom sets, and even those girdles which would flatten my 30 inch pot into the 24 inch sylph it used to be.

Was it yesterday's news which told of the Africans machine gunned by police (white, of course) while protesting action against ID/permits required of them? And that women and children were among those hit by the staccato death? What would McCall's mean to these?

And when I take a breath of spring like air, just warming up around the edges even with snow still piled high, and wonder what deadly atomic particles might be in this fresh, free gift and necessity of life, then the pretty girls and precious personalities pale. Or I wish they would. There is an incompatibility between the world of McCall's and the world of lunch counter demonstrators in Montgomery, hungry Indians who have never had a more private room than a train station bench, and production of chemicals for warfare in Fort Dietrich, MD.

Both are real worlds. Will the harsh one destroy the slick one?

3-29-60

I must make up my mind. How does one, when one doesn't know? Do I want to write or do I want to have written? The last part, I know is true. Is the first part also? Sometimes I'm sure it is. So here I am—34 years & 10 months old, never wrote but one story in my life, and that a direct steal from Mary Poppins, and I think I want to learn how to write! I do too well in this course. A "C" would perhaps knock me back into reality. Taking correspondence course with Miss Hovey?

I want to try to write, but I think I purposely hold my mind from coming into real contact with writing ideas because I'm afraid it will fail in dealing with them.

Don:

I shared, with Lois, this feeling of apprehension in facing reality. Unfortunately, I didn't recognize it when I should and we never discussed it. In my work I was often called upon to design medical instruments for specific purposes. A project in development was in safe harbor—once finished it was immediately evident whether it was a failure or a success. The risk was real. The temptation to keep developing and not bring my mind to face finalization was real.

Lois:

Do I have the nerve to set one hour of each day for practicing writing? To use the basement for it in summer & on days when the kids are home? If I do this for the rest of the year would I know if I have anything to say and any ability at saying it? I think I would. And whether it turned out plus or minus it would be a useful experiment.

Don:

During the years 1960 and '61 Lois took correspondence courses from the University of Iowa. She wrote many short stories that were usually returned marked "A." Marginal comments by instructors where complimentary and sometimes suggested she submit the piece for publication. And she did, but none made it into national publications.

These were also the years when we were bringing our old farmhouse up to modern standards. Two of the upstairs bedrooms had brick chimneys extending through the roof. Removing these meant starting outdoors and working down into the rooms—brick by brick.

The walls were in good condition, but the paper on them was not. We worked hard, and the kids pitched in to the best of their abilities. Lois was continually conscious of the competition for time between work and writing.

Lois:
4-4-60

Ha—wallpapering (steamed 100 layers off Fri. eve & Sat. all day. Don home!), removing paint, painting, gardening coming up, messy house, chimney to remove (Dave made great progress Sat.). You see, busy, busy, no time to write! Oh, such prolonged unresolve! Keep living—notice!!

Don & I have drawn very close in last few days, have communicated many internal feelings. Don't feel inclined to write it yet.

4-12-60

A pulpy mass internally. Is this all sexual excitement? Certainly much of it is. Lady Chatterley and her Keeper have done me wonders. I do love their freedom. We have some of it, we also have a way to go.

I should have saved this book for a dry time. Don laughed yesterday morning, telling me I had had sex 5 times in the last four days and two times in the last four months. That isn't literally true, but I know well what he meant. And last night again we had a time. Tonight? Yes, yes, my body cries out now. But I am aware of its fickleness. And I'm trying to learn to live through both times, "The thick & the thin," as Mellor says. If it won't at a given time, if my spirit "looks down from the top of my head" and feels disgust or disinterest at this amazing process of contortions which can be so much more, let me be, leave it be, till the tide turns, as it always has, and always will?

There is much truth and accurate description of feeling & sensation in this book. How does a man know so much about a woman? Is the sensation of desire and orgasm identical in both sexes? I always assumed there were some differences of degree at least.

To think it's taken me 34 years, 11 months to grow to love & know sex with as little fear & as much joy as I do now. Am I slower than most women? I don't know. Have I gone as far toward freedom, have we, as two people of our backgrounds & temperaments can go? No, there are some acts we haven't done. Are there feelings we haven't felt?

To know that women sometimes hate sex, hate the indignities of it for a few seconds (or weeks) at a time and yet want it and need it and love it, is most comforting for me to know. The scenes of sex pure & beautiful preceded by stumbling in either or both minds are real & it's comforting to know they are real enough for literature, therefore more than real for just me. (The scene in the forest where he puts her down "like an animal" for such an end of joy) Oh, God, it is not wrong to feel so sexy. It is right, right, right. Except what??? When he leaves? Is this what is awful about age: But better to have had it fully, even intemperately before it goes, than to never have had it at all.

The one thing I remember about the Kinsey report is that unwed mothers, while often regretting the child and the ensuing complications, never regretted the act. Never? Well, usually this must be true.

4-29-60

The cow milkers have gone out. And I am still living with myself before anyone else, so it's unpleasant for us all.

Darning lesson today, Christian Ed. meeting tomorrow, also club work night, School & Home night Thurs.—are these so hopeless or am I? Finished Heart Funding yesterday & was vastly relieved. How long can such a woman maintain sanity?

Is it God I need? Which God? In what clothes of interpretation do I put Him?

George Herbert loved God so, believed in him so, how could he have had problems? Yet much of his life was spent in misery because he felt "Unemployed," that he hadn't found the true God chosen vocation.

5-2-60 8:45 p.m.

OK Genius, write something superlative & soul searing! Such frustration must be handled better. For two days I've been a model of domesticity and maternity—whisking & cleaning, forbearing and kind, but yearning, yearning to be doing something else. Writing? Working for a cause that really pulls me? What cause is more important than keeping an orderly house and being an aware and attentive parent & wife? These are important. They are not the only important jobs in the world, but they are mine now & I'd better like them. Like what you have to do & you're a person. Hate what you have to do & you're a wound up toy, ready to snap & whir chaotically at the least extra or untoward event. Sounds so easy, just determine to like it, turn on a smile and carry on. Ah—and can I find the energy, mental & physical, to practice writing one hour a day?

Using one's time! No courses given in this—it's too hard & too personal. But how important it is. And how badly we all do. Am I driving Davie too hard? Must watch to find if this is so. He's awfully weary these nights. The cow will get easier for all of us, I think.

5-10-60 5:20

Oh ye of little faith & less knowledge, either get rid of your foolish ambition & rest easy with yourself, or do something about it. Reading Mayra Mannes and Susan Glaspell makes me know how little I know. Mannes has complex sentences, but clear & sincere. Is it their rhythm that makes you know it's good writing?

Isak Dinesen in "Harpers" says doing a little every day without faith and without hope is what gets things done. How amazing and how new. Raised on pap of positive thinking and no original thinker myself, how would I know how true this is until I see it in print, thought of by someone else.

Is it possible to live a normal, housewifely life, have energy enough for husband & children, and superimpose learning to be a writer over this? This is my fear. That it is not. Is there a cycle necessary of all attention to family, then sneaking in of writing (or worse, thinking about writing) and then the guilty feeling from laxness? Then is there any relief? Why can't I love, and laugh with our children the way they are? And let them be themselves? What am I afraid of?

Mr. Counselor, you didn't help me know how to deal with this. Communicate what? Oh, if God could be less religious & more real perhaps I could find him. Or if I were less distrustful of religious things.

6-14-60

The wedding. Friend's House (Des Moines) rooms were full. Hanna & Phil entered to be seated. Ross, as soon as meeting was settled, spoke briefly about Friends weddings. Wilmer read the Monthly Meeting Minute granting permission for the marriage. Silence, 10, 15 minutes. H. & P. stood & repeated that so brief statement: "In the presence of God and these friends I take thee, Philip, to be my husband, promising, with divine assistance, to be unto thee a loving and faithful wife as long as we both shall live. Each signed the marriage certificate, Hanna "as is customary, adopting the surname of her husband." After the two appointed (by Mthly Mtg) witnesses had signed, Wilmer read aloud the whole certificate. Silence settled once again on the group. Merle spoke of the circles of influence coming from a good (Christian) home, and of how each one was responsible to help make a better world for families to live in. Someone prayed that they not be spared human problems, but that they be given strength & sense to deal with them. A man spoke on the eternal rightness of marriage, male & female in creation. On significance of first worship together as husband & wife.

No kiss, no ring in ceremony, no corsage. Hanna dressed in ballerina length white dress embossed in delicate pattern. Edging around neck, sleeves & hem of tiny 1/4 inch wide loops. Minute buttons. Over minute fabric covered buttons. High scoop neck, no bra padding. Small, firm breasts in a kind of now-you-see-it now-you-don't shadow underneath.

Timelessness—no haste. God is a spirit. That of God in every person = Spirit. Man is spirit. Compatibility of spirit, the link with the eternal & inexplicable in the vast universe and the physical needs & desires of humanity were made manifest at this Friends wedding. Dignity & joy cannot but add to depth of inner experience.

A boy said he saw them kissing. And they disappeared.

Man is spirit as well as physical. Consent of Meeting & parents recognize that mankind is apt to be misled by passions. While a marriage beginning with no passion may seem a meager start, passion disciplined by group scrutiny may have its values.

6-24-60

Aunt Helen has been here 4 nights & 3 days. She is a wise & knowing visitor, knows how to help and fit in unobtrusively. Attractive! Yes. Dave is enamored of Aunt Helen. He cried "privately" to himself after she had gone. In his journal he wrote that she gave him 3 precious things: the wooden word puzzle, the tic-tac-toe, and a sense of peace & a "new place in life." I'm a heel for peeking at his writing, but it is most satisfying to see him expressing some of his feelings. I know he has them, perhaps more intensely than others, but he keeps them well corked.

Six little girls to feed pancakes (Jan's request) to this a.m. Janie & Sheryl stayed overnight. Dave stayed at Paul's.

Last evening after supper, when all the kids were out playing, I went up to work on the paint removal job. Don, doing screens, caught me in the hall & took me into Davie's room, and took me—on the floor because up on the bed we were so exposed to the curtainless windows. It was nice.

6-29-60

Weary mentally and confused. Have been reading "Appeal at Fort Deitrich" propaganda and feel hopelessly crass & no good. These demonstrators seem to have such a close fellowship and an exciting life. What a remarkably happy combination—to have close friends and allies in thought and the resulting security as well as a daring & dangerous life on the frontiers of non-violent resistance. Surely it is not all sweetness and light, but surely, also, it makes opportunities for many satisfactions not so easily obtained in our mundane life. Always when I read these things I feel like a "wanter," as if my life is engrossed only in concern over house decorations & dining room chairs. Will I ever outgrow this conflict?

I want to be all things & have all things. The life trapped in possibilities without enough realities?

To be a writer, sit down & write. There is where I fail, I don't sit down, and when I do, how slowly it goes, but I have a better understanding of the importance of getting it down in any form, and then revising, than I used to.

Ruthie's tonsils were taken out yesterday & Dave had eyes examined at SUI clinic. Gets his glasses Friday. I'm so glad for him, because he's been quite handicapped visually, I know. Ruthie was her own brave, quiet little self & got along fine. Didn't spit even one drop of blood afterward. I didn't know it could be such a bloodless process. Today she's up & around, a trifle subdued & speaking cautiously but not at all limited in communication. Yesterday was a comedy of shuttling across town & river between the two hospitals, the glasses company, meeting Don at noon, Dave to Hubbard's to mow their lawn—it went on endlessly & I was bone weary last night. Went to bed at 8:30.

Do I cheat our kids? Do I cheat myself? What do I want to do & be? Am I too obsessed with sex mentally and not easy enough about it in its actual physical manifestations? I would be delighted to be like the dopey girl in the story, so physically stimulated by her husband's touch.

Feel worthless. Here comes Don & no supper. Better get busy.

7-4-60

Too many impressions. Now, this instant in IC park—Davie mowing Hubbard's lawn, girls playing, 4th of July crowds. How could such a day be in Iowa? Slight breeze, warm enough to be comfortable in shade, but delicious warmth of direct sun is not too hot. Feels good. Always wish I could store this penetrating glow against the coldness which hurts. Have stoically turned my back on the pool to write here at a shady table. I love to watch the swimmers, very few real swimmers, and the divers. Two little boys were diving & bubblingly making faces at Martha through the observation windows. I love watching the indolent girls with their straps down so casually while the boy casually splashes their thighs. And of course, we all know blood is boiling under the playfully cool exterior.

The couples necking in the park, two couples (together) about 5 yards apart under blankets. One girl working at getting the blanket spread over his buttocks without rising from her own prone position. I get upset when couples do extensive necking in teams—shows a lack of the seriousness, which I deplore in myself. Yet I know that for me passion will always have to be a private affair. Then why am I so inordinately pleased when Don caresses me in public. Because any woman wants others to know that someone finds her desirable and likes her.

Funny Don. He wondered if the couples were married! "Married people don't neck on the ground in daylight." "They might," he replied." And married people are never unescorted by children," I added. "Don't be bitter," said he lightly.

8-12-60

Such a funny internal day. Have not done one thing & now have a headache because of my perversity. Have been troubled about doing nothing while the world explodes around us.

Don's vacation starts Mon. We plan to do great things in the line of papering, painting & plastering. Refreshment comes from giving, not resting. Rest comes from a different outlook.

Discipline, discipline, discipline—organization. I will never get beyond the dishes and the washings if I do not practice these. Why, when I practice them do they hound me, run and ruin me so that any deviation or failure in the schedule (like lovemaking, etc.), frustrates instead of refreshes? Am I just incapable of such demands for adjustment? Yes, I guess that is it. I must learn to live with myself as I am while I happily work toward being better. Must do dishes before supper time. Help—headache—is it really from inactivity, or have I been inactive because of impending headache? Ha. Crazy woman, wish I admired you more.

9-28-60

On skimming that last entry, I remember that the headache was real, (a comforting thought to a neurotic) and I was beginning what turned into a three week bout with flu. Fever and headache on our trip to Des Moines & to the folks & camping & while papering & painting. I'm really rather proud of the way I kept going & going while always light headed & weary. But I suppose the fever must be as responsible as my own will for I find that a low fever of 99-100 makes me light hearted, unworrying & sexy. The 102-103 fobs lay me low though.

This is a great day, the beginning of my acting out what I have been thinking months about. At 9:30 a.m. I sit down & write. It will not be easy. It will be torture sometimes, and that's what I'm afraid of. The problem of using one's life time is the basic theological problem? Anyway, a very important one.

Our house is attractive! Should I list all we've done this summer?
Upstairs:

Repaired big plaster spots.
Painted hall ceiling
Painted all woodwork in hall & bedrooms except Jan's room. Steps too.
Papered 2 bedrooms & hall.
Papered & painted toilet room.

Downstairs:

Plastered dining room & front room ceilings & painted them. They are a beautiful light cream, rough texture.

Painted woodwork chocolate brown in both rooms.

Repapered both rooms, very pleasing, quiet papers

Don built a book shelf-record-radio built in and a crutch to hold up the sagged ceiling. Handsome & useful unit.

Papered kitchen walls, painted ceilings & some of the woodwork.

There are still many minor jobs to be done before we are back together again, complete & new. But we do look nice. I am too fond of the place to have to move in a year or less.

Oh, and we have 8 new dining chairs.

10-31-60

A perfect Halloween night. It has rained almost continuously since Sat. night and the wind whistles around the corners of this house, rattles windows. The maples have lost a lot of leaves, but there are still enough remaining to make the ocean-like cycle of crescendo-decrescendo swoosh.

Feel contented in a work achieved way—got the dining room cleaned top to toe & floor waxed. Feel isolated, also in a kind of uncomfortably contented way, from Don. He is working very hard this semester & finds it tough going. I do hope he gets his masters next June. He says he's quitting school whether he gets it or not.

Don:

These _were_ busy years. I had started a couple years before on a Masters degree in electrical engineering. I was working full time, taking classes, and studying as much as possible. I had made arrangements with my university employer to make up time I spent attending classes by working on Saturdays. It was a good arrangement and allowed me to graduate the same year our youngest son was born.

With five children, I needed a private place to keep my books and study. In our primitive basement, beside the furnace, I set up such a place. This placed a heavy burden on Lois—more child care than she deserved—but she survived with grace. I had never been a coffee drinker, but this was the setting that changed my habit!

We had immodest visions for improvements in our house. We juggled priorities, so that one phase of our lives was never at the top for long. The children grew, the house became more comfortable, and the education of father, mother and children continued apace.

It was an age when there were areas along the Mississippi river where no one cared if a family parked and camped for the night. We were an hour away so accomplished this outing a couple of times each summer—pitched a tent, unloaded our cooking gear, played games, and watched the barges on the river until late at night.

Lois:

Have been very busy, planning tercentennial program for Meeting, having short-story study group (Miss Hovey, my correspondence teacher comes to dinner with us on those Mondays), getting the SS class paper ready to print, cleaning house, etc. All this so I'll be able to "live" when I get "caught up." You'd think I know better, & I do rationally.

I may go to Washington for 5 days the middle of Nov to the Pilgrimage & Vigil. It will certainly be a new experience for me, and I want to go. Don's folks can't come so it means asking others to help with the children. And I hate to be obliged to anyone, but I must be getting better (less prideful) because I find it not impossible, just uncomfortable, to think of this.

I think I can go among all these Friends from over the nation and not feel crushed with guilt & worthlessness. I want to try it and see anyway.

11-17-60

Washington & back. So glad I went. For the first time in my life went among people who "do things" professionally or avocationally and kept my self-respect & identity as one person intact. A real triumph. The vigil was a success for Friends & did help batter the "respectability barrier," regardless of what governmental or popular impact it had. It was truly impressive to see 1,000 people walking two by two in calm silence around the Pentagon.

12-17-60

This is a tough one this week—every night some school or church activity. Will I thrive? Or just survive without getting depressed? Must do so!

Lying in bed half awake & half asleep, half formed shapes, incomplete ideas & thoughts, is it a waste of time? Yesterday got up & then went back to bed after half an hour for half an hour & felt more rested. Get the guts together & get up when wake up, that is the best & least wasteful of energy.

Tummy aches—oh boy, what a day ahead.

CHAPTER 9

LIVING THE MIDDLE AGES

Don:

We were now early middle aged, living in the 1960s, and in the first house we had ever owned—heavily involved in making it more livable and raising our five youngsters. After an urban city childhood, Lois had adapted miraculously to rural living. We seemed compatible, but very busy. I wonder if the busyness was an escape for me to avoid the more difficult aspects of my personality—expressing inner feelings both to myself and to Lois—and of equal importance, expressing to her my appreciation for her wifely care and love for us all. She didn't seem to appreciate her own efficiency and attention to the daily needs of house, grounds and family. The chance to develop our own country home was a challenge we both accepted with joy and anticipation.

The yards were overgrown and the house had a broken window. Raccoons were living upstairs. A beautiful, huge soft maple tree stood near the southeast corner of the house and gave merciful shade during hot summer days. We bought the place cheaply and went to work.

The source of water was a "dug" well about 30 inches in diameter and 45 feet deep. It was brick-lined and probably a hundred years old. Water was about ten feet down. The top was rotted wood so Lois demanded a safe top for the well before she would agree to move five, by then, young children onto the new place. With an old steel implement wheel cast in cement, I made a concrete top that could barely be moved an inch at a time by two men. With that in place, no child could possibly fall into the well, and we moved to our new home. My "hobby" for the next fifteen years was remodeling and improving our living conditions. Evenings, weekends and vacation time were mostly work time for me. I gradually acquired the necessary tools to do most any construction job. Much of the time, at least in the beginning, Lois' great need for order was grossly violated. She was long suffering and patient as we planned each project, then undertook it and finished it. Outside, we cleared the grounds, developed garden space, tore out old fences, and gradually pushed the unruly area around the house farther and farther away. We graveled a loop for a circular driveway. Much of the hand work and drudgery got the kids, as each grew old enough to help, involved, and was a way for the family to share responsibilities.

Inside we remodeled the kitchen, took out doors, cut in new doors, made office space out of the downstairs bedroom, and built in a telephone booth. We carpeted some floors and put vinyl on others. We added a bedroom above the kitchen and replaced the steep, curving typical old-farm-house stairway with a modern one with a landing and low rise steps. In one corner of the kitchen we built a breakfast nook with west and south windows. The kids soon named it "the pocket." There we ate, played games, visited, argued and sometimes entertained guests.

Our new home had no bathroom, but did have a flush toilet in the corner of one bedroom upstairs. My first project was to get a full sized bathroom built. The house had a small space, off the kitchen, which had been used as a "shoe and boot" room. I leveled the floor, and plumbed for bathtub, sink, washing machine and toilet. With new linoleum on the floor and Formica countertop our standard of living was greatly improved.

The little, unincorporated town called Springdale was home to about thirty families. A small country store, on the only corner in town, carried a limited assortment of groceries, and various household items. Our purchases were penciled onto our page in the tall account book and we settled up every two weeks. People were friendly and welcoming and we loved them all.

In this town, where we lived for most of our later years, we associated easily with our neighbors, some of whom had little education. Communication was often on the local gossip level and concerned with who was doing what and the health of the dogs, cats and horses of the community. We were a community like millions of others the world over.

The annual summer hog roast was a well-attended event. Every family brought favorite dishes of every flavor—games and gossip took up our time while the porker rotated slowly on the spit. Finally when the self-appointed town mayor pronounced the meat edible we gathered around.

Lois:

7/28/62

How write a portrait of a year? More and more the most important items are internal, especially as one's internals grow so noticeably as mine are! Yet a glance at the dates marked on the calendar show how busy our external lives have been.

January:

I think it was at Aunt Edna's funeral which was on the last Saturday of January that I became really aware that I was much overdue for falling off the roof. We were appreciated more than we deserved for coming up to New Providence. It was a first funeral for the kids and I felt guilty using it mostly as an educational device for them, since Aunt E. meant nothing to them. So many family complications and tragedies were represented there in Uncle Roy's children and grandchildren, and our own family, still in a kind of peaceful unit seemed more hopeful. And wouldn't it be a joke if we should have another one?! Later at the graveside in a bitter wind and balancing on frozen chunks of snow we met a friend who asked me how many kids we had. I'm always proud and embarrassed to say five—and don't let it ever be six, for heavens sake, I thought.

February:

Second semester registration and three weeks overdue. I was hysterical all right, but not that hysterical. Standing in line in that enormous field house, feeling faint and sickish, I knew then. But I registered for 12 hours, four courses, thinking such a schedule might help me from going crazy. I couldn't keep to it though. I dropped the two library courses within a month. They were my favorites but required reading beyond my dizzy abilities.

October 11, 1962

Roger was four weeks old yesterday and he's such a joy—the child I seriously considered aborting, that Don talked to Dr. Conner about the chances of aborting the child I feared would be a boy. Now I fear I'll develop a mamma passion for him which may spoil us both. I look at his perfect features when he sleeps and weep inside.

I am hating myself for a fool this week, but trying to "keep my sense of humor"—Don's admonition. After vacillating all summer, I decided to nurse Roger and have been doing so. This last week with outside activities rushing back on me I decided to wean him. He's getting along fine and I'm getting along fine too, physically. Yesterday was very uncomfortable and leaky. Today I have a perfect figure, but the soreness is much less and production is obviously down. For a wild moment I wondered this a.m. if it were too late to try to get back to nursing again. It seems so awful to have such a magnificently performing body thwarted from doing what a strong part of me wants it to do. Why didn't I let it keep doing it? Lack of confidence was one big reason. Constantly I was aware of holding myself down, needing rest, etc. Now I am not so sure rest and good diet are so all important. How much rest have women through history who nursed a year or more gotten? Vanity was another reason. Would I get flat and saggy breasted? (I soon will know.) This is a dilemma because the best figure I'll ever have will leave as soon as the present engorgement and swelling go down. Embarrassment is another reason. It is difficult, almost impossible for me to nurse in front of other people, men or women, partly because I'm just plain prudish, partly because I think nursing offends some. Why can't I be brave enough to live by my own convictions over such a basic and simple matter?

I had thought I was going to stay home this winter, be truly domestic and maternal, nurse our last baby, sew and cook, be the ideal wife and mother. Well, what is the ideal wife and mother? I don't want to be a selfish vegetable like Mother L. I am still trying to digest what Don said recently about his wanting a wife who was interesting and active in affairs and independent. He seems to have such affection and respect for Mother who is none of these things that I have always assumed without thinking that she was the kind of woman he would want his wife to be, and I've tried to be somewhat like her, or am I like her without trying? Sometimes I feel so trapped with kids and home obligations, and yet I feel so frustrated when I attempt more. No—school last year was a real lift to me. I look forward to Saturday classes this year. But I quake at the thought of working full time or even half time. Housework I can probably hire enough of to keep us orderly, better than I do perhaps. But who will just be here for the kids? Tradition and custom of a generation ago held me tightly. Don's sister, Margaret, who grew up with a far more motherly woman than I did, has worked all her children's lives and still keeps sane. Guilt is the burden, that I don't devote my all to each one, a husband and 6 children. Ridiculous!

June 6, 1963

Four loaves of bread, a quadruple batch and two single batches of cookies and an angel cake today. We are not spick and orderly, and I despair of becoming so. How does one transcend the work in the summer or even do all of it without being pushed?

Knitting, star study, kids' band, reading. I must keep these in mind. Four projects that deserve some time this summer. Mosaic? Washing, ironing, food and maintenance must not be allowed to swallow all of my time.

Dave is at loose ends already, doesn't complain though. Driver's ed. begins in ten days and it will be good for him to get out among peers. He has a lot of reading to do and should review algebra and German this summer, but that's not very exciting fare for a fourteen year old.

My diet has hit bottom today I fear, too much baking. If I could just show a loss for encouragement!

Roger has been so good, lots to watch and lots to entertain him, of course.

Don waits for word from Beckman in Palo Alto. I can't really conceive of his being hired there, or rather of our moving there. So much is shabby and scroungy here and yet to leave seems almost to flaunt goodness in the face. We have it so good it would have to be worse if we changed. This idea is firmly fixed in me, a real coward's philosophy, perhaps.

Reading *Nausea*, 1938, leaves me cold while recognizing the skill and clarity used in describing abnormal Sensations. Do I understand significance of the book? No. Have read avidly and senselessly last two years. Remember none of it. Except *Fate is the Hunter* by Gann, and that mostly because Don and I read it together. First whole book we've achieved together in marriage.

Forty five minutes of rest and writing-refreshing.

6/27/63

Camped on the Mississippi one weekend.

Thirty-four days, no rain, getting dangerously dry.

New upright freezer, roomy, nice. Busy filling it with peas and rhubarb.

6/29/63

Don and I talked a long time. I am realizing more and more in my comparatively recent mental health how much this is his doing. When he feels like a failure and when I wonder about it, this is an impressive reminder to me. The time, energy and love he has spent on me are immeasurably large. His job is not very satisfying to him usually and he feels out of place among all the MDs, no engineers. He needs more recognition than he gets, his virtues are so quiet and undemanding I forget to give him a little of that which he gives so freely.

Don admires my conversational ability and I have to remind him that I almost never have an original idea. I'm a reader and an absorber, not a creator. The delight to me is that I'm so much freer to use what brain I do have. Fifteen years ago I was so busy comparing myself unfavorably and hopelessly to everyone around me, and then hating them for their superiority, that I hardly functioned beyond this emotional cycle. Today I am a person with a lot of flaws, but better able to accept and even in some cases overcome. I think a less sympathetic, less helpful husband might have caused me to deteriorate instead of heal. I was unable to go and do otherwise, though I wanted to. It has been and is a process.

7/3/63

Marvelous feeling of well-being.

Church Pastor was here, leaving 7 books for me to read on modern theology and existentialism and Kierkegaard. Will I really be able to understand them? I was pleased that he remembered my interest. We were talking again, mostly joking, Sunday p.m. Don sighed, and said he just gets so fidgety after one paragraph of that stuff. It's not a language he knows (nor do I) just as his engineering and math books might as well be/are in hieroglyphics. I told him of the sociology of the family course lecture I heard where mutual interests were rated of highest importance in a survey of engaged couples and yet tests showed wide lack of basic interests shared. One of nature's jokes. Don says we do share the basic mutual interest and the rest have to be built in the process of daily living, which is another mutual interest.

Don got a $2,000 raise for next year!! Wow, what a morale builder. No wonder it's been such a joyous day! This doesn't solve all of his work problems; I hope it will help. It will considerably ease Dave's tuition problem next year. It fires me up to get more courses in library before I have to go to work.

7/9/63

Three extra girls here today. All had a good time, I think. Jan practiced with Gwen for 4H.

Have thought today what a really full and satisfying life I have. What's all the fuss about sex? If I can't keep interested, so what? I'm tired of worrying and wondering about it. If the gift of passion is gone—goodbye. Is this a usual age 38 female feeling? It doesn't seem to be Don's.

7/17/63

A haircut and set for me today and I look so nice! Am going to try it without a perm a few weeks to see how well I do. Self-discipline of rollers and pin up time!

Also today the bank sent a notice of granting the $6,000 loan Don asked for to pay off our mortgage and make improvements. We are hoping to add an upstairs bedroom and a basement room and re-roof in a month!! Next year we want to redo the kitchen. Ah, that will be the day.

Jan and Gwen got red ribbons for their 4H demonstration. Elaine and Helen both seemed genuinely concerned and surprised that they didn't place better. Helen worked so hard with them; she was the most disappointed, perhaps.

Visited swim class Monday after Jan's demonstration. Martha and Ruth are tops in their class. Naomi fell by the wayside because of not back floating. But she is getting it better, and she's fine on her face and opening her eyes, perhaps that's enough for first year.

Margie, Carolyn, Ruth, Naomi and I went swimming for Naomi's birthday. We had cupcakes and drink in the park afterward. A peaceful, easy party for me. And I needed it. I'd been feeling so pushed with berries and 4H and well, what, just mothering and wifeing.

Roger has had measles. For a week he was sick, terrible cold and constant fever. He's fading now and much more his happy self again. Also beginning to eat solids. M and N will catch them I suppose.

Last p.m. bugs got in and ate us. It was hot. One time in the night when I muttered some complaint, Don said a bug had bitten his balls and he had a blister, "and you think you have troubles." That struck me as funny and I got to laughing, tried not to and only shook the bed. This a.m. he really did have a big irregularly shaped blister right where he had said, also one on his inner thigh.

We enjoy Gann's *The High and the Mighty* together, not a great book, but a great sharing, which we need. I'm not going to keep a chart of optimum times; superstition and fear of documenting passion might forever destroy this elusive gem. But I wish I did know more about it and us and could find the proper mental set for it. I think so many sex info articles are written to further the American dream perpetual harmony and satisfaction and are not necessarily true in letter and/or spirit. Is the union and abandon I/we long for, and even sometimes achieve, only a dream, which starts building early in childhood when one finds himself a lonely entity, often the object of disapproval or indifference?

4/21/64

Oh, how frustrated and sorry for myself I feel. Caring for kids seems such a futile job. Certainly it is moneywise and it doesn't satisfy my inner needs. They constantly thwart my desire for neatness and order and I get mean. Not an active meanness, but cold withdrawal which is probably more destructive to their little psyches than an angry bop would be. My days are full of things to do. I do accomplish some of these things each day, yet why am I never satisfied? What do I want a day to contain? Until I can answer this question there is no hope. Service to others? I do achieve this on a very small personal scale. Time of my own? I do get some of this. Perhaps I take more than many women do with as many responsibilities as I. I don't use this time systematically. I usually read-gulp-anything easy and self-escaping, and I ought to have a program of study.

Don was in Chicago last week. By Friday when he came home I was depressed. The second car, for transport to work had to have a new (rebuilt) engine and all of my earnings are buying it. This hurts. Resentment seeps out. Yet how unfair. Never a word from Don when my teeth cost so much to restore. I do wish we could get better adjusted to our salary. It's always such a struggle and we seem to have less things than others who have less salary. Are our Scattergood attempts unrealistic? Is it worth it to spend so much there? Will the kids who go there be enough better able to live than those who go to public school? It's a relief to have Dave there. I do not worry about his social or his scholastic achievement. I can be removed and think of the opportunities he has and not see whether or not he's utilizing them. And we have no conflict with him now. Later?

One of the most unpleasant aspects of parenthood is going through adolescence again with my daughter and to a lesser extent with the son. Since those years were so terrible for me, I find the same sick hopelessness welling up when I see Janet in a similar situation. After six children have grown, perhaps my own problems will be well understood and absorbed!?

Don:

The oldest four of our children attended Scattergood—Dave and Janet entered as freshmen. Martha and Ruth transferred in after some time in the public school. Scattergood School had been such an integral part of our lives for the past twenty years that we made assumptions that our kids would automatically attend. We believed in the mission and work and farm oriented atmosphere. Our experiences and relationships there had been good for us and we assumed they would be the same for our kids. A biased attitude I'm sure.

Lois:
4/24/64

Our two cars are now in tip-top shape $400+ worth. I don't know what we would have done if I hadn't had my earnings stashed away. They weren't even enough to cover it all, but they took off a large bite. There goes my new stove.

As of now, grapefruit, eggs, skim milk for three days, then 12-1400 calories/day until 115 lbs. Also, outside work or 15 minute workout/day. Twenty-four hours in every day, need exercise to feel better. Know this. Why does the human put off or get too busy to do what needs doing and even when one wants the results of the act?

3/13/65

Kersey's 55th birthday. This has been a horrible day. Probably just menstrual mood, but it has been gruesome. Do other women carry on a continuous dialogue within themselves? I feel as if I would be such a better mother if I could enter wholly into the person and task at hand, but nearly always there is an entirely separate business going on in my mind. Sometimes I agree with myself, sometimes I disagree, scold or make fun of self, but this inner conversation is real and constant. Or is it only when I'm unhappy and dissatisfied? Is that all of the time?

Don:

Lois was an habitual "talk-to-herselfer." She often forgot to notice who was around so I often caught the drift of her conversation. I never tried to interfere or answer but had the opportunity at times. Occasionally she was stopped short knowing that I was listening. I did kid her about having to talk louder while running the lawn mower in order to be heard!

Lois:
3/15/65

Yesterday went to U. Library to study for the correspondence course. I love to be sitting studying where people all around me are doing same. Childish? Escape?

3/16/65

Lunch with three younger than four! No wonder grandparents enjoy children so much. They know each stage is only a preparation for the next and usually the children are only temporarily large on their landscape.

Becky, an outspoken three year old, doesn't want rice but ate more of it than of anything, except the red fruit Jello. This went down by the tablespoons full held onto the teaspoon by a grubby but dexterous left hand. The stretching capacity of the oral organ is as amazing as some of the other more concealed parts of us. Crawling under the table to tap feet and enquire of the owner, "is this you?" getting up to get Kleenex, once for nose duty and once for cleaning unwanted egg from the spoon, (we are fastidious), turning on the light, and getting up once just for exercise were only four major movements in a meal of pure motion. Even when not doing anything that can be defined as doing something she is in motion, kinetically, cellularly, even her straight brown hair signals action and go.

Ricky, four months younger, is much more passive, an ideal audience. His dark shadowed eyes, the temple veins that visibly beat, making his life seem so vulnerable, crinkle at the corners and sparkle with gaity; he is always delighted to have something to laugh at. At Becky he laughs and laughs his slightly hoarse chuckle.

Roger, ten months younger than Rick, is still rather a baby, but he tries. He laughs too. And he copies. Under the table with Becky. Over to the light switch with Becky. And he repeats her witty sayings. "Do you like to eat boogers?" "Sometimes I use a Kleenex," says Becky as she licks her finger. Ricky and Becky exchange a look of complete understanding and comradeship having paid verbal homage to the social rule and acted on the universal fondness for salt.

2/28/67

It amuses me that whenever I have a sexual revival I also have an urge to write. What peculiar form of exhibitionism is this? Or is it a creative outburst? Sometimes life seems too good to keep. Most of my journal writings seem steeped in sex problems and joys. But there may be fairness in this. To our children I am certain that I seem to be a grouch, care worn, neuter creature, absorbed with pans, brooms, laundry and financial fizzes. I suppose that one of the chief reasons for the generation gap is that parents never communicate their very active inner lives to their children. But how can you tell your 14 year old daughter that you had a marvelous time last Sunday, making love twice under their very noses?! It wouldn't do at all.

We had been planning to go to Des Moines for the weekend, just Don and me. But it turned very cold and windy on Friday. Friday evening Don decided that too many pipes could freeze or the furnace might conk out without him here to watch over the mechanics of life. I was disappointed, but also relieved. All week I had been anxious about the trip, fearing that we would both be disappointed sexually and adventure wise. We have had no practice in painting the town red, not even pale pink. When I confessed this anxiety to Don on Sunday he said he had been determined to prove that he could go on an overnight holiday and leave me alone. Sat. p.m. we took the kids over to Scattergood to see "Raisin in the Sun." Jan felt blue, no date.

Sun. afternoon we took a "nap" and had a delightful end to the sexual drought I had been living under. Then we got up and went in to IC to see the movie "Dear John." I was so glad that we were not edgy when we saw it. I had been afraid to see it, because I feared feeling inadequate, but at that moment I knew I was not. Don asks the good question. "Why couldn't the same story, the same love making, the same getting to know each other have been used for a returning sea captain to his wife, instead of to a stranger?" Granted enough absence, therefore novelty, I think it might make a good tale. No, the child, you would not get a sitter for your own child, and the irresponsible spell would not be allowed. That is where it would fail. And this is where parents do fail sometimes, we do not leave our children enough for our sakes. For their sakes I suppose it is easy to leave them too much.

CHAPTER 10

OUR DECADE OF THE EIGHTIES

Don:

The Christmas holidays were just past. Our house had been full. Martha, now in her late twenties, and her partner at the time, Donna, from Florida, had been here. Dave, our eldest now in his thirties, and Brenda and their daughters Tanya and Heidi, ages seven and five, from eastern Pennsylvania had brought our daughter, Ruth, from Philadelphia with them. Roger was living in the basement.

Lois was a member of the Scattergood School Committee and had some major responsibilities in the selection and appointment of a new director during those years. She was appointed clerk of our Quaker Monthly Meeting for two years. I was on the building committee and it was during this time that we remodeled our Meeting House and doubled the seating capacity. It was a lot of work, but a community effort and very enjoyable.

We owned two residential rental properties in Iowa City with our daughter Naomi, now in her twenties, in charge of renting and collecting. One house was already a duplex, 533-535, and we decided, in 1983, to remodel the other one and make it a duplex also. It became 519-521. Roger was a beginning carpenter and budding architect enrolled in the Architectural Design program at Iowa State University. He was hired to supervise the job by the contractor we hired to build the new duplex.

Lois:
1/4/81

Two degrees above zero. Walked to cemetery. Cold!

"A high brow is a person educated beyond his capabilities." Me? Am limiting food intake, would like to get back to 120 pounds. Holidays were a real bloat.

Rog's room smelling like pot, small stash under the bed. Tried to talk to him at breakfast. He very negative and removed. Worried. Do not want him to turn into a dope head. Uneasy enough about his hours down there with Connie. Don seems to think it's OK. I've always hidden my sexuality, even when I shouldn't, so I don't fight it, but still—I wonder.

Next Wed. evening, swimming lesson night. I think I've decided to try again. Important: Do Not compare body or skill with anyone. Do Not care if not "swimming" after 10 lessons. Be glad for opportunity to exercise. Goals: turn from back to stomach and vice versa, swim width of pool breathing and propelling somehow.

How to evaluate Christmas holidays? Over all, successful, I think. I hadn't even thought of Martha's coming, but Don did, and looked up some flights. Then 12/23 called to say they were taking a plane next morning.

They both live well, spend money for personal things. Donna admits she could never go to school because she's not willing to give up her present life. They live in a 2 BR, 2 bath apt., hardly your attic student. Ruth resented this, or resented most that M. showed no interest in her, asked not one question about her life.

2/5/81 Thursday

When I stopped what I was doing and got Rog some supper last night when he got home about 8:30 he said, "Thanks"!!

I've applied for a half time job as assistant editor for a "scholarly journal" in the department of economics. It really intrigues me, something more demanding than this job offers.

Sunday 2/22/81

Didn't get the job, not even an interview. Have rented a Selectric to see if I can train myself to pass the clerk III (50 words/min) test.

This has been a crazy month with temps in 60s. It's also very dry and we hear dire forecasts of drought. But yesterday evening it began to rain and it gently rained all night and all of today until the last hour when it has turned into wet and sticking snow.

3/3/25-31/81

Home from visiting Martha in Florida and Don's brother in Texas and into cleaning and gardening binge. Rog called from Martha's, very sunburned. Seemed some subdued, hope not sick. Jan & Don out to get [garden] cultivator and visit, Naomi also. Always nice to have 'em come. Interviewed 2nd time for RA job, one of final four, but didn't get it.

Feel down about job.

6/16/81

I miss writing, but how to get back to it and keep as busy as I do, which I also need. Here it is summer already and no record. Yet my head is fairly straight without it. If I don't need writing as therapy I neglect it, yet miss it. But do I miss it as a discipline or as a free blow-off? The latter, I fear. The two hours a week I watch Masterpiece Theater I could write. So much easier to watch The Golden Bowl, Cousin Bette, the diet is rich.

Rog graduated from high school May 30. We had an open house afterward, well attended. I invited all of Springdale. Felt good about it afterward.

6/22/81 Monday, 8:00 a.m.

Rog and a friend had charge of pre-meeting discussion yesterday. Rog initiated it, did very well. If I could see him as others do—He IS handsome, and why should a mother expect to understand (or vice versa) her son?

Having super trouble "centering" TO WRITE. In quotes and capitals because it is an important thing I want to do, must do, if I'm to be eligible to attend the writing workshop I've already registered and paid for. It says right there on the application form, submit ten pages of your writing two weeks before we meet. How to activate the slumbering urge? How to dare add to the printed verbiage of the world? Recently I've been reading Tuchman, Merton, Hardwick, even a skim or two in the Bible. If publishers would limit their choices to such as these, readers of the world would be better off. But what would all the lousy writers do? Why do they write at all?

I am trying to gain understanding of why I like to write, or why I believe I like to write. Since for so long I am unable actually to do it, more than for cursory journal entries. I'm no longer even certain that I do like to write.

When I was a child my mother frequently sat for mornings in a small armless rocker at a small desk and wrote letters, mostly to her three sisters and her two daughters. She was an unhappy and unwell woman during the 12 years that I knew her, and I think some of her happiest, or most satisfying hours were lived at this small desk, her own spot in the world.

I must have learned from her that a desk of your own is a precious thing. I wanted one, and one Christmas I was given a child's desk with a chair so straight backed it pushed you forward, off balance. The hinged top lifted over a storage space. It was stained (pine, I suppose) a rather garish yellow and designed with stark sharp edges, not a soft or rounded line on it or the chair. I loved it, took delight in cleaning it out, sorting things into neat stacks, big-little books (I never had more than a few), school papers, pencil box…

I never had a desk truly my own again until this one that Dad Laughlin made became mine. It was the one thing I asked for. Made of walnut with four drawers on one side and a top drawer in the middle, it is much grander than my first, but styled much the same. Dad L built things square and sharp edged also. What surprised me was how important and satisfying to me this desk instantly became. My special place in the world. And how had I not known I needed it for all these years?

There was another desk in my life, our lives. The first thing that Don ever built for us was a pine desk when we lived on Scattergood farm. We had no furniture then, and it became the most impressive piece in our small farmhouse front room. Its bulky rectangle served for many years as container of important papers, household business and letters. One drawer used to hold children's books, crayons, papers. It was finished with a clear sealer and wax and for many years I took great care to keep it clean and polished. It gradually darkened and the soft pine wood became gouged and scarred from the use and abuse of eight of us, and my pride and care for it diminished. It is now in Don's office with drawers full and top covered under piles of his papers.

I will always honor it, and remember the love we had for each other as we built it (I was chief sander), but it was never truly mine as this desk from Dad Laughlin is.

Does a desk a writer make? Oh, no. But having a writing place to feel comfortable in makes it more possible. Margaret has a room and desk and piles of orderly papers on it and file drawers, and a typewriter on a little slide out table, a dictionary and book of marketing possibilities for writers—how could she avoid writing with all of these? A true writer will not be stopped without a place, but surely he suffers from its lack.

One certain reason why I like to write is because it feels good to sit at my desk, my spot in the world. The grain of the walnut, the Chinese vase with pencils and Bics in it, the basket with letters to answer, the desk tray with clippings and notebooks, the dictionary, the lamp, the obsidian chunk I found in the road and use as a paperweight and through which the sunlight gleams amber: How did I live before I had these precious things for my own?

Do I feel I must write in order to deserve having them? Possibly.

But long ago, before I had these, I wrote. Therapy. Someone gave me a diary for a birthday, probably the tenth. The five lines per day were a source of frustration. My compulsive nature was distressed when each day could not be compressed or expanded to fit exactly into that space.

I gave up and wrote over the neat printed dates, perhaps five pages one day and nothing for weeks, and felt I had betrayed something, —the book?

Don was my diary during late HS and college. No wonder I loved him so, I could write to him about anything, and twist it to put me in a favorable light. I was concerned in those years to be honest, but I know that much of what I wrote was to elicit his approval. Or perhaps more importantly, I would denigrate myself, often humorously, so that he would respond with reassurance that the flaw was not serious. Five years of letter writing-courtship, I know now is a very dangerous entry to a marriage. How did we fare so well?

Stashed away are six or seven spiral notebooks of journals kept during our marriage. I haven't had the courage to go through these. I know they are repetitious and self centered. They were therapy, which kept me alive for many years. Besides a few corny poems of early marriage and two short stories of twenty years later, they are all I've ever written, not counting letters. Oh, and one article, which was also embarrassingly therapeutic, but printed in "Quaker Life." So much for the good taste of small religious periodicals.

10/27/81 Tuesday

[My sisters], Teresa and Naomi visited us last week, a truly momentous occasion. We had a lot of good times and some close sharing but not a lot.

T and N are definitely "older women," not merely middle aged. I feel still middle aged, drat it, early middle aged, but it's so difficult to know how one appears to others. I've got to begin accepting "older" as fitting me. Drat.

I'm working (there hasn't been enough to do really) full time for one month, so have had to miss a lot of swimming lessons. And this last time, my 3rd in the beginners class, has been the best, feel as if I'm making progress. Have actually gotten across the pool a few times, and I do want and intend to keep some kind of consistent try with it. Have been exercising with some regularity in the women's gym at noon. Am also down to 120 lbs., which is where I want to stay.

Don has gone to NY for learning about a new $100,000 mannequin he'll be responsible for. Will return Thursday. He's been very busy with solar collectors all fall, once we went three weeks eating only 2 suppers together, he coming home after work only those times. I get bored and lonely at home alone all those evenings.

Don:

The mannequin was a marvelous display of electronic excellence. It was a teaching aid for medical students, and played audible heart sounds into stethoscope-shaped earphones. Different tapes allowed students to listen to normal heart sounds as well as those from a diseased heart. It was a full-sized human body with a realistic silicone skin over the sponge rubber torso. By placing the stethoscope on the appropriate spot on the body the appropriate sounds were heard.

It was a beautiful and challenging combination of electronics, hydraulics and mechanics. I loved the technology.

I went to New York to help finish the construction, and learn the details of its many systems, before it was shipped to us. Each one was hand made, one at a time by a very small company specializing in animated circus characters. It was a satisfying and educational trip.

Lois:

Don is also working on a large solar collector for us.

I think we ought to be paying more attention to each other and/or to our relationship, which is us. I've become kind of neutral, make almost no demands on him, go my way keeping busy. But in our everyday comings and goings there isn't much excitement; neither of us is putting much into it.

Rog seems to be settling into ISU life. He's been home several weekends. I've been less active with Scattergood since the director resigned and went away. That was a bum year. I like working with the adults and being on the committee.

Don is to speak to the students Nov. 14 on being a Conscientious Objector-past and present. I hope he'll put some thought and planning into it.

I'm just rattling on here to keep from going INSANE. Except for relieving Pat at switchboard I haven't done 20 minutes of work today. It's really awful!! Ten more minutes and I flee, take the riders home and then spend a lonely evening or come back in to hear the husband of a writer I admire. —Hortense Calisher—Curtis Harnack. Is it worth the trip? Lonely either way. Also Simone Signoret in a film at the Bijou at 8:30—lonelier yet.

Sun. eve. Nov. 22 5:15

Restless, bored, anxious. How come to terms?

I have observed it many times in other women. The public appearance in clothes that don't match, the bulky sox, the shoes only for comfort, or even work shoes not changed, the hair let go, with the ducktail or the section uncombed or matted, the side that was slept on not forced into symmetry with the rest. I used to wonder why or how a woman would let herself go so dowdy. And with it all a demeanor of lonely independence. She can be subdued, isolated, or she can be rather aggressive, but the underlying and basic emotion is "what the hell, there is no hope." I am understanding better now.

And what is it she has given up all hope of having? I believe it is romance, adventure, new experience, opportunities dwindling to zero. This syndrome often hits in the forties; the kids are gone, the husband is the same old guy he's always been and he's not about to change much.

I've been fortunate, or have I? I've tried to initiate some pizzazz, and succeeded partially for a while, but it was largely illusion and hope of more adventure that kept me going. The actual events were not that often nor that transcendent. But now, in mid-fifties I am sharply aware of the aging signs, and of the rejections to my overtures, and I find myself joining the host of women who have given up.

But I'm not real comfortable with them either, yet. After the full acceptance occurs, then is there peace of mind? Do dreams and fantasies still pop up to trigger discontent with reality? I suppose they do. But having once accepted, it MUST get better. That's when the serenity of age begins, having accepted the losses which one has battled against losing.

Swimming—my body and theirs. Aged, aging, youth. The woman with the missing breast.

After two days at home I know how seriously I have to have something.

Jealousy, deal with it, write about, jealous of youth. Lack of kindred spirit friend, male or female. Write about.

Get your act together, Lois. Become one unified person, that's what maturity is. No more dreams of adventure, just be Mrs. D. Laughlin. I've begun knitting a lot when home alone. That's a big step forward. Also eating a lot. When I hit 130 I'll have it made as the perfect middle-aged house slob!!

Don:

We made many trips to Pennsylvania during this decade. Dave's two girls were grade school kids and liked to visit grandma and grandpa too. We did many things with them—often sleeping in the yard at night with the dog, which they seemed to love. One year we rented a pony to have on the place for them to ride.

Tanya and Heidi were with us the summer the Soviet/American peace walk stopped at our place for rest and refreshments. They walked for a while with the nearly two hundred or so members of the groups. These years were perhaps the peak of the "nuclear age." There were hawks on both sides who felt severely threatened by nuclear weapons in the hands of the other. Both sides recognized that these weapons were protection only if used first. "First strike capability" was the word of the day—we sought such and the Soviets did the same. Many of us thought of our two positions as a "balance of terror" and that it was not a sound basis for peaceful coexistence.

The walk across the United States was by a few hundred peace-concerned Soviet men and women, joined by an equal number of equally concerned Americans. It was a grass-roots symbol of the growing concern and alarm over the threat of nuclear war. It was one of the early signs of the political thaw between our two governments.

Lois and I offered our place as a two-hour stopover for rest and cold drinking water. We were very pleased when the offer was accepted. With the help of interpreters, Tanya and Heidi fashioned a Russian welcome sign to tie on the back of our big dog, Max. He wandered freely among visitors lounging in the shade and was lovingly greeted.

We made trips to help Dave with building a new bathroom in his house, and trips to install a solar water heater on the roof. We attended Tanya's graduation from college and Dave and Brenda's twenty-fifth wedding anniversary.

We enjoyed these trips, sometimes with grandchildren, and sometimes by ourselves. As long as my sister and her husband lived in Toledo, it was always our halfway overnight stop. After they moved to Colorado we took a more southerly route and a motel at the halfway point. On rare occasions we made the sixteen hour drive in one stint.

Until her death, we always saw Ruth when we went east. She and Dave lived an hour apart.

Lois:

1/8/82 at home in Springdale

New fridge arrived, pleased with it. Don spent all day re-wiring, installing it. We now have shelves where old wall fridge hung. Very nice. Zero temps all day, howling wind and drifting.

Don:

Shortly after moving into our house in Springdale we found a unique, used, wall-hanging refrigerator. We enjoyed it for years, but it was small and our family outgrew it. The new standard upright refrigerator meant we had wall space, which had to be covered—shelves were the answer.

Lois:

1/10/82

Minus 28° F this a.m. 30°. in our room. Bless electric blankets. High wind and drifting snow. All are urged by radio to stay in. Rog struggling with 50 ft. drift to get out and see Connie. Don working on radio, much improved. Has been out of whack for ages. No [Quaker] Meeting.

1/11/82

Dug out about 9:30. Passed typing test @ 58 wpm.

3/18/82

37 Years today! AAUW tonight. Got group to sponsor Nuclear Freeze Meeting. Will have to do most of it myself. Scares me, but will do OK. Home to Don after 11:00. Almost swam length of pool.

6/82

I'm going to take another 7-hour day, the third in a row, so I can watch the Joffrey bunch rehearse again. I got some of the women here to go during noon hour.

I've been sleeping alone because of poison ivy and haven't really minded. Kind of free. But I want to get back into the marriage bed before a single becomes normal. It's scary to find myself a sexual loner. But perhaps I'm not, because I've thought about it the last couple of days, which indicates what—that I am uncomfortable in it.

Have had some feeling of life futility in recent days. This used to bother me a lot. I don't think my life has become so much more productive as that I've relaxed, accepted what/who I am, and my limited life most of the time.

I think I might have made it as a hanger-on in an intellectual circle if I'd grown up or ever been exposed to that milieu. And my craving for idea talk might have been satisfied. But being able only for the edge of that world, would I have felt forever depressed and valueless compared with the leaders? Reading New York Review's personals reawakened my recognition, need for someone to talk my language with, who brings out my conversational flair, who responds innately to me, who I don't have to explain things to—that takes the fun out of it, and I've been doing it for 37 years. Yet when I'm impatient and disillusioned, disappointed by it, I also know that Don's steadfast, stable, plodding personality has been what helped me survive some very bad years. Or did it? Was he part of the problem? I must work this out.

8/13/82-8/15

Writers' Workshop at Scattergood School sponsored by Pendle Hill for Quakers begins. Have I done a lot of the "work" already, or am I repressing what I need to work on. Feel fairly cool and calm. A few times had a momentary feeling, "Can I stand this all day?" This being the alienation feeling. But it never lasted. Writing exercises were fun and interesting. Good ideas for more consideration. Came home to Rog & Don who had put up most of collector bldg. Rog napped & so did we after loving well.

9/2/82

The first journal line I've written since the writing workshop. After weeks of distress I suddenly realized this week has been one of peace and contentment. Why? Barb has not been working on my crew and work is a joy, 100% less tension. And I'm just comfortable with myself. Why?

10/23/82

Sex again in a.m. Insatiable man. Scattergood barnraising for Don all day. I stayed home and trimmed shrubs & trees all afternoon. Perfect day. Prepare for weekend trip.

11/14/82 My first Monthly Meeting as clerk. Gulp. Ugh.

12/5/82 Surprise chili supper for Don's 60th Bday. Went well.

Don:

The birthday party was a landmark occasion for me. Lois, Janet and Naomi had planned well—many friends came. The kids declared they would plan a party for me every twenty years from now on! So far they have kept their word.

The summer of '83 was busy. In May Jan and her husband, Don went with us to Martha's graduation. We drove to Chicago and flew from there to Ft. Lauderdale. Martha, and friend Bob, hosted us for the weekend. They were both nervous about graduation, but the long ceremony went well. Martha, at age thirty, had a college degree!

The loan for remodeling our rental property was approved—our contractor friend and Roger staked out the new addition and construction began with Roger, age twenty-one, as foreman on the crew. The job wasn't finished when Iowa State College took up in September so he stayed out a semester to see it through. We felt so blessed with our youngest son—well, with all our kids—they were all leading independent and productive lives.

Lois turned 58, Dave 35, Ruth 29, and Naomi 28 during the summer months.

Lois:

12/28/82 Thursday

Shopped in CR with Janet. Had a good visit. Jan evaluating her marriage sees well, but not all. Hasn't realized the shocks her husband Don has had losing his job, aging. She recognizes his lacks better and still appreciates his great help to her over the years. Fears she will grow beyond/away from him. What then? "Ruth says, Don [her dad] and I not 'soul mates,' she's right." Spent $100 on a jumper, blouse and dress!!

9/83

First day on new, one day a week job at College of Nursing. Continue at Registration Center also. Summer over, hottest, driest one I've known. Duplex goes apace. Nome has moved into 535. Chicago arts trip with print study group. Wonderful print studios visited.

10/83

Woodwork in duplex goes slowly!

This fall has been incredibly busy, building the duplex, hand crafting the oak woodwork, laying carpet till late. Got our grant from AAUW to put on our conference in Cedar County. Gulp.

Don:

The AAUW Conference on International Interdependence was Lois' idea. She brought it to the group and they accepted it. She was appointed chairwoman. She helped raise funds, find a place to hold it, and contact guest speakers. The details were in her lap. Thus began weeks of worry and work.

The conference was well attended and well accepted. She was secretly proud of her ability to pull off a significant public discussion of an important topic at a time when the world was not at rest.

Years later, in a mild display of satisfaction, she occasionally mentioned that conference when the topic of international relations brought it to mind.

Lois:

12/83

Dave's family and Ruth supposed to arrive 12/24. Coldest weather in 50 years or more, minus 60° wind chills, minus 25° temps. We had a nice remainder of the week till late New Year's Eve when Dave's left. Half a week is really about all I can manage without getting depressed. Great to see Ruth who is still bound to Tafa.

Duplex is finished! And half rented to two guys.

Don:

Tofa was Ruth's Zimbabwean friend whom she had met at Temple University. He was a PhD student. They saw each other often.

Lois:

1/84 first week

Rog called, back from Gator Bowl, OK. They froze. Will stay with Connie, a sort of open milestone. Working at College of Nursing part time.

1/84 third week

Mary Grefe cancels speech for our AAUW conference on World Interdependence. Despair here, but Beverly Everett can do it, cheers. A lot of anxiety over the coming AAUW conference. Also enjoyed few weeks of guitar lessons with Dale Thomas.

4/84 second & third week

A surprise honor with jokes for me at AAUW. Most thank you's mailed. Fight cystitis. Snow on ground on 22nd, Easter Breakfast at Mtg.

We go with Nome to PA, stop overnight in Toledo at Margaret & George's.

Go to Philly for Ruth's graduation from Temple University. Stay in room of one of her absent housemates. Ruth too thin. Drove to inner city. We went to the University on trolley and train with Tafa and Terry joining us. Much tension between Ruth & Tafa. Ruth graduates summa cum laude. Parrish House puts on party for Ruth. Lots of people come, all races and cultures.

Been a good week.

6/84 third week

First Laughlin reunion begins. Martha arrives. Dave's arrive with Ruth. Tanya wearing head cover, a jolt. All family home first time in 5 years. 12 for dinner. Martha takes girls horseback riding a couple of times. Other Laughlins arrive, most stay at Scattergood. About 26 total.

Don:

Dave and his family belonged to a conservative Brethren Church. Their tradition required women to wear a head covering when in public. It's a symbolic gesture of the Biblical injunction assigning "men as head of the household." Lois was jolted to see how much Tanya had grown up since last visit.

Lois:
8/84

Have been reading *Wu Li Dancing Masters* and *Keeping Women*. Calisher, whose story collection, *Absence of Angels* gripped me years ago. This one has been a pain to read, requires effort sometimes too great for the worth of the thoughts. Story of an unhappy woman. So what's new? Jessamyn West's *The Life I Really Lived* is wonderful. Her style and characterizations are hard to beat. I wonder if Anne Tyler was influenced by her. Want to read her *Woman Said Yes* again.

Helped Jan wallpaper her bathroom, Naomi too. We had fun, very slow but perfect job.

11/84

To DeSoto Wildlife Refuge with Alfred & Helen. Saw 1000s of snow geese, dinner theater, "Fiddler on the Roof". A nice day & lovin' 2x to boot. Wow, do we need more vacation time. First snow, stayed on ground as we came home.

Go to Dave's in new Datsun truck. Take croquet set for Christmas. Ruth comes on train. We drive her back to Philly, have theater & dinner night, fun time & good visit with Ruth.

Long visit with Jan. Ruth depressed, lonely.

1/85

Don sick all day, fever, flu. Bought this nifty little book to keep my life in order! Nome has rented one room of 521, 2 to go.

Practice AAUW speech after supper. Realized I don't have it jelled. No theme, whatever, is just a hodge podge, and I've spent hours on it!

Horrible day of deep depression, feeling incompetent. Don at Meeting House all day.

Program went so well I was sorry for Eleanor. Ah life. And what a good relief today!

Meeting cancelled. Half-cup water frozen solid in our bedroom. Don dug out drift ready for work tomorrow. Wrote a lot of letters. Talked to Jan, she's really liking her new management/admin job. She plans to visit Ruth in Feb. Max becoming a house dog!

Called about Crisis Center training—55 hours. Need to decide, class? Other volunteer? Not crazy about volunteer work. Also energy seems low, get tired.

Long cold day, snow black with dirt. Don with idea I use bargain flight to Calif!! Called old college roommate, Mae. She very warm and welcoming. Will go to LA first time since graduation to see college kids—39 years!! Momentous. Polished Meeting House stair rail Don made, very pretty, heavy oak 6" wide.

2/85

Bright sun, 15 degrees. Writing letters inviting myself to see people. Hope I get plus responses. Roads drifting in. Don got stuck on road north tonight, gone an hour and a half to get Max who broke away for Mayhew's female. Damn dog goes berserk!

No school, blowing snow, pump drifted in, no water this a.m. Don dug it out, but it closed again by midmorning. Gray, gray, cold. slept in till 8:00. Have thought a lot about clothes to take. Can't imagine warm weather and not wearing triple layers.

Can't believe I'll be in LA in 48 hours. Live it up and enjoy every well, strong day I have.

Don:

Lois was picked up at the Los Angeles airport by Iowa friends from long ago. She visited her cousin, Sterling, then a friend from Taiwan, Liu, hosted her for a day or so. After a reunion with her college roommates of the forties she took the bus to her sister Teresa's in Berkeley.

Lois:
3/1/85

Arrive LA on time. DeHavens showed up about 20 minutes late, kind of a lost feeling.

3/7/85

Rainy, cold. Mae and Bob [Mae's husband] picked me up, took me to Whittier College. Didn't recognize much on campus. Didn't recognize Liz [college roommate]. Visited their daughters' houses. Financial references are all you get here, not your introspective sort.

3/9/85

Whittier College reunion lunch at Mae's, 7 of us. Carol [college roommate] still beautiful, happy, and, fulfilled with self. "Well, he just likes me." AAUW too "radical" for Bobby. Ye Gods. Pat pale and very wrinkled, long divorced from Tom. Anna dignified and quiet. Mae snow white hair. All of us trim!

3/10/85

Leave on Greyhound at 8:55, a big relief! But really glad for past week. Would never live in Southern California. Ralph, Teresa, and Eric met me at bus station in Oakland. Ralph made two serious driving errors, (pulled in front of left hand turning car), Teresa very tense, Ralph super defensive and angry when she tried to direct.

3/12/85

Teresa & I take BART to museum of modern art in SF. I spend glorious afternoon alone on cable cars, Ghirardelli Square, fisherman's wharf, supper at Houlihan's. Waiter seated me in back corner by kitchen door. I moved myself to small table for two beside window with glorious view of bay and Berkeley hills. At Gir Sq spent $100 on mobiles!! For Jan and Martha. Also a design store full of exotic, expensive stuff new to me, loved it.

3/18/85

40 years! Don sent 13 red carnations with baby's breath bouquet with funny note! Teresa & I took BART to SF, then Sausalito ferry. Had lunch at swank dockside restaurant in Sausalito. Talked of husbands and sex. Ralph jealous and suspected T of infidelity, never true, darn it. Impotent now. Gorgeous day, cold on boat. Feel sad for T. Ralph so dependent, demanding, jealous and selfish—

3/21/85

Clear, warm, see whole bay area from T's house. T & I walked up into high houses in a.m. Kersey took me to airport. Had a nice guy to Denver, a satellite engineer. Denver to Cedar Rapids, an ego nut, finally just read and ignored the bore. So good to see Don. Don suggests night in town. Glory!

3/22/85

Had wonderful night in Holiday Inn, downtown Iowa City. Breakfast there, back to bed. Then home to reality.

4/19/85

Burned in ditch, had to call fire dept. Cuts from climbing over barbed wire fence three times trying to beat out flames when they went into Herman's field. Don doesn't know yet.

5/17/85

Kersey and Bert are planning to come to wedding. Lay in sun, had slight overdose. Pounding heart, nausea, blackout almost, pouring sweat. Laid on bathroom floor till better. Blood donor might have caused? Mowed for two hours.

5/22-25/85

Friendly Circle shower for Connie & Rog. Cleaning & gardening like crazy. Strawberries are thick, freezing 'em and eating.

Turn 60. Surprise Bday breakfast for me put on by Don, Jan & Nome—stupendous! Springdale folk and Mtg folks. People brought picnic table in their pickups.

Gorgeous morning. I was working in garden, so was really surprised at all the traffic in front of the house.

Don:

If Lois had had anything to say about it she would have turned down the idea of a party to celebrate her sixtieth birthday. But she didn't.

Our local daughters, Janet and Naomi, and I secretly planned a community breakfast for a Saturday morning near her birthday. The whole Friends Meeting and the whole town of Springdale were invited. Two or three came with picnic tables in their trucks. We set up in the yard on a beautiful, quiet May Day.

She was in the garden, when cars began to arrive, working and digging and with dirt on her hands and face. She was mortified at being found in such a condition, but it took only a moment for her to become completely absorbed in the joy of the morning. She enjoyed the time and was secretly proud to be the brunt of jokes and fun.

Lois:

5/30-31/85

Kersey & Burt arrive from California. 14 for supper. Had home music program, good fun.

Don:

It is customary, in our rural society, for the groom's family to plan the wedding rehearsal dinner on the evening before the wedding. We knew it would be a large crowd so we first planned it in the beautiful city park in West Branch. Late in the afternoon the wind was still too high to keep tablecloths in place, but, characteristic of Iowa, early evening often brings a great lull, and it happened that day.

Lois:

5/31/85

Rehearsal dinner. Very strong winds all day, decided we'd have to use the Masonic Lodge. Don, Jan, Dave & Brenda arranged tables there. Took Kersey & Bert to IC to visit Don's place. When we got back found the kids had taken stuff to park after all! I was terrified, but wind went down and it was very nice in spite of slow cooking on grill.

6/1/85

Rog & Connie's wedding at 4:00. All went well. Rog squeezed my hand when he ushered me into the pew, a nice personal highlight. To Muscatine for the reception. Dave's and Ruth left from there about 10:00 from the dance.

6/7-10/85

Painted red on front porch, looks great. Sun bathed and read new "Harpers," luxurious loaf all afternoon. Mind churns pros and cons of unorthodox love life. West's "World is Made of Glass" haunts me. Woman has to kill for sexual satisfaction, and portrayal of Jung's life more unsettling, more real to me. Pick buckets of lettuce before it gets bitter. Don spun it in washing machine! Pick last of strawberries. Lousy mood.

6/11-14/85

It dawns on me that Rog probably won't be around much ever again. I'll miss that. Cultivate Connie is the answer? Felt very sad when came home, Rog is really gone. Now it hits me. Connie's family will be his base. Don good comfort.

6/15-18/85

Reading. *In My Father's House*, Solomon. Moves me deeply. Pros & cons of polygamy well expressed, and religious struggle, wow.

6/23/85

Don feels need to be more active in peace movement.

Don:

The French withdrew from Viet Nam after a defeat at Diem Bien Phu in 1954. In 1955 the U.S. took over their "advisory" duties with the South Viet Nam army against the North Vietnamese. By 1965 the number of advisors in Viet Nam had grown to 23,000. This was the first year that combat troops arrived in the country even though "advisors" had been fighting for ten years.

In the United States the war was very unpopular, but still went doggedly on. In positions of power it had many supporters. Of course, all manufacturers of military gear, from shoes to war planes, had an interest in keeping it going.

Sometime in 1966, during the Johnson administration, a group of concerned citizens started to meet for a half-hour silent vigil in downtown Iowa City. Every Wednesday that I could I spent my noon hour as part of the group. We ranged in size from three to forty as we handed out a flyer on the immorality and futility of the Viet Nam war. The vigil continued faithfully for seven years, and was disbanded only at the conclusion of the war during the Nixon administration in 1973.

The war really ended because enough concerned people were elected to the U. S. Congress to say no to the president's military aggression. We felt we had had a part in switching the mood of the country.

Now, more than a decade later, it seemed little had changed. Reagan was now illegally supporting a corrupt regime in Nicaragua, which represented wealth, violence and power rather than the needs of common people. What could an individual do in times like these? I didn't know but felt the need to get involved if possible.

Lois:
6/27-30/85

Witness for Peace meeting, long. Nice bunch, don't know if I want to commit. More general peace push appeals more than Nicaragua to me. Cleaned Roger's room, just couldn't face it a few weeks ago.

Rog dropped in unexpectedly. Connie has ball game. Got him to sort his stuff. He took some of it. Says he likes marriage better than living alone! We went through the pics and I ordered $100 worth.

7/1-4/85

Don's huge solar tank is up to 140 degrees. Hot water system not connected yet. Bought a new electric water heater. What a relief. Have to relight the present one each morning and sometimes it goes out during the day, gets boiling hot or goes out.

8/1-11/85

Rog and Connie arrive to stay at our house first time, and I forgot fresh sheets on the bed! Jan drove with me to Toledo, Ohio, to get Tanya & Heidi. Jan dealing with her summer/fall marriage. Dave left in a.m. to go back east and we came home with girls.

Hiroshima 40 years ago, went to memorial ceremony, kids enjoyed. Took kids to pool.

West Liberty Fair, good horse show, rode baby elephant. Dave's girls both seemed to really enjoy seeing livestock. Played Clue before bed, slept out. Rog worked here all day, girls take turns riding on mower with him. Slept out, stars great.

To Adventureland with girls, fun time. Stopped at Rog and Connie's, saw campus, had pizza supper with them. Girls on plane to Baltimore at noon, like two little girls from 19th century.

8/22/85 to end.

Soft rain most of day. Don & I great get together, changes whole world after a long spell being unable to give or get. Why? Self punishment?

Trying to hold off anxiety for next week. Live it a day at a time. Spent all a.m. on new typewriter. Will be OK when I learn electronic tricks. Slept outside, misty/cloudy. Max cuddles! Also Don, of course. No give for love making on ground! Too old for this?

Progressive dinner for Scattergood folk, was nervous all day, but went very well. Don a real help getting party on the road. Uptight, couldn't sleep, played guitar till after 1:00. Then slept.

Teresa's Birthday. To be appreciated when old, marry an archeologist, joke from Ralph.

9/2-6/85

Depressed all week. No sleep. Despair. Called for shrink appointment. Feel more relaxed and normal than have for months! So why need counseling, just need an appointment!! Don apprehensive about it.

Slept like a rock for a while in the afternoon, after two nights on the ground. Cooled off in dormer room. Did a lot of desk things with fan and cold drinks all evening.

Don:

Our house had neither room nor central air conditioning. We made use of ceiling fans and desk fans. We slept outdoors on many hot nights where night breezes and cooler ground were a blessing. It was often too hot to sleep in a sleeping bag, so we slept on top of them. Our back yard was private so we seldom put up a tent. We didn't bother to bring out a mattress and it didn't take many nights to remind us that the sleeping bag was not thick enough.

Lois:
9/17/85

Have lost my big orange Shards II journal. Keep wondering who's reading it! Ye Gods. Embarked on counseling a couple of weeks ago. [Counselor], 43 years old, two teenagers, theological background, left ministry. Spent "hot tub" years hopping into one therapy after another in Ca. First interview, general background for each of us. My anxieties predominant. Conclusion: I would like to continue for me. Counselor wants Don to come, too, which makes sense. Don reluctant, but not unwilling.

Is your present marital status open for talk? Of course, how ignore what is? Going in to work in a.m. Don had asked what I was going to talk about. (Have felt so good have a hard time remembering problems.) Felt foolish going, but [C] made it real and easy. We talked about power. Don has more than I do, [C]. But do I exercise as much as I could? Power = decision making, making changes, persuasion, spending money. What is Gestalt therapy? In 4:00 a.m. session with myself last night I thought of more power signs: refusal to communicate or respond, withholding affection, have forgotten other. These are negative powers I have used. Can he not hear the hostility in his voice? He certainly hears it in mine, but I do also.

Also Don's inability/refusal to admit/recognize motives/feelings. Examples: talking to A, pinching nerves in my knee as "affection." These are negative powers, also.

Can I bring these power things up today without crushing Don? Fear his vulnerability more than mine. I've felt like zilch so many times so long that I feel tough as nails in one way—enduring. Don hasn't ever felt especially down or up, just is. Hasn't questioned self? He gives a speech in Chicago this week. I sense some anxiety.

Today in session-therapy-what is it called. I did a family gram. It brought back so many memories, I'm exhausted. I get stuck, writing journals about some problem over and over and over. [Counselor] says he can help me get unstuck. Sometimes the waste of my life makes me cry. The years of never feeling free, spontaneous.

This may be a very interesting fall, and wrenching, if Don can be made more aware of his quirks, defenses, etc. I've gone on the premise that I need to understand, change, accepting that Don simply can't/won't. He's always insisted he's satisfied with self and doesn't care to investigate. Now I find myself worrying about his vulnerability. I don't want to destroy his confidence. But isn't change what we both want? I fear he may think more in terms of changing me than himself. And sometimes I feel so strong because I've humbled and gritted through a lot of personal mental anguish and he hasn't.

Had lunch with Nome today. It's nice she comes and sits with me on Weds. Telling me about her friend's son going down the tubes fast. Makes me realize how lucky we were/are with our kids, and how lucky they were to have parents, even as flawed as we. I told her we were seeing a shrink.

I've volunteered to spend Monday afternoons at the Iowa City Community Theater, not exactly a star role, anything from cleaning toilets to using computer for ticket sales. But after the fright of my first evening with 'em I felt brave to go back to the work night. Helped set up the risers for audience chairs. Not exactly acting, but possibly an entry.

10/85

Resenting Don's solar fixation, told him so. Also lots of vague anxiety/depression. Still sleeping out frequently. Dropped off of Iowa City Community Theater volunteer. All one day writing about childhood for [counselor]. Useful? Housekeeping jag.

Don:

Lois often had a much better grasp of the many compromises necessary between idealism and reality. It was too easy for me to be dogmatic and uncompromising with my idealistic bent—whether it be renewable energy or a healthy diet. She was more realistic in facing the expenses and labor involved in my idealistic paths and was, for example, more willing to compromise in the choice of food for the sake of cost and effort.

Lois:

10/28/85

Today [my counselor] floored me utterly with the serious suggestion/prescription that I travel, make a trip, go through the process by myself. This to give myself a "horn of plenty" in my life, after lots of "deprivation," especially while growing up. Well, it's such a jolting new thought, to have a "developmental" need to do something like that now. And it scares me, could I do a really big thing alone? Where would I go? How much should I spend? Ye gods, I have a tight head from the mere possibility. Cruise? Not a middle aged groupie, at least not only that. But could I do everything all by myself? How much loneliness could I stand?

The numerous choices boggle my mind. The important thing to remember is to choose and do something, what, is not as important. Paris, Vienna, England. Mexico, Italy, Quaker Country. Freighter, Eurorail Pass.

Don:

Lois came home from this particular session with our counselor in an excited state of animation. She was not worried and didn't even have her usual self-doubts about the proposal. She met it as a challenge she had not thought of. As she told me of the possibilities, I knew immediately that my role was to stay out of it. And I did.

She didn't rush into any decision as she pored over all the travel literature she could get. She kept me informed of her thinking and the pros and cons of all possibilities, but no hint of a decision. Our history had always been to plan trips together, but this one was different. She was on her own and thrilled by the challenge.

Lois:

11/85

I go to Quaker schools' conference for Scattergood Committee held at Pendle Hill. I fly to Harrisburg where Dave & Brenda meet me. Stayed with them a day or so, did sewing for Brenda. Then train from Hanover (45 minutes from Dave's) to Pendle Hill. Get off and begin to walk in wrong direction with heavy suitcase, man working in his yard sets me straight. Conference high-powered, serious, organized. Two roommates, both head of day schools. Ruth and Jack come to get me after final lunch. Black, 54 years, econ professor, but not recognized when she called the number he gave her! Hope she'll heed my questioning. He is nice. She's not "in love" and she dates other men. Says he's a lousy lover. She has lost the organizing job, needs more help, also not the right personality for it. Wish she could have a better place to live, so dark. Ruth to work, I to loaf and sorted conference notes and handouts. Will have to report to Scattergood committee. Long walk. Ruth & I out to supper and to gay film, "Buddy." Dying AIDS partner. Wind and very cold coming on seven block walk home after we got off the bus. Have had wonderful visit with Ruth. To airport by public transportation from station Ruth took me to. Home to CR, now to settle down again. So ends the trip, really loved it.

Don:

Ruth was our fourth born child and exhibited unusually independent traits from birth on. She was a beautiful child and could try our patience no end. As a baby in her highchair she could suddenly become unwilling to accept the status quo and stiffen out straight and shoot out under the tray onto the floor in the blink of an eye. This rebellious trait stayed with her to the end.

As a freshman in public high school she became disillusioned with common attitudes of the friends she made. She yearned for more depth to her friendships and less emphasis on clothes and status activities. She transferred to Scattergood School as a sophomore.

After graduation there, she lived with my sister and family in Toledo, for a semester as a freshman in Toledo University. This didn't suit her, and she returned to Iowa City. She seemed a restless soul and worked at various things. She was interested in farming at one time and worked on a cooperative farm in Iowa for a while and then an apple farm in Ohio one summer. She was an idealist and felt that there should be little distinction between men and women. She considered herself capable of doing most any man's work, but later on accepted the greater physical strength of men.

She left Iowa to join a group forming "A Movement For a New Society" in Philadelphia. Within a year she became disillusioned and formally left the group, but stayed close to the friends she had made. She associated with many men during these years, and often broke her heart over them. Her murderer may have been someone she knew.

She had a propensity for falling in love with men and sadly few men responded in a satisfactory way for her, but she often held on to memories of them. She seemed to be on a continual search for direction and purpose in her life and for a soul mate with whom she could share the person she was. Her urge for commitment was a strong priority. She was a philosopher and journal writer, and had graduated from Temple University a year before her death. She loved the printed word and longed for informed discussion on many topics. She seriously questioned the economic system called "capitalism." She purposely avoided owning a car and traveled the city by bus and bicycle.

At the time of her death, shortly before her thirty-first birthday, she was working part time for "Friends Journal," a Quaker magazine in Philadelphia. She intentionally limited her work so she would have resources left to do community service; she was carrying on classes for poor, inner-city women in household appliance repair.

Lois:

The conference was a success for me. I didn't wow anybody, but I was present, responsive and even initiated introductions a few times. Best of all I was not sick inside with fear and anxiety and inferiority. Ah, growth & maturity?—so wonderful. Sorry mine is delayed 30 years.

Ruth & I had good visit last night. She is seeking something to commit self to (30 years younger than I with same problem) She recognizes her fear of failure, the lack of self confidence, the too strong recognition of skills lacking in comparison to others.

I've decided to go with Witness for Peace to Nicaragua.

Don:

Witness For Peace was founded in 1983 in response to the U.S. funding of the Contras in Nicaragua who were carrying on "low intensity warfare." It was a politically independent, nationwide grassroots organization of people committed to nonviolence and led by faith and conscience. The social theory was that a nonviolent presence in a community lowered the violence of the invading military regime. There was substantial evidence that it worked. But it meant intentionally being in a potentially violent area.

WFP activism may have averted an all-out U.S. invasion of Nicaragua, and certainly contributed greatly to the effort to cut off U.S. military aid to the Contras. In 1998 a Nicaraguan peace settlement was negotiated despite the Reagan administration's efforts to prolong the conflict. In 2008 the group celebrated its twenty-fifth anniversary.

Lois was totally committed to this trip and accepted the possible danger as a built-in part of the program. I may have been more anxious than she.

Lois:
12/85

Zero temp and blizzard 12/1. Roads icy. Don took 2 hours to get to work on Monday. WB hosting stranded travelers in school gym. Schools, appointments all canceled. Don & I good talk, why we stay together? He's determined.

Got call at work that I'm accepted for Nicaragua trip.

Naomi's graduation from College of Nursing.

[Counselor] appointment. Get out of negative thoughts cycle. How change? Don doesn't think things are sad as I do.

Don & I to Cedar Rapids in bitter cold on Christmas Eve. Rented motel, ate at fashionably late hour. Walked across three empty parking lots in howling wind from motel to restaurant. In the morning ate at only place in town open, played Scrabble with new game. J & D came out for soup supper, played Hearts down by basement fire. Martha called in afternoon, sounded good, seems to be enjoying Nome's visit.

Meeting of Nica group, several gray heads. Impressed with young minister going for 2nd time with his 17-year-old son. Will be strongly liturgical and Catholic, but I can hold my own.

1/1-5/86

Have been lazy all week, getting up at 8:00 or so, exercising for 40 min., studying Spanish, reading Witness For Peace stuff. Concerned about looks on trip! Hair, on head how to manage, on face, same. It'll work out but takes thinking about. Have loved this break, just busy enough without Christmas hassle and just enough alone.

1/13-19/86

Good meeting with [counselor], feel so lucky to have such help. Told me to act a downer to see if Don can tell. Is this for his awareness or mine? I feel he's gotten more aware during these sessions. I'm still learning to "vent" to others. He more dependent, vulnerable?

Tried acting down for Don. He said he recognized it.

1/27 to 2/2/86

How do Don & I communicate? We're both trying to share more/better.

So much to read about Nicaragua and Costa Rica. Registration gang had a party for me! Surprise shower of gifts, mostly fun. DI interview also published. Awful pic! Article OK, could do better next time, I hope.

Bought jeans and boots for Nicaragua. Have 100 lbs. of med supplies besides 35 lbs of paper. [Editor], Tipton Conservative, called, wants articles, has speech contact for me.

2/3-9/86 Begin Witness for Peace trip to Nica.

Mon. Naomi drove me to Des Moines. She has Nursing Boards Tues. & Wed. Training intense, sense of being evaluated and tested all the time. Commissioning service at close of All Pastors Conference in Des Moines convention center. Arrive Mexico City 2:00 a.m. Pile into taxis to go to La Casa de los Amigos. Walk in city in the morning, one whole wall of large hotel gone from earthquake, rooms exposed. Return to find flight cancelled. Many calls in Spanish, plans to stay over, then get flight out suddenly, pile into taxis again. Two stops in Honduras, Tegucigalpa is one. Arr. Managua, forever customs process. Arrive WFP house late, supper and bed.

Visit four government people. Felt really out of it, declared so at Reflections, cleared air. Leave for Condego, stop at Estali.

2/10-16/86

Overnights with families. All day in Estali. Dirt floors, doorless latrines, stick walls, lumen electrico woman, tire fire. Sleep in school house, to other camp with Austrians, walk up to guard hill, Mothers again after supper in smoky hut. To coffee picking grounds, guard singing, bird calls/signals. Back

Back in Managua, visit Iglesia de Santa Maria de Los Angeles with vivid, violent murals.

2/17-23/86

To airport hoping to get on 9:30 a.m. plane. Actually leave at 11:30 p.m. Arrive Mexico City about 3:00. Sleep really well for four hours. Arrive DM 10:00 p.m. So good to see Don. Night in hotel, good. Arrive home noon after dropping Don at work. Unpacked. Dreading writing and reporting.

2/24 to 3/2/86

Saw [counselor] without Don, he forgot to come. In art museum met a wonderful woman who talked with me about some art videos we watched. She expressed for me the dilemma of our over stimulation. It was a gift of a visit.

3/3-9/86

Writing letter/statement for WFP. A hard job for me. [Counselor] at 4:00, last time, hate to let go. He's there, a comforting thought, but really hope to wing it alone with Don. More writing, slow, slow, phone calls to Congress.

3/17-23/86

Speak UCC Tipton. Went OK, some organizational lapses. Don critiqued me. Lutheran minister laid it on me to educate groups all over the county. Wish it were fun. Went to Cedar Rapids afterward for anniversary, motel and movie till 2:00 a.m.

41 years! What a day. Bought a CD player and 4 discs. Bought an angle saw for Don and heavy Chicago kitchen knives from Kubias Hardware sell out. Reserved plane tickets to go see Martha May 14!

Best talk I've done, used few slides I have.

4/2/86 Wednesday

So many things have happened since last entry (in red book). Giving presentations about it has been difficult. I guess it's stage fright, and I also realize now, years after the fact, that it's part of the feeling I bore day after day when facing classes. No wonder I could never feel comfortable teaching. I feel nauseated with fright before these events! I've done five now, at least two more to do and I should be easier about them. But I'm finding each one is a major challenge. When can I rest, having done 7 meetings, a radio talk and letters to the editors and a news interview? I wish I could.

I've stopped seeing [counselor], I miss it. The other night when I was separate from Don he said he didn't think it had done us any good—I wasn't any more interested in him, had too much insecurity (speaking engagements show this.) I felt really bad about that. I've got to pay more attention. Especially now that he's going on partial retirement, 50%. That is a new milestone, sad/happy combination. He will have more time for Titronics Medical Instruments and Pleiad Industries and I hope it will be what he wants. He's having some satisfying/exciting times getting an instrument produced through Medtronics in Mpls. and his company will produce a chip for it. Could be a real business.

Now that I've had a taste of travel, I'd like to do more. And I think I'd enjoy it more without Don. Although we had a really nice time for our anniversary. I had to speak in Tipton the night before and he arranged an overnight for us and we had a great time visiting, shopping, eating out. We bought a compact disc player. But emotionally we have a gap, he feels it, I feel it, we do not connect in an important way, in spite of our close feelings. I don't know if we have a greater problem this way than other couples. We might.

Don:

Men often don't realize the real needs of women. Women think of sex as a relationship while men think of it as an act. I think of an old adage from out of my past: men give love to get sex while women give sex to get love. There is a grain of truth in that but it is not complete. Genuine love does not always produce satisfying sex, nor does good sex necessarily lead to a loving relationship. Life is too complex for one aspect to deeply control all other aspects. I have often been thankful that very seldom have all the sections of my life gone sour at the same time. If my love life is on the blink, at least my garden is green and lush with all the weeds under control. I may be having trouble at work while my love life is warm and comforting. In a sense I am fortunate to have a complex life.

I think I have seen it work like this: For any two people trying to live closely together, in the beginning of the relationship one might say "It's raining hard outside, isn't it." The other replies "Boy, it sure is. It's raining cats and dogs." Thirty years later, with the relationship on a much more familiar basis, one might say "It's raining hard outside, isn't it." The other replies "No, it's not. It's raining cats and dogs." There is a sad and profound difference between these two replies.

Why do we let ourselves get into the position of instinctively rejecting our partner's claim, before whole-heartedly agreeing? Is it lack of respect? Is it carelessness? Is it arrogance? Is there such a thing as "over-familiarity"? Do we let over-familiarity breed lack of respect?

So what is love? I remember, on more than one occasion, often deep in the night, telling her I loved her. She replied, "I guess I love you too."

The Christian Bible states the best characterization of love that I know of. The thirteenth chapter of First Corinthians is a remarkable list of how one lives among humans in a loving way.

Is love, therefore a way of behaving? Is it an emotion?

The Hollywood model would have us believe that we "fall" in love and that guarantees happiness. It does not and should not be expected to. It guarantees that we have a responsibility and that may bring wonderful satisfaction and source of happiness. Years of raising children is a major, encumbering, responsibility, but a wonderful satisfaction and source of happiness. The children themselves are not the source of one's feeling good, but one's response to them is. We find our own "good feelings"—it is not the obligation of a life partner to make one feel good.

Lois:

4/9/86

We had a good trip home on Mon. Stopped at DeSoto Wildlife Center, saw coots and northern ducks. Had nice time together. Yesterday I goofed all day. The poison oak patches are better but terribly itchy. Was on the phone a long time over a small snafu in the AAUW bus trip plans. Also visited Jan on way home from meeting a student about radio documentary on Nicaragua. Stayed and ate supper with Don. He stayed in to work at TMI.

Don:

Lois was a lifetime member of The American Association of University Women. For years they carried on a money-making project of sponsoring a bus trip to Cubs games in Chicago. Year after year she was appointed to head this activity. The bus was usually full, but often not so until a few days before departure. This always worried her. She spent many hours on the phone to fill the bus.

Lois:

4/29/86 Tuesday

Don & I are going to Ames, Viesha, Friday to stay overnight with Rog & Connie. Sunday I go to Whittier to give a Nicaragua talk.

Last weekend was super busy with guests for two meals. Let's slow down and smell the roses. "Fools rush in where fools have been before." "The older I get the better I used to be."

Don was told yesterday that he can't go on half time for six months or so. Three MDs are leaving and they need him there. He said the reason for the refusal was so complimentary he didn't mind too much.

5/1/86 Thursday

Tuesday night Don & I returned from a really nice week with Martha. She has a NICE place, Bill is nice, and we all had a good time most of the time. Florida is not my style, any megalopolis is not for me, just enjoy the village pace and crowd of IC so much, and question whether I could ever feel easy driving anywhere in bigger cities. Bill loaned us his jeep and Don drove that on two trips for us and did fine. It was a fun vehicle to be in. Martha gave us her room for the whole time, which was super generous. Water beds and jacuzzis are probably for more playful, sexy people than I. The bed was better than the floppy bags, but I like our firm foam better for love and sleeping. We used the jacuzzi once. Don fixed her gate latch and we hung the old quilt of Grandma Hunt's.

Beth tells me how awful to be in your 40s with no man. Well, awful at any age. Yet freedom from is also nice. Don is not happy with my ability to do without, I know. And I do love it when it happens. Don says I should make it happen more often!

Coming down on airplane, Don says is erotic (not going up). We laughed at that.

6/1-2/86

Rog & Connie one year anniversary. Call from Philly just after I got home from work—Ruth found dead in her apartment.

6/9-15/86

Return home from Philly on 10th. Rog & Connie home for weekend. Ruth's ashes came.

Don:

Lois called me at work as soon as she got the call that our daughter had been found murdered in her apartment. Later that evening, at home, the Cedar County Sheriff stopped by to tell us that the call we had received from the Philadelphia Police was not a crank call. This was standard procedure and we appreciated it, even though we had accepted the finality of the message.

In the next few hectic days we made plans to drive to Philadelphia for her memorial service. The group there in charge—friends and the minister of the Church where she sang— agreed to hold off the service until we could get there. With an overnight in Toledo, my sister joined us for the rest of the journey. All of our other children arrived in a short time.

There were details concerning Ruth's life and death to attend to during the few days before the funeral. We met with the undertakers to arrange cremation and for the ashes to be sent to our home in Iowa. The Philadelphia police had impounded nearly twenty of her spiral bound journals in the hope of finding some clue leading to her murderer. We spent considerable time with them trying to make arrangements to release the journals to us. But to no avail. As long as the case was not closed they were to remain locked up with them.

Ruth had acquired a large circle of friends during her short life in Philadelphia, and the large, massive inner-city church was packed to standing-room-only for the funeral. The large choir, of which she had been a member, provided the music. The brother of her best friend was the pastor in charge of the service.

Ruth's ashes arrived from Philadelphia shortly after we got home from her memorial service. We kept them until a suitable time could be found for burial. Finally, with the whole family home for Thanksgiving that year we gathered at a small Quaker cemetery, across the road from Scattergood Friends School, and laid her ashes to rest.

Lois:

Another cemetery in my life is Hickory Grove, across from Scattergood Friends School and part of the long history of Friends in this neighborhood. It is even smaller than Springdale's but true to form, it is in the middle of the section, no, it's in the half mile center of a road bordering the section. Interstate 80, which connects the nation from east to west coasts, had to make a curve in its construction in order to leave Hickory Grove untouched. The roar of intercontinental traffic is now a constant in this rural spot.

Here, in Hickory Grove Cemetery, the ashes of our Ruth were put directly into the ground one cold day when all the family was here. Don had dug the hole for it ahead of time. I had written a brief eulogy which I read into the November wind and the noise of traffic on I-80. I can't find it now, and I felt then that it didn't matter to anyone but me, even if they could hear it. Each one has his own memories. When Don poured the ashes from the carton into the ground he momentarily broke down, and his children spontaneously reached out to him with support.

It was a relief for me to put her ashes in a place with a name after having them in the upstairs hall cupboard all summer. I halfway wish we had bought a more elaborate marker, naming her parents and siblings. On the other hand she stands alone, a mysterious, unique person. I toyed with the idea of scattering her ashes into the Mississippi, a child of the Midwest and of the world, disseminating human essence from prairie to ocean. But I'm conservative. I wanted a place and a name for her.

Don:

My mind goes back to intense discussions with Ruth sitting at home sipping coffee, on her trips home from Philadelphia. She was adamant that all institutions should divest their investments in South Africa because of the apartheid practices there. She was much better informed than I, and could argue forcefully for struggling people on any continent.

She was a strange mixture of naivety, brilliance and deep love. When she got back to her seat after the graduation ceremony from Temple University, she asked her mother what the notation "Summa Cum Laude" on her diploma meant!

It is impossible to imagine what she would have done with her life had she been given more time. She was well acquainted with the jungles of inner city

Philadelphia, but she was a risk taker with the people with whom she made friends and it is hard to say how this might have played out—or did play out.

It was unbelievably difficult to lay the ashes of a beautiful, young daughter to rest in this peaceful cemetery.

Lois:

1/4/87 Sunday

Teresa called yesterday, warm invitation to come out, also a plea?

Later: Should catch up on this year before it gets any older—actually haven't written since Fall. Does that indicate such good health and busyness that writing is not necessary? Partly true, I'm sure.

We spent that weekend with our Quaker social group, our first time to join them. This is a group who grew up together in the Yearly Meeting, became parents of Scattergood kids, and used to camp out together on the way home from getting their kids at summer vacation time. We were staff at the school, or not "in" with the group enough to be included. Most are a few years younger than we are, which is not so significant now that we're all older. It was fun, glad we went.

2/1/1987

Sharmon Hawley Nash, forties college roommate, just called from Santa Cruz. I'm so delighted. I wouldn't have recognized her voice, but she said she did mine. I really look forward to seeing her, the one I liked best of all at college. She said she left her husband because of his alcoholism. He died three years later and she "became a dedicated teacher," never remarried.

Teresa has been urging me to go out and I've bought tickets for March 3.

2/11/87

Teresa called last Saturday morning to tell me Ralph had a stroke on Wed., but was home and already recuperating. But she really needs help, he falls. Maybe I can help her get some new patterns established. It won't be easy. She says his mind is clear and as willful (selfish) as ever.

Don has been so busy with TMI, fixing the manufacturing area and making dopplers. He's also now in another related company that he thinks will go. He will very soon go on full retirement I think, as soon as he can finish two projects that he's doing.

He's better off than I. It is really hard for me to feel productive at home after I've caught up with the basics. I need an ongoing, demanding personal project. Some volunteer work, as in hospital, might be the thing. But I don't want to be scattered into 100 dabbling activities. Need: social contacts, mental stimulation, produce something visible?

Don was nice to me last night in my hurt and humiliation, and I didn't let him know how much I appreciated it, too embarrassed. I was thinking last night in defeatist terms, which are deeply grooved in me, of how at FGC, when I wanted so much to dance, to be chosen, I wasn't. College, HS, Jr Hi, before that? People see me, don't like what they see, and ignore me. I know this doesn't always happen, but the feeling of it is there forever, I guess, even when sometimes I feel really attractive, more than a 61 year old should.

2/18/87

My father would be 102 today. What shocks me is that I think he died on his 85th Birthday and that's 17 years ago!

3/17/87 early a.m. at sister Naomi's in Orland, CA.

Bob left us TV zombies watching "Murder She Wrote" and went to bed about 8:30. Bert said she couldn't possibly go to bed till after 11:00. Naomi bravely stayed conscious through it all. I slept on the sofa, finally slept after 3:00. It was warm though, wood stove cozy. Walked around their square, two miles of almond and orange groves, valley houses, mountains in distance.

On the trip to Berkeley with Kersey and Bert, Naomi several times made a big point of identifying Mt. Lassen and Mt. Shasta. She's very aware of and knowledgeable about geography of where she is, has always learned names of streams, mountains, key points, used to make me feel dumb. She gives and gives and then crashes for a needed rest. She is happy and secure in Bob's love for her. They have a mellowed pattern, long developed. Bob makes strong, belligerent statements, Bob damns and all; Naomi responds with "Bob-O," modifying and softening—

3/18/87 at Teresa's in Berkeley

Forty-second anniversary. Thought of calling Don at 6:00, 8:00 at home, but didn't. Visited with T. Learned of Kersey's vomiting at a dinner years ago when Teresa mentioned the house of Dad's estate from which K was stealing the rent. T is like Margaret, quiet, meek but gutsy interior.

Time hangs heavy here all day. The long walks save me. Ralph, the former sparkling conversationalist, almost never speaks, just sits and stares or sleeps. Am strongly hoping for a day by myself in SF. Should be using this time to think about the rest of my life, what do I commit to? Want to travel. England, Europe.

Don:

This was the second time Lois had been in California on our wedding anniversary. I knew she needed to visit her older sister. Teresa had been her mother when she was young—even into the years when we were dating. I felt easy with her now repaying the care. Teresa respected her and loved her dearly, and Lois, thirteen years younger, was a comfort to have around as she struggled with the problems of an increasingly senile and sick husband.

In another sense it gave me a chance to send her flowers, or make a call, which I probably would not have done had she been home. It felt good to send my love through such a long distance, and reminded me of years before when I had courted a young girl over the same long distance.

Lois:
3/21/87 7:15 a.m.

Weird night. Did I have a heart attack? Sometime before 4:00 woke up and went to bathroom. After back in bed became aware of cramping pain around lower chest, rising on a wave of increasing tightness to include all of chest and up into neck and right ear. Inside of ear hurt for a long time after that, and the entire pain just stayed there, steady, relentless for a time. I didn't get breathless or weak or sweaty. I leaned up on one elbow and that seemed to relieve the grip of it somewhat. After a while the pain (discomfort might be a better word; it was never unbearably intense) lessened and I tried to sleep, but another wave hit and raised me onto my elbow again. This time I tried to feel my pulse. It was steady and I think possibly a shade faster than normal, which was not surprising since I was anxious about all this, but I would lose it, 7 beats, blank, 23 beats, blank, 34 beats, blank 3 beats, blank. It occurred to me that I might be losing it because it wasn't there.

I'm reminded of a wonderful story of a gutsy woman dying of cancer, *Life Before Death* by Abbey Frucht. I just finished reading it this week. At the end "we are standing around watching my body and the stethoscope must be broken for there is no heartbeat in it."

By this time the cuckoo chirped 4:00 and I was eased and painless and tried to get back to sleep. I heard the cuckoo do 5:00 though. It rained in the night, very gray and more today? The metal chimes on the neighbor's balcony rings a constant mellow sound that Naomi liked better than I.

I don't know whether to be inactive today or walk as usual. I don't want to be sick or die here! Home heart attacks are my motto! And what would Teresa do with another invalid to think about? One of the thoughts I had when afraid was the childhood prayer, Now I lay me down to sleep, the Lord I pray my soul to keep. Ye Gods, regression—"Oh , there's no place like home for a heart attack" instead of "for the holidays." That melody ran through my mind in the night.

Thursday I spent with my years-ago college roommate, Sharmon. I like her. She's much more matronly, conservative than I had thought she would be. Such a vibrant, humorous, golden haired beauty in college.

3/21/87

I hope I'm some fun/stimulus here, who knows what helps or hinders. Ralph is patient, tries to be. It must be very hard for such a power tyrant as he has been to be weak and dependent.

3/22/87 Sunday

Ruskin, "There is no wealth but life." That may be true, but life is not always wealth either. Ralph's is gone. Thomas's essay on death, "The Long Habit," means more to me than the above quote; Thomas admits that death is not bad.

3/22/87 I'll be home with Don in 48 hours! Glory!

The routine here is unbelievable and awful. Teresa, bless her, has not had a cooked potato yet, burned 'em dry one time but they weren't done yet. Meals are nutritious and absolutely predictable, and I'm too much that way, too.

Ralph has no usable skill anymore, no zest for life. Life has become a waiting game, waiting for the end, and the shorter the wait the better.

3/23/87 8:00 a.m.

When most all options are gone and age is high, dependence is almost total, then death should come fast. Leave some life for the care giver. Although being so needed may be what keeps her going. T realizes she needs friends, needs out sometimes. Belongs to no group, oh yes, the talking stick group at Unitarian and Women's League of Voters. Has one friend, seldom sees.

Don:

Lois ached for her sister as she watched Ralph and Teresa's lives winding down. Her greatest fear for her sister's husband, and herself, was months of lingering dependency before death finally came. During this visit she could see what might be ahead for Teresa.

She had expressed many times in her later years the hope for a sudden and clean death. She wanted to be able to take care of herself until death arrived. In real life, in the twenty-first century, she achieved her goal. The time between total dependence and death was only a month. I was easily able to care for her during those final weeks, and she accepted what care she needed with grace and thanksgiving.

Lois:

5/4/87

Wake with thoughts of "Death of the Heart," (on last night's Masterpiece Theater) and Ruth's journals. The two journal yearbooks I found in 533 attic. I helped her move things there as she left her Iowa City life. Each spiral notebook covering one full year, June to June. I've been so thinking of how, if, what to edit her life. Could I do it? Should I do it? She wrote her life better than anyone and she figured things out at 22 that I was working on at 40 years older. Could I bear the cost of really going through these things? First would have to go the guilt of the voyeur. She went through many deaths of the heart. Or is there only one and after that we are so tough that death has provided for survival? I read the book years ago, thinking it long, wordy and with nothing happening. Also thinking I should, if as intellectual as I'd like to be, have deeper appreciation and understanding of it. The drama did this for me. It was true, nothing happened, yet everything to the neophyte, open heart. Portia reminded me of Ruth and all young girls who see clearer and more honestly than their elders. Anna saw, after reading the diary, but she had no love.

All these thoughts were with me when Don wanted sex. I told him afterward the transition was too great for me to achieve, but he's understanding and kind. And I'm glad he likes my body even if my mind is a hindrance too many times.

I'm seeking, seeking a sense of order and peace, which has been lacking for a long time. I think, hope, that dropping two days of work at College of Nursing will help, a lot. I have a disgusting urge to do ordering things like re-do the address wheel. If only something would be permanent and finished. How can I need this so much? The impossible. And picking cuticle, really deep and close to the nail is another symptom of distress.

I've always assumed a journal is private, to confess the worst of me, to admit it and deal with it. Also I'm always aware, too aware, that I may be writing for future readers. With the 70s journals of Ruth I don't ever get the sense that she is writing for others. She's working out, intensely, the person she is and the person she wants to become. How can I get over feeling like a spy to read her? I need permission. It will be hard enough to do it with that. Who can give me permission? Hannah? Margaret? Don? The other kids? Marilee? We read some excerpts at Merilee's house the week we were in Philly, and now I feel kind of aghast that we did.

5/22/87 Friday Greensboro, NC. Laughlin Family Reunion

5/24/87
Thirty miles from Indiana border, going home! How does grief work? Riding along singing, thinking Heidi's taking voice lessons may be she can give me some tips. My mouth cavity is small. Interest in voice makes me closer to Heidi than to Tanya with flute, because I can do nothing with that instrument. Cautionary thought, don't let Tanya feel left out. Tanya has Ruth's flute, Martha has Ruth's guitar. These last three thoughts were almost not conscious. An unconscious thought possible? At the thought of Ruth's guitar the wrench, the twist in the chest and the internal moan which I can let sound when alone. It's only a few seconds of spasm, but so awful.

The next two weeks, get through them somehow. First anniversary of Ruth's death. Which is best, time to fully experience the pain, wallow? Or keep so busy there is no time for full impact? Of course, the obvious is to find a middle course. Do some of each. Ruth I loved you so much, not knowing how much. Be gentle with self, relax, lean on the everlasting arms in Biblical terms, rest on the flow of the inevitable and true; it's like a pad of air, the painful and joyful, they are there in endless mix and flow and will sustain if I let go and trust them.

June 4,

Wrote the above pulled over on the roadside. Got home on my birthday. Jan & Don, Rog & Connie came for supper that night. Awfully glad to be home.

Don got word from Philly detective that we can copy the journals of Ruth, but they can't leave the premises. He suggests we copy them when we take the files back home in July. I dread going into Philly. Who do we see? Where stay? I hope I can stay healthy/active 20 more years. It will be a long time before I can read those notebooks.

6/11/87

Rog & Connie stayed over last night to get an early start, 4:00 a.m., to Chicago where Rog has three interviews lined up. He's created a fabulous portfolio, hand lettered/designed. Both dear kids, do wish the world's best for them.

Don:

In the two years since Roger's wedding we, and he, had matured and changed a lot. There was now no thought of his becoming a "pot head." Connie had become a most leveling influence in his life. We honored her for taking over. His work in architecture was outstanding and we looked forward to their trip to Chicago for job interviews. Their future hung in the balance, but we had no worries about the outcome.

Lois:

Slept like a stone last night, even slept soundly after I heard the kids leave at 3:50. Reward for night before when I was wide awake till after 3:30. It happens sometimes after great sex, usually not when it's just routine gift for Don. Wonder what the syndrome is? Don's theory is that I don't have it often enough and the shock is too much! Of course his cure is obvious, and probably correct, take time to be sexy, quit driving self. But how fit everything into a day's amount of time and energy.

6/12/87

Am trying to discover why so depressed when Don came home last night. We came home for supper. He picks me up after and delivers me to work now, and I really miss the walk from Hancher, a change since his retirement. He left immediately after supper to come back to Titronics Medical Instruments, working hard on some development 10 to 12 hours a day. This is retirement? I spent the evening making stew for potluck tonight, cleaning kitchen, took a walk 1.5 mi. very slow, very tired. Sat with ice on back while watched "Mystery" for an hour. Went to bed at 10:00. Reading when Don came home shortly after.

Was I mad at him? Disappointed from lack of attention? Just feeling the futility of life? This feeling comes on me even when busy with projects. I'm a human animal who cannot always overcome the recognition of our basic insignificance in the whole universe, but I shouldn't let the futile sense make me a dud. Maybe presenting the plus face is the best service to others. But how act plus when see no plus? Aaaugh—

6/15/87 Monday

Busy last week Rog and Connie came back from Chicago with two job offers. His portfolio is a work of art. It will be interesting to see which job he/they choose. Chicago will be a new experience for them. They are both practical and saving types. I hope they have some fun there.

7/31/87 Friday, 8:30 a.m. at Dave's in Pa.

This past year I've aged ten. Illusions of youth, illusions of middle age, even, are shattered. I'm dissatisfied with self: appearance, personality, goals (what goals?), sorrow over shortcomings as parent and wife, also fatigue over both, wish to avoid responsibility, yet no joy in contemplating freedom. Back and foot pain have been real and hindering this summer, really restrict freedom to move and that's a real set back and step into agedness. Have to accept this. Have become inactive, unadventuresome, avoid challenge, glad to avoid speaking at YM, may have to do it yet. Find now we may leave here Monday.

Don sitting across reading Dave's letter to Ruth, cries. Well, he keeps so super busy in the world, luck, nature more than discipline. I see I'll have to increasingly force myself to keep in the world as I age. It becomes distasteful to me and I become afraid—of traffic, of crowds, of change. YE GODS!

Don:

Visits to Pennsylvania were now different. While I loved the visits with Dave and his family the time we usually spent with Ruth was conspicuously missing—no drive into Philadelphia, no meeting her at the train. Heidi loved to sing, and she and Ruth and Tanya often played flutes and sang. But not now. The place in my heart where Ruth had always stood was now empty. It had been a year since her passing and memories were still vivid and raw. I assumed they would dim and heal as the years went by, but never disappear.

Dave had written a letter to Ruth, posthumously, expressing his love for her, and I was deeply impressed. I kept so busy, "in the world" as Lois said, that it was easy to keep my deep emotions hidden. In that sense, with her greater ability to express her inner feelings, Lois probably lived a more healthy emotional life than I.

Lois:

I've been copying songs and chords for two hours from Tanya's camp book and keeping a cold pack on my foot and knee. Guess I'll forego walking till I find out which is better, rest or exercise. I am trying to do a few flexies/day, but feel terribly inactive.

Just before we left home we learned that Nome has moved out from Bill's. I hadn't expected it quite so soon, but I'm sure it's best. She's moved back to IC. I'm sure she's upset and depressed. She told Don he was #4. I can only think of three. All of which I'm glad she didn't marry. But where will she find a good man—the commitment as part, a major part, of what makes each one grow up responsible. And the longer they experience uncommitted relationships the less possible the committed becomes. Is that true? My heart aches for her.

I'm reading Ardyth Kennelly's *Peaceable Kingdom*. Read it many years ago and it has always stuck with me, not only the flavor of the polygamous wife dilemmas but the humor and humanness. She's a marvelous writer, would like to know more about her.

Don:

Her good friend, eighty year old Marjorie, had talked Lois into going with her on a group tour to Europe. They had traveled together before, but never to Europe. Lois was apprehensive, but still looking forward to a new experience.

Lois:

Am not really thinking much about the European trip. Doing no reading and minimum prep because I don't want to be disappointed. Go cool with no expectations. A group tour with Marge and a bus load of other 80 year olds could be a real drag. I hope for better, some youthful 60 year olds?!!

11/2/87

And where did Sept. Oct. go? Have been sending out info of the Friendly Woman and haven't had much response. A meeting set for the 14th may tell me whether there is enough woman power to make it go. I'll have to do much phoning next week.

We have a new furnace, after two months. Used a lot of electric heat during early October when it was cold! Today is 70, what a shock when it drops! Still no shower. Don is building a "nice" bathroom in the basement. I don't think we need it, but he needs to build.

The Swiss trip was good. I'm awfully glad I went. I do like to travel and the tour has many advantages. No use pretending I'm an adventurous knap sack type. The nice accommodations are helpful to the over civilized. Marge has unusual stamina and alertness for an 80 year old, I think. I hope I can do as well.

Don and I are enjoying each other, good news. Don pleased at his fitness rating we went to; we were older by 35-40 years than everyone else there. Think of Ruth a lot, sometimes much pain. Got the Don/WB School books finished, quite pleased with them.

Reading time. Mona Simmonds' *Anywhere But Here* and the biography of the Mabel Loomis Todd and Austin Dickinson affair, fascinating. Plenty of action, but a lot of the affair on those Victorian notes. Dad's Emily would fit into that world of notes, appearances, entertainments. How to keep a passion permanent: Have obstacles, drama of deceit, alone against the mores. I think they truly didn't feel guilt? But they knew they should in their time and place. That so many knew or guessed and tacitly accepted, even helped, is remarkable. And David Todd, the threesome? And Emily Dickinson. What did she know?

Connie and Rog have bought a place for about their rental rates; they are very financially minded, took me thirty years to get where they are. I deplore too much interest in personal economics, but I'm also a hypocrite about my interest. They are open.

Don:

For many years Lois had subscribed to a magazine called "Friendly Woman." It was a quarterly Quaker journal first started as a newsletter in 1974. It was passed, every two years, from one Quaker group of women to another in another city. It was a periodical containing essays, fiction, poetry, commentary, and art.

After weeks of discussion among her friends in our Meeting she decided they had the capability to carry on the publication for the next two years. She organized and headed the group. After their application was accepted the Meeting was required to become a legal non-profit organization in order to have non-profit mailing rates. It all came together.

Lois:

The "Friendly Woman" first meeting went well, seven of us. And yesterday Annie T. told me she would join us. Yea! Now if I can get Lisa BW and one or two more we'll be fairly well set.

Don works night after night in basement on the bathroom we don't need. No shower since mid August. I miss it, and have a hard time not resenting the whole project. It will be a nicer basement and very nice bath, with a hall into greenhouse, Don's pet. And the new furnace is a plus.

Have felt really bad about me and Don and yet no deep depression as in the old days. I just roll along through it—losing true feeling? He's so nice, millions would give anything for such a good husband, and I have no intention of separating, unless he should want it. How do I respond to a man who misses the obvious point of a play (Time of Your Life), no, not the point, but the very plot. It's just so hard not to feel disappointment and scorn for his obtuseness. I've always had trouble with this. It's just a particular spot of perception he lacks, pops up in social (real and literary) situations frequently. I suppose I totally lack a spot of perception for his interests (electronic circuits) but he has fellows he can share that with. I would like us to have some parts of our minds in common. I may be wrong, but I think it would make it much easier to respond physically to him if we had minds more in common. Well, I've struggled with this for years and sometimes, like now, the gap between us is more intensely and painfully realized. There is no solution. I've looked for more congenial men, no success. They're all only looking for bodies.

Don:

Many problems in a marital relationship are solvable with effort, patience, devotion, care, and often counseling. But I suppose, in many conjugal relationships, there comes a time when both realize there are problems that cannot be solved. One way to face this situation is to make a painful split. But a less painful solution may be for each to realize they can just live with a nagging problem and count the blessings from the rest as sufficient to hold on. Lois and I lived on the latter.

She came to realize the "particular spot of perception" that I lacked would probably be with me for life, and that she had, as she said at one point, "the same old husband that wasn't about to change much." Realizing these things put a damper on our relationship, or rather gave a direction that we did not control. She often reported, with initially great enthusiasm, on the classes she was attending, but they were too far out of my sphere of understanding to satisfy her. I listened, and did the best I could at response, but it was not sufficient. For part of our lives we lived in different worlds. We both knew this and accepted the pain.

We both lived with her ever-present self-deprecation and perpetual fight against depression. They colored our lives and relationship.

When I first encountered her depression, within the first few years of our marriage, it was totally new to me, and I was of no help to her. Even if I had known what was happening to us, I doubt if I had the experience to properly help. I didn't know that she was depressed and took her distance from me as a sign of something I had done wrong. I could get no answers, and suffered alone as I searched for what was between us. Two or three days could pass with no verbal communication except the necessary—"please pass the butter."

But in those days life was far from bleak and lonely. We enjoyed the new challenges of farm management, teaching and supervising student life at Scattergood Friends School. We made life-long friends among staff and students. Our talents were stretched to the limit as we learned to live with each other and be competent in our faculty positions.

Following our Scattergood years we plunged into home and family building. With an old house as a major challenge and a rapidly increasing family we were constantly busy. About child rearing we had few disagreements. She was by far the better disciplinarian, and because of that I easily, but guiltily, felt that I shirked my responsibility.

In the remodeling domain, most of the creativity and work came from me. But we consulted and planned together as each phase was undertaken. The disorder was the bane of her life and I always felt under pressure to get things cleaned up. She was patient and knew intuitively that mess was necessary to get the work done. But mess is also part of one's personality, and many times I failed to see that a mess created a separateness between us. It went on for years.

Lois:

1/5/88 Tuesday

Holidays are over. I've felt very harried.

The two weeks in the east went well. We copied eleven of Ruthie's journal notebooks, and visited with police a couple of hours. Marilee says one notebook is missing, the last one. I haven't checked dates or tried to sort out. I didn't ask questions of the police or anyone, so will never know some things. But would it help anyway?

I'm having a lot of trouble feeling driven and trapped by family: the Laughlin reunion in May. Doing Christmas, doing Thanksgiving, doing New Years, the last six weeks of every year blur by. Don assumes that I'll do this, do that, will know where he left his thermos, his gloves, why does he? How much right does he have? I have to exert more independence to reduce my resentment: I could insist I drive to work alone sometimes. I could let the house go more. I could exercise, practice guitar and write when other people are around. Why am I so timid about doing my interests? Partly a fierce secretiveness in me (why that?) that makes me not want to share, partly a feeling of hostessing, need to subdue my schedule, my desires to fit theirs. Partly excuse for laziness. Partly fear of not being good enough, of being ridiculous.

It's January and I see the year already as a series of obligations: open house and host for all holidays, canning food, garden care, YM, the reunion, having Tanya & Heidi.

Even the big and glad news, Janet's pregnancy, suggests possible obligations I don't relish.

Balance, how find it, how not get swamped and depressed? Those obligations don't take so much when taken each one at a time. It's my attitude, of course.

High temp today is 0° F. Yesterday was up to 10 degrees or so. Don continues to work every day and sometimes extra on TMI instruments. I never know how much his illusions and hopes color the reality of the business. What will he do when/if there is nothing like this to work on? And what will WE do? Are we delaying the problems inherent in retirement? Of course. For as long as possible. Yes I have, expressed anxiety, unease, selfishness, entrapment.

1/6/88

Have just read this book through, rather heartening really, I do cope/survive. Now, just add some fun. Welcome to a new book. I love the crisp clean pages. Farewell 1987! Not my favorite year. Will there ever be one?

1/7/88

Had "delightful" time at Cadwalladers for supper. Everything they do and have is just right, including their attitudes, their religion, their retirement. Iola did admit once that they feel uneasy with one daughter's life; she and her children enjoy "shopping too much and too often." I can accept that concern, implications reach wide, but hardly a killer deviation in our culture; the non-shoppers are the freaks. I told Don such perfection and joy became a bit stifling after two hours and I wanted out. He says it makes him want to see them more often. Logical—surround self with good examples of how to live and be. Why do I run and hide, literally, from what I admire;

Today is peaceful, at rest with self. Aging face & body, unruly, ugly hair, fears of leadership ("Friendly Woman" meeting on Sat.), overwhelmed by tasks and obligations, concerns about kids. All of these I can see and feel unshaken—today. Hurray for today.

Camping in Alaska

Arctic Circle

Tuk

CHAPTER 11

OUR ONCE-IN-A-LIFETIME TRIP

Don:

For years, off and on, we discussed the possibility of making a journey to Alaska. We wondered about a commercial trip but agreed it didn't offer the freedom we wanted on such a venture. We felt perfectly capable of planning our own route and schedule. We had read lots of articles and flyers about touring Alaska via the Alcan Highway so thought we knew something about the pitfalls and pleasures of such a trip. A good atlas showed us many ways to get there and places to explore.

Not the least among our considerations was the concern for the carbon emissions such travel would cause. We wondered if we were entitled to that much frivolous contamination of the atmosphere. We went through all kinds of rationalizations, and finally justified a long trip on the grounds that it was a once-in-a-lifetime affair and that we were living environmentally frugally in all other ways.

Our plan was to use our small, long bed, pick-up truck with a topper and camp as much as possible. I built a plywood floor above the wheel wells for a thin mattress and our sleeping bag. Beneath the platform was space for food and cooking utensils. We attached ropes to some of the boxes so they could be pushed forward under the bed and easily retrieved. Lois fashioned curtains for the side windows for a bit of privacy and we traveled in style. The space above our mattress did not allow for sitting up on the bed, but by careful squiggling we could change clothes horizontally. It was primitive living, but it was our arrangement and we felt the chance to be independent and on our own was well worth the sacrifice of convenience and some comfort. The small truck had lots of glass windows and the unobstructed view proved to be a welcome advantage.

We planned the trip in conjunction with a family reunion to be at my sister's in Estes Park, Colorado, in the middle of September. Our route was to take us angling northwest across Iowa into Minnesota and north to the Canadian border. Then northwest across central Canada to pick up the Alcan Highway at Dawson Creek. The farther we planned from home the less specific we made our routes. We hoped to make some decisions as we went along, as we saw opportunities and conditions to warrant them. But in general we would camp in a few places in Alaska, visit Denali National park, ferry our truck down the west coast of Canada, drive the west coast of Washington and Oregon and California to Lois' sister, Teresa's place in Berkeley. A two-day visit there then north east to Chico, California, to Lois' other sister, Naomi McLain, then east through Reno and Nevada and into Colorado.

At my sister and her husband's beautiful mountain home, looking out toward Longs Peak, we would meet up with my brother Jerry and wife Coralie and several cousins.

Just before the time we had set to leave, the stick shift transmission gave out and needed replacement. That wasn't easy, as we couldn't really afford a new one and a guaranteed used one was not readily available. The local garage finally located one and installed it only days before our planned take off time. We were told to take it for a short trip test drive. The Alaska trip turned out to be the test!

In addition the tires needed balancing, at least, or maybe replacing. So, on the day before leaving I took the truck to the tire shop for new ones on the rear and balancing on the front. But driving home that evening the fronts were still vibrating, so I scheduled a replacement job for 7:30 a.m. on our way to Alaska. The mechanic assured me we could get it done promptly but the verdict, when we arrived on schedule the next morning, was very different. We agreed on the spur-of-the-moment to skip the tire change and head out.

As caretaker-of-the-car, one of the things that really worried me was the fact that we were starting on a long trip with many unknowns and without a spare tire. I had nightmare visions of being stuck beside the road, many miles from civilization with a flat tire. We had a good spare under the truck bed, suspended with a chain and ratchet. Normally one would insert the jack handle, crank it down and crawl under and drag out the tire. But not now. The night before our departure I checked on it. Years of salt and dust in the mechanism had rusted it tight. No amount of penetrating oil and coaxing would loosen it up. So I reluctantly gave up and went to bed for a short night before the big day tomorrow.

A peaceful and relaxing trip was so dependent upon all the machinery working reliably and well. I had vivid memories of an occasion many years before when a friend and I had worked most of the night on a very old and dilapidated car to get it ready for a mutual young friend who was taking her two young boys—grade school age—on a trip to Alaska. I remembered with satisfaction that she had made her trip of faith with no problems—not even a flat tire. She had run a lot of her life on faith and it had worked well for her. I felt Lois and I were doing as much.

We had little conflict over these many uncertainties and both succumbed to the excitement of a new adventure at our advanced ages of 69 and 71.

Lois:

8/10/94 Leave Springdale 7:10 a.m. in yellow Datsun pickup.

Arrive Linder Tire in Iowa City. New back tires put on yesterday & another trip to balance front tires. Don still not happy with vibration, so in for new front tires. Don worked till nearly midnight underneath trying to release the spare tire. No success.

Ooops, Change of plan. Linder can't do tires till 10:30. We decide to drive the egg-shaped tires to Alaska. No available spare, but we're no worse than before we knew it was frozen on!

So many small niceties didn't get done for this trip with the truck in hock getting major repairs. New transmission had to be ordered, not expected when D. took it in for a checkup.

Rog with Darren, Tyler, Katie & Erin were over for a while last night while we were getting packed. I was making window covers for the topper. Don was packing in. I wish we didn't have the stove. It causes about 3 boxes of cooking supplies & food that we did fine without last year. And it makes me feel compelled to do more food prep & cooking than we did then.

Arrived at Maplewood Campground about 8:00 p.m. after supper in a dingy hole called the Farmers' Table in Dent, Minnesota. We'd never know about Dent, too small to be listed in Atlas, if we hadn't chosen a roundabout way to find Maplewood.

"There's not much to see in a small town but what you hear makes up for it." On cash register.

Fat woman with loud laugh, space user. Fat man with 2 new knees, can't climb a ladder, "can still look," used to be handsome gone to flab. Beat up old American Boy look used to teach school, "two years in Crystal City, North Dakota."

Didn't sleep too well, 1st night in truck. Shower helped restore life this a.m.

Day 2 8/11/94 Lv. Maplewood State Park 7:10

Sumac just beginning to turn. A barred owl visited our camp in early twilight. Very curious but not enough to come down on ground for cracker Don threw. Also heard & saw a chipmunk chipping on a rotten stump. Blows out cheeks & makes his chip chip sound. Just now, young deer by roadside. Strips of mist over lake & hollows. Another long-eared, mule deer. Lakes/ponds everywhere. Wild rice, acres of it. Sunflower fields, masses of blossoms worshipping the east.

Enter Canada. Bought Bing cherries, $5.95 for a couple of delicious pounds. Supper in Grandon. Poured rain, storm had been building for hours. Truck parked half block away & in a deep puddle when we came out of restaurant. Sky clearing & sun out when we got back to camp. Feet sopping. Camp sopping. Nowhere dry but this cab & the back of the truck.

We had glued on the Velcro strips for privacy curtains before the rain. Climbed into bed, (can't sit up) & read People of the Deer till 10:30. Slept, best I've done for three nights.

Day 3 8/12 Lv. camp 5:50 a.m.

Alarm was set for 4 but I begged Don to turn it off when we were up at 3:00. I hate to pee, can't squat deep enough to avoid spattering my ankles. Don says I sound like a waterfall & can be heard all over the camp. He waves his around to squelch the noise. Well, no way I can wave my butt around.

We're losing money using US $. Some won't exchange. Don goes crazy, drives me some, trying to figure mileage using liters. So chilly after supper no place to go but to bed. Light till nearly 10:00. Curtains work well, must remember to remove on right side for rear view mirror.

Day 4 8/13/94 Lv. camp 7:10

Forgot towel in cold shower. Used T-shirt & wash cloth. Lunch at park for boats, fisherman. Getting tired of cheese sandwich, apple, milk lunch, although do no better at home. A quart of milk bought in evening does well for breakfast & lunch. Now eating off the endgate for breakfast after being on road to allow dew to dry some.

Valley View Visitor Center really nice, exchanged our US $ into Canadian. Warm outside & hot in cab. Wish we could store it for tonight.

Lots of hills & hummocks today, then a valley, then back to hills (foothills of Rockies?) Pines, birch. Truck has no oomph on hills. We may do the Rockies in first gear. Will cook a supper tonight, see how it works. Don thinks the burners are very low power. They are!

Dawson Creek celebrating Fall Fair & Rodeo this weekend. Town is jumpin'. Zero Mile Campground is quite full. Set up Naomi & Scotts' tent, very nice one, took us 30 minutes!

9/14/94 Sunday

Leave Dawson Creek, begin Alaska Highway. Stop at Munch Lake, Double G Service, 446 mi.

Cooked pancakes for breakfast. Tent bed not as easeful as truck because moved in only one layer of pad. Heavy dew, packing wet tent, etc.

I do OK scurrying like scared mouse to get shave done while no one else is in bath. Envy women who come in at 5:30 with hair in place! I'm wetting & combing mine because last night's loving really screwed it up while it was still wet from washing.

A good day 1 on the famous highway. It soon turned foggy & rained/misted/fogged most of the day as we climbed & dipped through these northern Rockies which are not as rugged or high as in Colorado. The variety of wild flowers is astounding. At lunch break I went back into a cleared "No Trespassing" zone (lumber or road equipment center, tracks of huge machines) and picked 6 different kinds of blossom in as many seconds.

Animals seen: Dead caribou on the road. I wish we'd stopped to see it close. Later a mother & fawn in the road. Mother licking & pawing at the stuff on the shoulder. Don thinks salt content in it. The fawn ran across the road through the ditch & into the timber when another camper came by. Mom stayed, taking short runs up the bank on the opposite side of the road where she blended so well that even seeing her she became momentarily invisible. White spots under tail and just above hooves look exactly like the rocks. Another time in true rain we passed two bicyclers chugging up an incline & stopped to see another yearling? (no antlers). Farley Mowat says Caribou are the only female of deer family to grow antlers. The bicycles scared her up the hillside.

I drove all afternoon and didn't get sleepy once. Too much driving attention required. Winding, rough, sometimes not much harder than gravel, but oiled or tarred and packed. Not crowded & speed comfortable. Behind a double tanker, speed too slow even for me. Sometimes no center line & shoulder very narrow & undeveloped.

We've been eating lunches on the tailgate if no picnic area is available. Tonight at Muncho Lake camp we had a real supper, chicken, rice & stir-fry veggies with a delicious sauce on them and a generous pot of tea for me. A three-table cafe with a three-stool counter, where an attractive woman with thick, long hair in a loose mother earth style bun a la 1960s, served and cooked. Work worn hands too much for her age. She was baking loaves of bread & cinnamon rolls & doing dishes, pots, by hand in a deep sink on one wall.

A mechanic here may be able to unfreeze or release our spare tire tomorrow.

As we came down the last pass of the day the sky cleared enough for sunshine & it hasn't rained here today. It has clouded, misted ever since though, very little wind & temp about 60. We'll sleep in truck tonight in a pine woods campground with the cleanest outhouses I've ever seen. Painted all white inside with skylight, even toilet seat & lid painted, and no smell!

After supper we climbed a really steep track used for what? I really feared coming down, had on flat slick leather sandals & my week knees make downhill difficult. Don held on tight & we made it. 9:20 p.m. & still very light even in heavy overcast.

Picked up a man & his daughter & gas can on their way down to Oregon. Mom & two other kids stayed in their car, a beat-up station wagon. Quite a load for the cab. Daughter had been to school in Alaska and the family is "getting together again." The situation seemed fishy somehow, but we dropped them off in Ranchiero, 20 miles down the road, and left the mystery to others.

8/15/94 Monday Day 6.

Alaska Hwy 97 all day to Yukon Territory, then stopped at Jake's Corner, 50 miles east of White Horse.

Rained in night and now. Fog drifts hide mountains. The garage mechanic released the spare. Don's glad about that. Coffee & huge fresh cinnamon rolls from cafe where they were mixing up the next batch.

Stop at Liard Hot Springs. Walk at least 1/4 mile of board-walks over marsh/swamp. A few other people soaking in the rain. We walked back to truck to get our suits & joined them. Parts were too hot to bear. My first time in a hot spring. Lovely!

Arrived Yukon about 2:00. Rain stopped. Last 75 miles or so in BC on gravel, muddy & loose. Big thuds of road against the under carriage.

Stop at Jake's Corner, (Yukon # 1, Junction of 5, the Dempster Hwy) A kind of museum of old machinery from Alaska Hwy construction in the 40s, old motors, boats, cars, wrecks of all kinds. View of rock peaks close by, 2 ravens on the sign. Called Jan.

8/16/94 Day 7

Visitor Center at White Horse, wonderful film of country. Attendant gave us hard sell on going to Inuvik, up the Dempster. Junk yard trip found a crank for the spare tire holder that we left at Muncho Lake when we had the repair!

Five Finger Rapids on the Yukon. Took an hour to walk down to the river. Seven flights of stairs & some trail. Dusty powder part of the way & sun hot. River wide, fast & green, flows north. Coming back up Don asked if such action doesn't make me feel raunchy. Me breathing like a heart patient! I asked him what didn't make him feel raunchy, hauling manure? He said the list was too short!

Roadside sadness: A black & white bird, not a magpie, circling, searching around its dead mate, swooping down to stop beside it a moment, then up into the air again.

While driving & singing "Thanks for the Memory" I remembered my mother referring to that song, the only time she ever noticed pop culture as far as I know. She said that the "burning toast & prunes" line were appropriate in conjunction with the "burning lips" part. I never saw her romantic or flirty with Dad.

Camped on a barren lot, free, a repair, gas station near by. Hid behind a trash barrel for my privacy, felt very exposed.

Don exercised at fire smoke in distance. Local guy said it had been going a long time, about 70 fires existing at present, only 2 being manned. Light till after 11:30, have read books in poorer light.

Don:

Smoke in the air in timber country certainly did raise the hackles on the back of my neck. From first hand experience, in CPS, fighting fires close to the blaze, I knew the dangers from tinder dry evergreen trees exploding like a giant can of gasoline. Sparks could jump roads and back-fire areas with the speed of a stiff breeze. The smell of wood smoke in the air always aroused an ingrained instinct to get a fire line established. Crazy, of course, since now that my feet were almost too heavy to lift, swinging an adz was pure fantasy.

Lois: 8/17/94 Day 8

Begin Dempster, 456 miles of gravel to Inuvik, Chuck Camp.

Lv. Klondike River Lodge 8:30 after check-up on truck. Idling rough, bothered Don. Wonder sky & mountain layers, most in valleys. Dark steel clouds alternate with clear blue patches of sky, sun a silver ball. Supper in Ft McPherson, a small co-op cafe & motel with 8 rooms.

Picked up Wolfgang, a German traveler with 2 flat tires. Took him to Eagle Plains. Born 1940. Has German wife who speaks no French. They live on the border of France & Germany, works at N. German arms Institute, supplies procurer. Has been to India, China, Mid East. Family left Russian sector and moved into W. Berlin, British sector after WW II. Father was military policeman, registered as Nazi because in the army. Says we should leave Yugoslavia alone, even though sounds cruel. Thinks Middle East a world threat, have to be armed against their ideas and those of the military.

Don:

Two flat tires on a rough gravel road forty miles from the nearest service station!! We were still running on our old egg-shaped front tires. Could we possibly expect our luck to hold out till we got back to civilization? We both agreed this trip had its insane aspects. But I was relieved that we, at last, had one available spare.

Lois:

At Arctic Red River took Louis Cardinal Ferry, McKenzie. Met about 40 vehicles the whole 450 miles. Sky and land of the day's trip too vast to describe. Arrived Inuvik about 10:00 p.m. in brightest sunshine of the day, in campground a mile or so out of town. Drove into town about 11:00. Kids playing in the street, people walking around, no need of jackets. Buildings are metal, on piling. Stopped a young woman to ask questions. She's been in "north country" over two years, here only six months, working for housing authority. Explained the great boxed in channels that run between buildings. They house sewage & water pipes above ground, insulated. Can't put pipes into ground because of permafrost. She'd lived farther north with no trees, here there are scrawny poplars & spruce. "Boring" Wolfgang had said. If a native commits self to live in a house for 10 years, it's his. Loan canceled.

Our campground buildings are white with blue trim, very neat, clean. To bed about midnight, slept till 12:30, mosquitoes thick. About 1:00 got up, ate 3 cookies (poor me) and doped with repellent. Presto, bugs vanished. Four campers across the way talked quietly at an outside table beside a pit fire till 1:30 or later. Sun just under the horizon then. When I woke up at 5:00 it was just above the horizon, don't believe it ever got really dark.

8/18/94 Day 9 Thursday

Hot shower, glory after dust of the Dempster. Truck rear covered with dust, all the luggage, the bed! Trying to keep everything covered. We have about 700 more miles of gravel before we're back to hard roads.

Got reservation for 11:30 flight to Tuk but it was canceled, high winds here, 100 km there. Have fooled around town all day, checking to see if flight a go. No. Will check again at 5:30, if not then, we'll go on first flight tomorrow if safe.

Bought gifts for family, real art pieces out of our range. But I think we have some nice things representative of Indian crafts and designs. Looked in several shops. Visited Igloo church, the research center (animal & tribal studies). No one in that building wanted to talk to us, but it did have flush toilets, a treat! Caribou hamburger for lunch. I wouldn't have known. Supper at same place, huge veggie sub. Arctic char dinner in hotels, $25.

Don:

Unlike Lois, I have a hard time relaxing and doing nothing. I have tried to learn from her, but it doesn't come easily. On the other hand, up there in northern Canada, a thousand miles from home, with her as company, it was nice just to be. The scenery was gorgeous, and the machinery was working well. I felt peaceful and safe. The distance between me and my responsibilities was a distinct advantage.

Lois:

Both of us tired today. Traveling, sightseeing is hard work, so is camping. But we are doing well. Came up here as an adventure since I've quit fooling around with men!! Don said the other was cheaper!

Came home to camp about 8:00. Wind still very high and very chilly. Nothing to do or nowhere warm to go except to bed which is cozy & warm. Began to rain seriously after spitting off & on all day. Had bought two used books in Inuvik library, Ellery Queen for Don & Six Women who did what they wanted. Schuman Heink (My mother listened to her singing on the radio) & Amelia Earhart were what caught my eye. Victoria Woodhull, an unknown to me, relates to the Henry Ward Beecher scandal. Digression. So we made love for Don & read & dozed and about 11:00 a fellow camper came around & asked if we knew our lights were on. We've had a terrible time remembering even with a reminder note on the dash. I got up and turned 'em off & brought rain covers & pain pill from front seat & spilled some cookies. It was raining & cold.

I'd been trying to sleep for an hour or more before the good Samaritan came by. Read again, still couldn't sleep. Told Don I might need sex now more than I did earlier and he began talking about how light the sky was. I know he didn't hear me.

8/19/94 Day 10

Still talking to each other. Don says still talking even if we can't hear each other.

Don:

I can't remember what our problem was so long ago, but in retrospect I now feel it was probably my fault. I have never been a very verbal person all my life and probably wasn't meeting her need for expression of more in-depth feeling on something important to her. It may have been our route, or someone we had been talking about, or some stranger we had just met. To the end of her life she kept an active interest in the details of peoples' lives, and could understand their feelings; I lagged far behind in such perception.

Lois:

Just left Fort McPherson on south trek back. Getting into tundra & mountains rimming the whole horizon.

Woke up late this a.m., nearly 8:00. Truck wouldn't start as we had feared. Don got the camp manager & he jump-started it and we dashed off to meet the tour group at the airport, rather than going the opposite direction into Inuvik, because it was so late. Two guys in a camper from BC followed us to see if they could join the flight, too. We thought we arrived at the right place, a yellow building, Arctic Air written on the side of a yellow sea plane docked beside it. Not one soul was around, just a friendly white dog with milky eyes. After waiting a short while we decided the place was just too dead, and the BC guys said the real airport was down the road. So we dashed for it, found the tour agent waiting for our money.

Plane for 8 took off for the 35 minute ride to Tuktoyuktuk over the endless McKenzie river delta. Saw Pingos. Met by Inuit guide & bus. 900 population. School through 11th grade. The guide had gone to 4 other places for HS years. Ice caverns for families.

Sent card to Don & Jan. Dipped hands in Arctic Ocean on a black rock beach. One guy from FL swam for a couple of minutes. Seemed no colder than my memories of the Pacific in San Francisco. McKenzie River makes an ice road for a few months down to Inuvik, otherwise no road.

The early warning tracking station built in 50s now not in use. Natives "work for government" doing?? Big point made of wealth of the group that owned Ack-Ack Airlines & other enterprises. Dry horns 2-3 years & send powder to Japan for aphrodisiac?? Visited Anglican log church, two craft shops. Weird tour.

Flight up was wonderful. Couple from Tennessee with 20 year old autistic daughter, defective & retarded much more than Eric, my sister's son. Cool couple from BC in the built up camper. She beautiful long hair loose over ears, sophisticated, earth type of 60s. She reminded me that seals are slaughtered needlessly and painfully as I bought a sealskin tablemat of little diamonds of pieced dark & light sealskin!

Now going through Richardson Pass, 900 miles of gravel, some very loose & deep on top of a ridge south of Ft. McPherson. Very windy, no shoulders, scary.

8/20/94 Day 11

Eagle Plains to Dempster. Dalton to Chicken. Camp at West Fork 50 miles N of Tok on Taylor Highway.

Leave Eagle Plain onto the Dempster, very dusty, sun obscured, also smoky, especially last 40 miles of Dempster. Ranger not disturbed, like man at Klondike station who said 100s of fires, few ever manned. Lunch on Engineer Creek. Saw fox with white tipped tail, grizzly eating blueberries at Stone Mt. Camp. Ranger girl brought out scope for us to look. Barred owl. Sharp shinned hawk? Ptarmigan (prairie chicken) A passing truck tossed a piece of gravel into the center of our windshield, permanent pock.

Off the Dempster, back on to #2 Klondike Loop. End of dust, smoke still bad. Approach to Dawson. Visitor Center good exhibits and a bathroom! Dawson really into tourist decor & services, puts West Branch to shame. Ice cream cone and across Yukon in ferry and onto Top of the World Hwy to Tok. More dusty road, even more steep & curvy than the Dempster, more deep drop offs.

8/21/94 Day 12

Wake up in camp after rainy night and two aborted sexties and fitful sleep to find I'd left my money belt at Chicken. Only 25 miles back so off we went over the washboard corrugated road again. Told Don it seemed to be the best treatment his genitals might get. Mine too.

Don:

Lois was close to seventy now and I had known her since she was fourteen. In some ways she hadn't changed a bit, and I loved her now for the same reasons I had first fallen in love with her. Her clever quips and teasing weren't sexual then but just as original and fascinating—a personality I greatly envied—so different from mine.

Lois:

Clearing sky. Busload of tourists at Chicken eating cinnamon rolls & coffee. So relieved to get my stuff back intact. Had $150 Canadian & over $200 U.S.

Arrive Tok, cold, windy, gas up, breakfast, wash 1,100 miles of dust, mud off truck at a free wash. We both worked 30 minutes on it, cold. Met couple from Hawaii doing same, and a single woman washing her truck mounted camper.

Long drive on to Fairbanks, cloudy & cold. Coffee in Visitor Center & tailgate lunch in cab. First campground mobbed, RVs arms length apart, no trees for tents, nothing, mobile slum. Second place, Goldhill, empty spaces. Set up tent, so cold. Don changed oil. I washed every dust covered item, many changes of water in our one cooking pot. Went to a car vacuum to clean out truck & ate supper in a beanery, soup & bread. In camp built a fire & made hot chocolate on camp stove. Keep more money in the car now & less with me. Spent $30 for a few groceries tonight. I'm having the Scotch problem, how much to spend. Gas & lodgings are on Visa but even so our cash seems to disappear. Good bed in tent tonight.

8/22/94

Slept in till almost 9:00, well, not always sleep. Camp stove wouldn't work. Bought part to fix stove, hopefully. Watch Sandhill Cranes & Canada Geese at wildlife center with tailgate lunch. Took 2 mile walk & bought Don a red corduroy hat there. Visited a sports store for those who buy the fanciest of equipment & clothes, very chic, very expensive. Did laundry at camp while Don worked on stove. Alaska salmon costs $18, we'll probably skip it, too much for one stomach. We ate in a little Greek joint run by Alaskans who fell in love with the Mediterranean on a visit & opened this place on their return.

Sun comes out about 8:00 p.m. for a few chill minutes. Cold & windy all day. Went to Alaskaland museum, great photo exhibit of the 1900s by Johnson. Salmon bake was closing up, went home, made cocoa on fixed stove & went to bed.

8/23/94 Day 14

Leave Fairbanks noon. Camp KOA 10 miles north of Denali entrance.

27 degrees this morning, ice in pan, feet a bit cold all night. Red Squirrel both mornings early throws down spruce cones from the tip top of the tree and working his way down at a fast pace.

Breakfast nice with fire & hot drink. Dressed inside bathroom of Goldhill. Owner says people think he's too woodsy & primitive and take their campers elsewhere!

Went to Alaska pipeline, passed up tour of gold dredge #8. Starter was dead when we wanted to leave. Don bypassed with piece of copper wire he'd tossed in for some reason! Started OK at gas station, think it's a fluke?!

To university lookout for sight of McKinley. Lookout full of construction & sky too hazy. Bright sun for an hour, then massive clouds move in again. Leave Fairbanks, least satisfying & fun places we've been. Wet & cold is part of it.

Arrive Denali about 3:30. Visitor Center like Grand Canyon, organized chaos & crowd. No campground or bus space for tomorrow tour. Reserved camp space & tour for Thursday.

When we tried to leave the visitor center the truck was dead again. Don worked on it, tried different things, no response. Then he spent several minutes scraping battery posts, & presto, problem solved.

Ate an all-you-can-eat salmon bake at a tourist joint, getting very cold & windy. Don attended a film at the KOA grounds & I crawled into bed in full view of the too close neighbors. Warm in truck & slept well in spite of climbs out to pee by the truck.

8/24/94 Day 15.

This is Christmas Eve in National Park land. Workers all have a blast before they leave for the season, started years ago in Yellowstone.

Forgot my shower token (bathrooms a long block from our spot) but finally had a hot shower after long trip back to truck to get it. Don's was cold. We cooked pancakes; I got into cab to eat, so cold.

Came up to Denali & claimed our camp space in Riley Creek Campground. Saw a film in the visitor center, decided to join a nature hike, 2+ miles, ended at dog teams demo. Took about 3 hours & I actually got warm enough to unzip my top, 4th, layer, but not take off my hat, since I've had it on since I dressed this a.m.

Dianna David, park ranger/guide was so nice, a skinny, soft voiced, willow-the-wisp like Ruth with a presence. She had about 25 of us identifying & tasting 6 kinds of berries: low bush cranberries, bear berries, blue berries, crow berries, bunch berries, soap berries. Told Indian tales, how the crane got blue eyes & how Mt. Denali was formed by bears digging the river, making waves for the raven. Waves into Denali.

8/25/94 Day 16

All day at Denali. Bus tour through park see tiny spiral. Rain again, still. Leave park, head south. Stop at Mary Carey (Alaska books) Lodge, electricity from their own generator. Rained all night, complicated loving.

8/25/94 Day 17

Still raining, heavy overcast all day. Mind of a mouse, dry clothes & warmth & clothes not worn 48 hours in wet are important to me. On road to Anchorage. We're both weary of Alaska. For me, vastness of nature is beautiful but I need some borders, more than most people? Certainly more than the adventurers & explorers.

8/27/94 Day 18

Breakfast with Lees & left soon after nine. We went to Earthquake Park with the heaves & humps preserved and walked an hour. Watched sea planes till noon. Tailgated lunch. Downtown again & bought gifts for little kids, shared carrot cake in coffee shop. Found Centennial Park Camp on second try, got onto a major highway at poorly marked turnoff first time. Also located Meeting House. Foggy all day. Saw Forrest Gump movie.

8/28/94 Day 19

Tailgate breakfast in wet fog. Turned shower on wrong person! Profuse apologies from me and cool acceptance from her. Don't blame her.

Sunshine!! All afternoon on trip down Denali peninsula on way to Homer.

Stopped at Portage Glacier Visitors Center. Film, "Sound of Ice" spectacular about glacial formation & importance of glaciers to land & wildlife. Ice worms! Icebergs in river. Film seemed more dramatic, moving than the real glacier. Tailgate lunch.

Arrived Homer about 6:00 Beach camping, decided to use after checking out municipal camp up on hill at far end of town. Public toilets are across the road & up the street aways. RVs thick but not too close. Parked with truck open to Ketchhrack Bay. Soft breakers to sleep to.

8/29/94 Day 20

On board the Tustemena or "Rusty Blue" or "Old Rusty." Homer to Kodiak. Sr. Citizen walk on bargain for $5.00. Several senior couples taking advantage of 10 hour trip. Departed 30 minutes late because so many vehicles to load & unload. We'll have 5-6 hours in Kodiak & return tomorrow.

Two couples from SD, daughter of one married to fisherman & lives in Homer. They've been visiting here a month. Are meeting daughter's husband, whose boat is to spend a few days in Kodiak. They plan to spend a few days on the boat with him. The daughter & 2 year old child are also along.

The second with a 5th wheel flew to Missouri to a sister's funeral then back to Anchorage to continue trip. Another couple from Florida. Don & I are out of style. He's wearing his holey old gray hooded sweatshirt. The others are in "outfits," the shiny sweat pant & matching top or handsome ski jacket with name brand jeans.

Sea Sick. Lost lunch several times during the afternoon, then had some dry heaves. Wet my jeans thoroughly. Mopped up self, washbasin, (didn't make the toilet the first heavy time), spent most of the afternoon in the bathroom curled up on a double chair sort of thing, dozing between bouts of nausea.

Arrived Kodiak 8:00, walked about town & wharf. Felt washed out weak. Supper in Chinese restaurant on 2nd story. Hungry but wary.

8/30/94 Day 21

Don saw whale spout. Otters, 3. Look so little out there on the glassy water. Water crinkled with smooth, like old lady's skin. Back to Homer about 10:00 a.m. Tried again to change ferry date from Haines. 100 miles to get there. Can't reach tomorrow's sail even if available space. Friday's had no space so we'll keep our Sat reservation. Alaska great for sportsmen, we've kind of had it & are eager to go south.

Camped again at Centennial Camp in Anchorage. Saw "True Lies," Schwarzenegger—stupidest 2 and 1/2 hours I ever sat through, although it was a pleasure to watch the girl who played the wife.

Colors distance, black, blue, mauve, green, glorious shades of each. Closer, spruces dark greens, yellows, tans & browns, aspen.

8/31/94 Day 23

Glenallen Hwy Anchorage to Tok. Warm & partly sunny all day.

Fizzled love early, Don felt bad. Slept till 8:00, tailgate breakfast. Laundry & food shop.

Matanuska glacier stop for lunch tailgate. Braided river & moraine, spruce & aspen turning. Slow road curvy and great wavy bumps (permafrost sinks?) some gravel.

Sourdough campground with private showers behind curtains & 4' by 4' dressing space! Matriarch of folks who run this camp, age 79, talked too long of her Alaska experience. So fluent, & so solidly, authentically herself. It was compelling. The SD couple who've been here before didn't come, they'd heard it. Don disgusted with her, partly because her sympathies were with the traders, not the Eskimo. Prejudiced commentary, "I never saw one in a hurry." She came as a bride from Wisconsin 50 years ago. Threw 11 bottles of hair dye onto tundra that had come in by dog sled. They ordered food in January for the year, got here in Aug or Sept. She taught in a government built school that had bathrooms but no water source in building. She & husband built flying business, had 5 planes. There's a funny outdoor museum here in the camp, old tea kettles & typewriters on posts.

9/1/94 Thursday Day 24.

Rained much of night, up after 8:00. Knee is really hurting when getting in & out of bed (truck) or even squat! Pain so sharp, leg gives way.

Tailgate breakfast, wet. Banana, orange, Cheerios & milk in cardboard boxes.

Warm still. Clouds beat Iowa for variety and quick changes. So vast here, mountains, clouds, sky, trees overwhelm. To know the state should fish a creek or climb a mountain, or watch a certain part longer. Same as in any place to know. I know my ash tree & my maple, know the sky out the kitchen window, can handle that. Tourists can never be part of a place.

For the past 15 minutes have been trying to understand Milepost maps from Tok to Haines. I get so confused. I'm really astounded at my inability to comprehend & orient myself in a place. Don learned Anchorage really easily. I learned a few moves by rote but have no idea how to get into them from another site. Sometimes I have a clear sense, better than Don's, of which way to go, and it's correct. But usually it's a fog in my mind & even checking & rechecking with map doesn't reassure or clarify. I just have to believe it. Pretty morale busting.

Big discussion about old woman's talk last night. Don can't understand why she brought the hair dye. I can understand that so well, a 30 year old bride whose husband liked the gray streaks gone. I can't understand how they could throw bottles (old sulfa, too) out on to the tundra. Don gets more like his dad, totally closed on a point sometimes. Me? Never!

This is the 2nd day of rough roads: Three hours of construction, pot holes & scallops on the old. Gravel & washboard. Top of the World hwy was some, but narrow, too. So far, 3 hours of 220 miles and biggest dump truck ever seen with female drivers. Picture album of the weird designs at the top of the black spruce, clumps on top of almost bare trunk, crazy leanings/angles, twisted tufts, especially where trees are most stunted. Black spruce equals permafrost below, somebody said.

Back onto old hwy with no shoulder & growth right to edge of road, a corridor of green, scrubby stuff. New hwy will have wide shoulder. Swath of trees has been bulldozed into huge piles each side. Yukon T signs encouraging drivers, "smile, fasten seat belts & drive with care,'" "Next year road will be better, hope to see you then." Narrow is really OK. Do people complain?

1:30 lunch stop at White River. Gift shop, clothing, restaurant, 2 cabins, toilet & shower for $3.00, cinnamon buns, sour dough brought in 1898!!?? "Check out by noon because we use the sheets for tablecloths at dinner."

Kluane Lake, blue & huge. Congdon Creek campground. Rest & walk along lake. Take two brilliant white stones. St. Elias Mountains on our right, west of road, snow topped. Supper in 3 table restaurant at Kathleen Lake. $18.00 for 2 hamburgers, 1 piece of pie, 1 coke, 1 coffee. ($1.00 U.S =$1.35 Canadian) Beginning teacher salary in Anchorage = $30,000, up to $55,000 for MS & experience.

On to Haines, won't get there till 10:00 p.m. or later. Going through tundra on Haines Hwy at dusk, multiplicity of reds, greens & browns, somberly colorful. Snow peaks in near? Sunset sky in gray & rose behind us. Looking down on snow peaks in one pass. Don says not actually down, a valley between us gives the illusion. Grandeur is a feeble word. Writer of Job, writer for the other side of the world seems to have expressed the implacable being, the hugeness, the indifference to the existence of humans. Are Quakers correct in accenting the value of the individual? Why does the individual concern self with preservation, well life depends on it, not mountains depending on human life, no, it does all relate. My understanding of the term ecology deepens.

We drove out of that spectacular mountain/tundra & kept driving another 2 hours to arrive in Haines at 10:00, dark & found a campground. I was so disappointed that we didn't stop to see morning up there. Don's priority is to get out of here. Drove 12 hours today. He is not good at just being.

Don:

Again, she is right. I remember this incident well. I was more than ready to get out of Alaska! We had seen more new places and brushed more different lives than during any other three weeks of our togetherness, and I was ready for the familiarity of our hum-drum life at home. But she wanted one more night to see the morning sun come up over the mountains. My regrets are deep over not letting this happen—I know I would have enjoyed it with her. We could easily have found a camping place along the road. And another twenty-four hours would not have dented our schedule in the least. I'm not good at just being. Her disappointment clouded our relationship for another day and I felt guilty.

Lois: 9/2/ Day 25 Friday. Haines, AL

Slept better than for several nights. Aaaaanger/frustration with self & Don & exhaustion. Rained most of night. Drove down to ferry terminal by 8:00. It will open at 1:15 p.m.! Drove on to Chilkoot Lake, past a salmon counting weir where a girl was hoisting dead fish out of it. 34,000 salmon had come through so far this year. The dead ones look small.

Saw two bald eagles, watched & tailgated breakfast by the lake.

Did get time of boarding upped 24 hours, will leave tonight. Also got a room, may have to pay for a 4 person room, $35.00 more, but agent left it open in case a 2 room is free.

Later. We did get a 2 room, an inside box, 6 ft wide & 12 ft long. Contains 2 bunks, a sink across and closet. Shower & toilet at one end. No window but ventilation OK.

Interesting to watch the other vehicles line up to board, and the people. Watching, embarking, trying to find our room again, stateroom deck is a series of mazes. We both got a bit disoriented, but figured out a # system. Even after 24 hours there were times I'd go in opposite direction at the top of the stairs on the observation/dining deck.

Card playing couple, playing at 6:30 morning of arrival in Port Rupert at 7:30. Good loving & sleep after midnight. Don up at 4:00 to see Juneau, said too dark.

9/3 on board

Took a Dramamine last night & lost all the morning, could barely move. Took a walk when we docked in Petersburg. Like hauling 1,000 lbs of me.

9/4/94

Prince Rupert dock to Prince George, BC, 450 miles, 10 hours. Arr. Prince George about 5:30, lost an hour from Alaska time. Nice campground. Spread tarp out to make a dry patch, worked well. Rained most of night. Rain on roof & tarp nice, slow drops, plops occasionally. Got to thinking of Ruth in night. Why didn't I make more of the little girl who wrote? She never felt loved & appreciated enough. It tears at me and no way ever to make it up to her.

9/5/94 Day 28 Monday.

Prince George, Hwy 97 south to Hope, B.C. 380 miles. Mountain roads, steep, winding & fast.

Sun came out, gorgeous Sept day, blue sky with large wispy strips of cumulus. Streams, lakes all the way. Valley south of Williams lake, irrigated pasture whenever flat, not necessarily level.

Saw a line with flapping clothes drying in the sun. Gave me a pang of homesickness! Homemakers, housewives of the world write. Some of us are not as adventurous as we are keepers of order.

Changed to a T-shirt from long sleeve double layer top that was comfy in Haines & on the ship. Now, looking at my elbow with wattles in the right rear view mirror. Ye Gods, how I hate the glimpses of sagging flesh I'm always running into. Remove all mirrors & make love in the dark after 60!

Spuzzum service station at Spuzzum Creek. Orchards, bought fresh tomatoes & peaches and a mini watermelon from a family of 6 or 7 children who run the business.

A lot of pines now as well as spruce. Bushes turning, not so much as on Haines road. Camp at Hope, vertical back yard. Tailgate supper of beans, tomatoes, bread & peaches.

In the bathroom: If you turn it on, turn it off. If you open it, close it. If you want it, ask permission. If you operate it, know how to use it correctly. If you break it, fix it or find someone who can. If you mess up, clean it up. If you borrow it, return it.

9/6/94 Day 29

Lv. Hope B.C 8:30, Ar Salem, Oregon. Warm! Ar. Lincoln city. Sun rose over the hill & through the trees. No dew, & my pee spots under the tree still wet. Up in the forest they were absorbed in the spongy, forest floor.

Suddenly a wide valley after a short pass. Produce, cabbage, sweet corn, broccoli & dairy cows. Chilliwack.

Mountains recede and disappear. The new American Gothic is a man & wife (very much wife) sitting on opposite sides of a pickup cab pulling a 5th wheel trailer house or in an RV. Both are staring silently ahead as three other lanes of traffic roar past. Don & I in our much smaller one-piece camper rig must look the same in that instant flash of passing. No pitchforks here. This is leisure time retirement in the USA. Hooking into a dump station is as near to pitch-forking or manure as these folks will get.

Camper guy in Fairbanks told us "drivers of $200,000 motor homes don't like trees." Willing to park 20 ft bare space apart, crowded slum.

Drivers of the one-piece motor homes, many pulling a car or boat or both with boat on top are the top echelon, 5th wheelers, some as long as semis are next. Those of us in the small pickup with camper top are the low caste. Vans are also above us.

Have been surprised at the quiet and separation in campgrounds. Expected more bon amie & mixing. We're only there evening, sometimes late, and leave early, so may have limited the socializing times. No talk in bathroom usually.

Hwy #5 is brutal, bruises the spirit. Going through Seattle & Olympia, 4 lanes all the way, 5 and even 6 for some stretches. The noise alone would be exhausting, without the speed. I drove 2 hours of it, ugh. Don't see how Don keeps going.

Lv for coast on peaceful 2-lane road. Ar Lincoln City, very tired. Dark. Don drove into a McDonald's drive through the wrong way because it was the straight ahead road at the intersection where we stopped. He didn't realize it wasn't the main road, sure sign he was tired.

We found a perfect motel room with kitchen in gray & rose colors and real wood panel & had a good rest.

9/7/94 Wed. Day 30

Leisurely breakfast in our motel by a lake with sun streaming in. Don made pancakes!

Now, 101 down the Oregon coast. Fabulous. Saw a whale spout several times & saw its back a couple. Cormorants as well as gulls. Seven pages of gulls in the bird book. Some of these are white, 2-3 year olds, some gray to almost black, immatures. California gull?

Drove into dunes area for tailgate lunch. Climbed one to top of wonderful huge beach, tan, fine grain sand, wonderful warm on feet. Met couple dragging drift wood piece. Four dune buggies roaring & smelling on a huge bare dune obviously used frequently. Much of the dune area is grown over with wild strawberries & shrubs & is protected from such use.

Finally found mantle to fit lantern in Coos bay. Sunny day for wave watching. I never get enough of it, need a cabin on the beach for days. Harris beach State Park Campground, wonderful woodsy, full, huge. Walked down steep zigzag path to beach about sunset. No shells on this beach, only driftwood and mountain size sentinel rocks. Lazy breakers. Light & color change all the time the gulls cry. Into Brookings for supper, nice one with candles & full courses. 10:00 o'clock & pitch dark in camp. Don suggests we leave early, eat breakfast or brunch at an outlook down the road.

9/8/94 Thursday Day 31 Brookings, OR to Berkeley, CA.

Don not ready to get up at 5:50 when I woke up from chatty woman in space next to us. She talked incessantly, still going when we pulled out at 7:20 in light rain.

California border check for fruit. Kept the 2 bananas we bought last night for breakfast. Down hill with lumber trucks. For two days & still today passing paper pulp & lumber processing plants. Acres of poles, cut lumber & mulch. Breakfast on a high, not very good overlook. A mile or so on could have been on the beach. So it goes. Last look at ocean breakers. Some redwoods on edge of road, first eucalyptis. Arrive sister Teresa's about 5:00.

9/14/94 Wed. Day 32 on the road.

Lv. Bob & sister Naomi's 7:50 in warm valley sun through miles of orchards, walnut, almond, prune, peach & some grape. Rice surreal yellow/green, all irrigated, of course. Hills hazy blue in distance.

Tired & cross. Just found out we've been going wrong direction to Penn Valley, 10-12 miles off, I think. Don going to see an electric car person again. Then on to Grass Valley & the Sierras. Farewell to bougainvillea & rhododendron hedges on highway, brown hills & dark green/black oaks.

Arrive Penn Valley. Bought lug of peaches & 2 casabas at a last chance fruit stand. Mountains come so fast. Windless days, have been all through our California stay. San Francisco was windy, of course. Such stillness is rare in Iowa.

Don just got picked up by the electric guy to go to his place. I need a bathroom badly, go into little restaurant where jolly girl is most welcoming. Buy a coke, get water. An 8 table cafe with Mexican theme. Patio mural on three walls gives pleasant fake scene of beiges, brick reds & soft greens & blues.

Woman in car next to us has no money, she's "first in line" after giving for years to food pantry. Demented daughter with red hair, ravaged face & body, driving a 10 year old Cadillac, "not ashamed."

Leave Grass Valley on #20 to Tahoe National Forest. Wow, was not prepared for beauty of desert. Got darker & darker while we discussed whether to try to go on to Ely or stop at a campground. Quite dark when we pulled off the road into the sagebrush. Stove wouldn't hold pressure, valve thing kept coming out. Don patient, added gas to tank, more tinkering, finally one burner worked enough to get pancakes made.

9/15/94

Leave Arizona-dry camp off the Loneliest Highway in America, # 50, 16 miles from Circle Wash. We quit last night when almost dark, drove off the Hwy on a trail into desert & stopped at nowhere with stars shining and not another light to be seen from any spot on the wide horizon circling us. Very dark & in bed before 9:00. Lovin' one sided. Don about give & take. We're out of balance & I don't know how to cure it. He says I can't take if I don't feel good about myself & I think I'm really not bad off that way.

Love to visit this desert.

Clinton talking tonight on Haiti. We'll motel it, clean up, even the rest stops today have been waterless, pit toilets, some very nice, but wipes don't quite sub for showers and we haven't since Mon night at sister Naomi's.

The vistas, petroglyphs, colors, textures, shapes, all under soft blue sky & a white 3/4 moon have been beyond my description. Passes that threatened to be too narrow to enter opened up. Wish I could haul out the grandeur & space into presence when at home. The Midwest is soft, rounded, the crags worn to black soil, gulches & canyons into creeks.

9/16/94 Friday Parachute to Estes Park

At least arousal is still possible for me. Ha! Live the moment. Up & at em, 8:00, packed up, walked 20 minutes. Breakfast at Jim's Cafe where waitresses wear T-shirts with Road Kill Message on the back. T shirt on a young boy, 16-18, "If it has TITS (in electric pink) it's—I never did get to see the bottom line. A small boy, 4-5 was with him having a wonderful time talking & being listened to. From something Don heard he thinks they were father & son.

I feel a bit drained & frustrated. Also a bit anxious about the weekend. I feel superior to some of our relatives and inferior to others. I must repress these feelings. Jealousy?

We've been going along the Colorado river for miles yesterday & today. Fantastic engineering of #70 into the mountains rocky crags, two long tunnels. Aspen are turning.

Lunch in Granby at a cafe with really good heads (not moth eaten & dusty) of Dahl sheep, mountain goat, deer, caribou, antelope, moose, black bear. Now start up the Trail Ridge Road over the continental divide. Granby Lake, Shadow Mountain Lake, gorgeous sunshine in the aspens. Trying to be UP. C'mon Lois, give!

Arrived Margaret & George's in Estes Park, Colorado about 4:00.

Don:

This is the Laughlin family reunion, which we had planned to be our last stop on our long Alaska adventure. We spent two days visiting siblings, and cousins, some of whom we seldom see. We did some slow mountain climbing on relatively unchallenging trails. It was a wonderful relaxing time, but we had been away from home a long time, for us, and ready to hit the road as soon as possible.

Lois: 9/19/94

We were first to leave. Down #34 through always beautiful Big Thompson Canyon farewell to the mountains. Then #36 to #80 & all day in Nebraska flats. Stop in Grand Island motel after search for oil, bought a case of it, so cheap. Walked 30 minutes or more in Morman Park by motel.

9/20/94 Tuesday.

End of 6th week. Bought milk & ate at Grand Island rest stop, a very nice one because of historical significance of 40 mile long, 2 mile wide island in the Platt, became Fort Kearney.

Hot, sticky. Shirt back is wet all the time. We're finishing "People of the Deer." Cold from Canada forecast for tomorrow.

Arrive home about 4:30. Kitchen sink and counter stacked with dirty dishes, some moldy. Floor filthy. He'd tried, (Jim, our house sitter while we were gone) vacuum cleaner in middle of dining room. Freezer in fridge has 4 whole with heads chickens, unwrapped, filling it!!

We brought in some things, unpacked a few. I did dishes for an hour & cleared some space on counters. I'd prepared myself for worse. Peaceful supper.

CHAPTER 12

THE TWENTY FIRST CENTURY

Don:

The last eight years of our lives lapped over into the new millennium. They were the years of our greatest sorrow since the death of Ruth, years of new accomplishments, and probably the years of the greatest change in our lives.

Lois' sister, Teresa died in January 2003. The following March, her California family scheduled a memorial for her. We made the trip by Amtrak and when we arrived home there was a call waiting for us from Darren. We called him back and learned that Janet had just been diagnosed with lung cancer.

The weeks and months that followed were filled with increasingly bad news. Jan was a fighter and determined to do everything that she could to keep herself alive. She was unwilling to accept the first diagnosis that it was fatal, and that palliative care was the only course. She wanted desperately to find a cure. "Dad you've already lost one daughter," she said. She had a fifteen-year-old son and a husband twenty years older than she. They had always assumed that she would live beyond Don and finish raising Darren. It was an acceptable circumstance for both of them. This was not to be.

She investigated other hospital programs for cancer patients. First she took courage from a hospital in Wichita, Kansas, offering special vitamin C cancer treatment. Then she made a trip with a close friend to a Native American healer in Arizona. Finally, she enrolled at the Cancer Treatment Center of America in Zion, Ill., with high hopes of finding a cure. Her sister Martha flew up from her home in Georgia several times to be with her during treatment sessions. Radiation and chemo kept her increasingly bedridden and inactive. Her sister Naomi, a nurse, helped her during her final months with necessary injections.

It was a spiritually stressful time for all of us. Lois and I were anxious to give every bit of support and love to our daughter, but we were uneasy with some of the cures she was investigating. One evening, visiting with her in her home, she told us she was leaving soon for a trip to a clinic in Utah offering special healing processes with essential oils. Upset at the prospect of her being the victim of a shyster, I spent the rest of the night on the Web investigating this clinic. I found a lot. And it was alarming. I printed the scathing reports about the scheming and dishonesty of the institution's owner—a medical doctor who had lost his license because of misbehavior, and took them to Janet the next morning. She accepted the findings and cancelled her appointment.

Our eldest daughter died April 12, 2004.

Lois had had little experience with hospitalization throughout her life, but as she grew older her knees became her greatest problem. She walked a lot, so it was new to her to have a physical problem with that activity. Her doctors kept telling her to use what she had as long as possible, and when the pain became more than she could bear, they could replace her knees with metal knee-joints. She finally, reluctantly, reached that point. In the fall on 2006 she opted to have both knees replaced at once. Many weeks of physical therapy followed. She worked hard to regain the movement she used to have, and I worked with her to keep up her courage to force herself to deeper bends each day. Within a few months she was again walking her mile without pain.

Lois:

10-10-06

I'm packed for a week's stay at Mercy—the backpack holds everything easily. Can't find a glasses case but have a box for the hearing aids and one for the tooth.

Nome hasn't told me but Rog says she plans to be with me after surgery.

10-18-06

Arrived home evening with list of pills & instructions. I now have a heart rhythm because of my tachycardia attack. I realize better that there were a couple days on the heart monitor floor when I was mostly not there or anywhere.

10-20-06

Swollen feet & legs painful. Regression since returning home. Haven't exercised enough to keep swelling down.

Was very glad to visit therapist at Crestview this a.m. where she verified the badness of swelling (Don had poo-pooed) & forced me to begin moving again those oh-so-painful movements.

Pain, pain, pain—I'm going back on the narcotic-Tylenol combo. I despise the spaciness but I'm wearing too thin on endurance. I keep feeling that I ought to be more healed, no muscle & bone pain. Fuzzy head coming back.

10-21-06

Good night's sleep, no meds after 11:00, but no relief from pain since breakfast & exercises just won't get easy.

Don's getting good at exercise help. He's essential. I haven't strength, physical, nor will power, mental to manage them all by myself.

Sleepiness and ease caught me & blessed snooze till nearly 2:00. Don came home early because I didn't answer the phone. I was lying!

Surprised at all the cards I'm getting.

Grace by Linn Ulmann, native Norwegian, set in Norway. Retired journalist & second wife 20 years younger. She's an M.D. & I can't quite believe in her adoration of her husband. She gives him the fatal dose & is convinced not to turn herself in by a fellow M.D. She had promised she would do this for him.

"There came a time when Johann realized that the world wasn't trying to tell him anything, that his body was saying nothing, that his pain offered nothing, that the body is flesh & flesh decays. It was simply there—all of it. He had no tacit understanding of the world. Sunshine was sunshine. Rain was rain. Flesh was flesh. Pain was pain—And a time would come & Johann would clasp his hands & whisper, "why?" And the answer would make no more sense than the question—"Because."

She promises to help him when all is futile. Relief is on Moi's face. Johann's death will be a relief. It grows light in the morning and dark in the evening. Dignity in these words. Not for Moi—for her it was day after day of pointless waiting. Only afterwards, after his death, would she be able to fill her days with purpose again, with tears, memories and comfort & reconciliation. His death would be her relief. End of Grace.

10-27-06

4th therapy session—Nicole—hard work & lots of pain. I don't know what level of knee use I'm heading for—age 60?—75?—50?

Dr. Hanna says "1 week of home recovery for every day in the hospital." That gives me a better perspective on my development. I'm back to depending more on the hydro—contains some narcotic which helps pain & increases spaciness. I'm learning to just breathe and pee—no more demands.

11-03-06

Today better than Wednesday. Am planning to go grocery shopping this afternoon with Don. He's in 827 now. He's been there and worked so much he feels proprietary far beyond my feelings toward a bare, unfinished house which I hope will be truly livable, no work left to do, when we move into it.

Herman's corn, across the road, was combined yesterday. Everywhere around us is now harvested & trees are mostly bare—not so colorful as some years—little of the brilliant coppers and reds. Don did a final mowing and leaf chopping in the yard.

11-07-06

Nancy and Pete brought lunch today. It does me good to have company.

11-10-06

Temp down to 20's tonight. I'm cold most of the time—chilled & shaky. It's melodramatic but I feel myself into such a decline that dying doesn't seem a shock. Pulse, lungs, blood pressure all OK yesterday. Lean, Lois, lean on the everlasting arms you don't believe in. The leaning into nature, into pain, into limitations is what I sorely need.

11-12-06

Walked to Herman's tree and back. This experience (surgery) has changed some core substances of me. Death is always close—maybe such awareness is a sign of maturity. I think so often of Janet's final weeks—how blind I was-how unfeeling, unknowing—self protective. Melissa and Geralyn were much closer. I hope, so much, they were enough—how alone?

Five weeks from surgery. Still sleeping on sofa. Don has been six weeks on the hideous couch in the office. I really don't see how he bears a wife who is so inactive. I must be a colossal bore. He's always kind, patient, loving—also ready for some sex which seems as remote—impossible—to me as trip to China. Also unappealing—that's the worst.

Don:

Lois evaluated our relationship differently than I did. Or, rather, she evaluated it and I didn't. I may have treated it like the old timer who said, "I told you, dear, when we were married, that I loved you. If it changes, I'll let you know." I never found her a "colossal bore" or hard to "bear," but I never expressed to her enough of what she meant to me. She needed more verbal expression of love than I usually gave. I felt it but it didn't come out. I don't know why.

Many evenings, after supper, we worked together to solve "jumbled word" puzzles. She kept a box of puzzles she had collected, and paper and pencils to work with. She enjoyed the fun time we shared, and the low level mental challenge, but it was not a substitute for a deeper sharing of serious political, spiritual, or social theories and ideas, which she needed. That was a real lack for her, during much of our married life.

Lois:

02-13-07

Tomorrow I see surgeon Myznik—I suppose for final check of the knees. They've done well. An angle sharper than 90° is always painful. I don't seem to progress about that. So going down stairs is iffy—sometimes do baby steps, certainly with a load like laundry. But going up is fine. And walking 30 minutes—no pain.

Lunch time—birds and squirrels eating on both sides of the house. Snowing lightly, mean NW wind.

Don:

This was a new experience for both of us. I had never had to be an intensive caregiver. She had never before been a longtime patient. I had always taken over some of her household duties after the birth of each of our children, but that was different and more short-lived. Exercises following surgery are absolutely necessary for developing bendable knees. We worked together to help her expand movement capability. She learned to say yes to the pain and lean into it. She found it acceptable because it would lead to painless walking.

Since our marriage in 1945 we had moved about six times. We had lived in Springdale for forty-eight years, but the house was old and nearly impossible to make energy efficient. The acreage was an increasing burden to maintain as we got older. One of our rental properties in Iowa City was also a very old house, in need of constant care, and the lot on which it stood was ideally sloped for the new house we envisioned. We were ready for a change.

Our local son, Roger, is an architect and contractor with years of experience in building the house of our dreams. All our stars seemed to be in alignment and pointing toward a move to the city in a new house. But such a move, after so many years, entails a price.

Lois loved our home in Springdale and I did, too. It was far more than an acreage with a house. Together, and with our kids' joyful participation (most of the time), we had brought it from an abandoned wreck to a comfortable home with lawns, gardens, sidewalks and paths. Our history was there. This was where our relationship had waned and waxed as we moved from our young, productive years to old age. It was the place where our major problems and joys occurred. Residence doesn't have to stay where one's personal history was developed, but there is a huge wrenching when one has to leave it.

What were we giving up? Space, for one thing. Lois had designed her kitchen after only a few years of living in the original one. My dad and I built it. Even as we moved out Lois called it her "new kitchen" forgetting it was designed in the seventies and that it looked its age to anyone else. She had cupboard space, closet space and basement shelves. Our attached garage allowed comfortable transporting form "trunk to kitchen" in all kinds of weather.

Our lawn had gradually expanded from small to large over the years and for many years Lois loved to run the mower during warm sunny days. Mowing always brought barn swallows swooping around the yard. It wasn't obvious, but we assumed they were catching food on the fly stirred up by the high speed blades. This she would give up.

Her space would be reduced, but nothing like mine. The spacious two-car garage had an overhead crane for the heavy jobs, and benches and shelves for work and storage. But most of all I had my "red shed" within a few feet of the garage in which I kept my "infinite inventory." Nearly fifty years of accumulated treasures—some of which I still needed to find a use for—were stored in its nooks and crannies—valuable things I could use if the need arose. All this I would give up.

We would give up fertile garden soil, and a western view of the setting sun. We would give up a wind break grove surrounding our back yard and our own well of clear, cold water. We would give up the dusty combine picking corn each fall in the field across the road from our front door. We would trade a car-a-week on our county road for a car-a-second on the main drag street going north out of the city. We would give up a free-ranging dog for a house-bound cat. We were moving from peace and quiet to hustle and bustle.

We knew all this and pondered the wisdom of moving. But aging was inevitable and reducing our space and responsibilities began to take on a feeling of luxury. Our new space would be adequate and comfortable but greatly reduced in size and care. The transition from the old familiar to the new untried was traumatic but gradually became acceptable.

So design began, the old house was torn down and the new house arose from the rubble. The year 2007 arrived and we moved in the spring. Now in our eighties, we moved into a brand new house for the first time in our lives. We settled in easily and accepted our new limitations as a blessing.

CHAPTER 13

OUR LAST DAYS TOGETHER

August 2008 was as normal a month in our lives as one could imagine. Our Monthly Meeting corn-freezing project was in full swing. Even though we now lived in Iowa City the old ties with our West Branch Meeting had not been broken. We now approached the town from the west after nearly fifty years coming from the other side. Every old familiar fence post and bump in the road from the east was now only a vague and forgotten memory. But new landmarks were fast becoming part of our mental landscape.

About ten members had contracted for one member, a farmer, to plant and raise sweet corn for us. On a Saturday in early August, we met in the early morning to pick, husk and process corn for the ten families. I went early to get in on the picking, while Lois came a little later to help with processing. We both worked till mid-afternoon to help get over three hundred pints of corn in the freezer. It was a wonderful community effort to furnish ourselves with winter food. Lois helped mostly with cutting corn from the cob, and then clean up. She worked hard, and we were both satisfied with the results and the fellowship with friends.

Also that August we attended a fortieth year dedication of a log cabin that had been built by young Friends at a timbered site by the Cedar River. When we arrived, we took a difficult trail from the parking lot to the cabin. Lois navigated well, but coming up some of the steep slopes she accepted help. I noticed, as I led her, that she seemed to walk to one side more than the other, but she enjoyed the day conversing with friends.

She had an appointment with her doctor on September 4 to discuss what seemed to be vague, but real behavior changes which we had both noticed. On the evening before the appointment we decided to walk to a restaurant for supper. It was about a mile—we had walked it often. It became very clear she was not walking normally. She was on my right and I had to continually hold her hand to bring her closer to me and not wander off the sidewalk.

The next day, as we described these events, her doctor immediately recognized the symptoms of "the only form of curable dementia that I know of," or so she thought. She ordered an MRI at a local hospital. After many delays it was done later that evening. The results prompted doctor's orders to check in immediately at the University Hospital where skilled neurosurgeons were on duty. They took more pictures and Lois was admitted and settled into her room by midnight.

The next day, a biopsy confirmed cancerous tissue in a large mass in her central forehead. It was too entangled with brain cells to be operable.

The next few days were a haze of consultations, second opinions and family discussions, and an overall deepening awareness that her life was nearing an end. The medical staff gave her six months, at most, and would offer only palliative care. They explained that anything that could be done would entail great risk. She, and we, made the decision for no heroic efforts to prolong her life. Tampering with the brain, even by the most skilled surgeons, could turn her into a vegetable for the rest of her life.

Once we made the decision to accept the inevitable, Lois stayed true to her character. "Well, I'm just going to enjoy the next six months being a crazy lady," she said.

Lois' home file has a large section on "Death and Dying." She had made herself a student of the subject. She had read books on how people die, and was familiar with the Hemlock Society and their philosophy. One of her greatest fears was that she would become helpless and lose control of her life. She knew of a friend who survived a year after finally becoming incapacitated from his disease. She was determined that this not happen to her. It didn't.

Lois' mental and motor skills began to deteriorate quickly. Martha visited for a few days in the middle of September and we bought two cell phones. We had the idea that whenever I needed to be away from home, Lois could call me if she needed help. It was already too late. She wasn't able to dial.

We both signed papers for absentee ballot forms. Her signature was so illegible that I questioned if would be accepted, but it was and the ballots arrived in due time. She filled hers out, and tried to sign it, but couldn't. I got my first taste of doing alone something that we had always done together. We didn't send in her vote. Her brain function was rapidly abandoning her.

Later in the month, our two older granddaughters arrived from Pennsylvania to spend a few days with us. It was a joyous time as they bustled about with all the energy of thirty-year-olds cleaning house, cooking, and helping Lois in a very personal way. In spite of the joyous facade, in the backs of our minds was the fact that this was probably the last time Tanya and Heidi would see their grandmother alive.

During these weeks, Lois' walking became more and more unsteady. From friends we borrowed a good walker with wheels and a seat. It was a wonderful help as I could lift her from her favorite chair and wheel her around the house and even outdoors. Early on she had enough strength in her legs to help lift herself from her chair; later she became totally dependent upon someone to help.

Within weeks her speech became garbled, her thinking skewed and she struggled to express herself. We struggled to understand. One time a friend came and brought a bag of apples which she placed on the end table near where the three of us were sitting to visit. A week later she returned while Lois was in bed and didn't see her. I told her our friend had been here and she said "Did the molasses get confiscated?" She was insistent, so I began to ask questions. What could she possibly mean? I finally worked it down to something in the living room and something recent. At last I asked about the bag of apples, and said they had been removed. She was satisfied and relaxed.

It is difficult to think of a bright, thoughtful woman, whose love of life was language and thought and human relationships, now finding these qualities slipping from her grasp. It is hard to know how much of her confusion she recognized. Was it speech confusion? Was it perception confusion? Many letters came from friends and I tried to read them to her, but she wasn't there—she just wasn't there.

Tanya and Heidi went home and told their dad that he had better come out as soon as possible. Dave came for his last visit soon afterward. Lois made her most insistent requests for help while he was here. She wanted me to help her die, and was disappointed when I said I couldn't. "Yes, you can," she said. At one point about two weeks before she died, with Dave and me at her bedside, she asked me to bring her seven plates. I was confused and couldn't tell if she meant tectonic plates or dinner plates. I brought a few plates from the kitchen cabinet and laid them on the bed beside her. She, lying flat on her back, took one and put it on her stomach. Then she said "Now, punch me several times." I complied and then she took a second and laid it on the one on her stomach. She said "Now punch me some more." After a couple of gentle punches she said in a disappointed but resigned tone, "Oh, it's not working." I think that was the last of her requests for help in dying.

The most heart-wrenching aspect of her final four weeks was her utter docile and accepting attitude toward what was happening to her. Only once did she react to her condition. Standing beside her chair, where she spent most of her days, she said almost in tears, "All I do is sit in this chair all the time." I cried with her, but we both knew it was all she was capable of doing.

She fell several times from her walker—she had no sense of balance and didn't know when she was leaning too far over. I was careful never to let her out of my reach, but in spite of my best intentions, she did fall. Once, in the bathroom she overbalanced while trying to count some pills she was supposed to take. Lying on the floor she continued to count pills and put them in the bottle—no emotion, no alarm, no hurt, no concern, no effort to recover, no cry for help. This was certainly not the woman I had been living with for sixty years. This total, passive acceptance tore me apart inside. I'm sure I was the last in the family to accept our separation. I spent those last weeks in complete denial of what was ahead. Of course, I knew intellectually she was dying, but emotionally I was far behind.

I am so thankful that I was in good enough condition to take care of her during her rapid six-week decline. Usually she helped in getting up from her chair or bed, but once she fell in the kitchen and there was no way for her to help on that smooth linoleum floor. I lifted her, but after that we took advantage of the Hospice respite program for caregivers for my recovery. Twice my children and I considered getting her into a nursing home, so I wouldn't have to lift her. Both times I just couldn't accept that separation and we turned the opportunity down.

Finally, on Saturday morning November 1, just two months after her first diagnosis, her breathing became labored and irregular. She would hold her breath for long periods of time before the next breath came. Finally the next breath didn't come. Roger and Martha were standing by her bed, holding her hand, brushing her hair, and telling her, "It's all right to die Mom. It's all right." I knew it was, but it wasn't. I was so thankful for their presence, because I could never have told her that. When we all realized that she had gone, Connie put her arm around me and pulled me tight—I was suddenly engulfed in an overwhelming sense of loneliness and abandonment even with most of my family in the room. My married life with Lois had ended and the mutual words from long ago came back: "Till death do us part."

POSTSCRIPT

One of the things that has become apparent to me in the years since Lois' death is the irony of my writing at all. She once said, as I was working on a magazine article about our new house, "Maybe it will turn out that Don is the writer!" Neither of us took the remark seriously. Now that it is too late, I would give a lot to be able to return to that time, and consider it seriously. After two years of struggling with language and words, in an attempt to bring our story to life, I am aware of the lost opportunity for a shared experience. It might have satisfied her eternal need for "things in common," which she often felt was lacking.

Had she not died I would not have read her journals, and we would not have had the common experience I now know was possible. Having traveled this road alone, I realize how much richer the trip could have been.

I have some deep unresolvable regrets.

At breakfast in our new home, we sat opposite each other with a toaster between on our small kitchen table. We usually had homemade bread which is heavy and has slices of varying thickness often hard to remove from the toaster. I had made a pair of walnut tongs for easy retrieval. Even with the tongs the slices were sometimes hard to get hold of. Lois often used the control knob to lift the whole rack up to make it easier for me.

I silently resented this help. Why? My only analysis is that I felt that the tongs I had made were sufficient—any help implied that they were not. What a tragedy. What a misconception of values. Why did it take her death for me to realize my errors?

In real life a minor passing incident—after death a deep abiding regret.

Is human nature such that it takes a tragedy for new insights to become visible? Perhaps. But I would like to think it doesn't have to be that way. That is why I have included in this story so many of those minor passing incidents that made up our life together. Sometimes I noticed, appreciated and learned from them as they passed. Others I wasn't even aware of. I hope the reader has seen what I could not at the time, and will piece them all together, and learn to discern the daily events of his or her own life more carefully, and appreciate every moment for what it has to offer.

If I were asked to name the one outstandingly best thing I did with my life, I would have a quick and easy answer: I found and married Lois and lived my life with her.

14140007R00118

Made in the USA
Lexington, KY
22 March 2012